Labor Movements and Dictatorships

PAUL W. DRAKE

Labor Movements
and Dictatorships

The Southern Cone in
Comparative Perspective

THE JOHNS HOPKINS UNIVERSITY PRESS
Baltimore and London

© 1996 The Johns Hopkins University Press
All rights reserved. Published 1996

Printed in the United States of America on recycled acid-free paper

05 04 03 02 01 00 99 98 97 96   5 4 3 2 1

The Johns Hopkins University Press
2715 North Charles Street
Baltimore, Maryland 21218-4319
The Johns Hopkins Press Ltd., London

Library of Congress Cataloging-in-Publication Data will be
found at the end of this book.

A catalog record for this book is available from the
British Library.

ISBN 0-8018-5326-5
ISBN 0-8018-5327-3 (pbk.)

Dedicated to Dick Drake

Contents

Tables

Acknowledgments

For support of this project, I am grateful to the Social Science Research Council, the Fulbright Commission, the United States Information Agency, and the University of California, San Diego. In addition to being thankful for assistance from the library at the University of California, San Diego, I am indebted to the collections and staff at the University of Illinois in Champaign-Urbana and the Hispanic Division of the Library of Congress. My work on this study further benefited from stints as a visiting scholar at St. Antony's College in Oxford and at the Instituto Juan March in Madrid.

Above all, I wish to thank my research assistants: Marcus Joaquim Maciel de Carvalho, Baldomero Estrada, Lisa Hilbink, Robin Linsenmayer, Scott Morgenstern, Karin Navarro, Wendy Prentice, and Eduardo Silva. By the same token, I owe a huge debt to Charles Bergquist, Joseph L. Love, Brian Loveman, Gerardo Munck, and Peter H. Smith for reading the entire manuscript and improving it immensely. In different stages and chapters of the book, I also received valuable comments and guidance from Alan Angell, Manuel Barrera, Jorge Barría, Amy Bridges, Guillermo Campero, Marcelo Cavarozzi, Gustavo Cosse, Martín Gargiulo, Manuel Antonio Garretón, Charles Gillespie, Isabel Gómez de Souza, Josef Gugler, Tomás Moulián, Carina Perelli, Romeo Pérez, Juan Rial, and Francisco Zapata. My secretary, Joan Brunn, also helped in countless ways. And, as always, my wife, Susan, and my children, Joshua, Elizabeth, and Katherine, gave me whole-hearted support.

Labor Movements and Dictatorships

Proletarians and Praetorians

How working-class movements suffer, subvert, and survive capitalist authoritarian regimes is the subject of this book. Right-wing military-based governments usually apply stern discipline to labor unions and their political parties. Normally appearing in semi-industrialized countries, these dictatorships typically impose antiworker economic structures, institutional rules, and political prohibitions.

In most cases, these despots succeed at breaking labor in the short run, but their success erodes in the long run. Those successes and failures reflect the experiences and assets that workers had gained in the democracies that preceded the dictatorships. They also shape workers' roles in the democratic governments thereafter. This historical perspective will illuminate how praetorian guards crush proletarians, and how the victims endure. Although laborers and other oppressed groups usually are unable to dislodge the dictatorships, they often are very capable of installing a thriving democracy after the dictators depart.[1]

The dictatorships studied here varied a great deal in their setting and history, but an essential common thread was their reaction against the working class. In every case, the pivotal role of labor should not be underestimated. These autocracies differed in the proximate causes of their takeover, in their precise bases of support, in the military and civilian organization of the governments they installed, in their specific economic and social projects, in their foreign relations, and in the way in which they made their exit from the presidential palace. In these countries, the armed forces and their associates took and held power for many reasons. These rationales included enhancing their own institutional situation, protecting national security, exterminating guerrilla movements, rescuing allies such as the upper class and the church, imposing a plan for national development, and installing a more stable political system. Nevertheless, to a significant extent, the existence of all these regimes was a function of their hostility toward workers. Rather than examine all the important aspects of these governments, all their intricate causes and consequences, this book will concentrate on their relations with organized labor.

In many ways, the antilabor stance of these despotisms defined their raison d'être. Along with other factors, it motivated their seizure of power, legitimized their existence, marshaled their supporters and opponents, underlay their model of economic growth, drove their social policies, and propelled their political practices. That conflict with workers also substantially affected their tenure and termination.

The dictators had several reasons for repressing the working class. They wanted to foster economic growth, encourage investment, increase competitiveness, curb inflation, and reduce wages. To do so, they curtailed union interference with market mechanisms. The authoritarians slapped down organized workers to establish order for economic growth, social peace, and political tranquility. To eliminate perceived threats to the capitalists or themselves, they declared war on prolabor parties and ideologies, whether populist or socialist. The armed forces concentrated exceptional firepower on any Marxist or revolutionary movements.

After eliminating any armed challengers, all the authoritarian regimes examined here saw labor unions and labor parties as their most dangerous foes. Those proletarian organizations were the primary ones that were hurt both economically and politically by the dictatorship. Working-class groups were the key antagonists who potentially threatened both the autocracy and its core supporters in the propertied class. Within the opposition, they provided the best-organized social sector, the element most capable of damaging the economy, the segment most experienced at resisting antithetical governments, and the most daring and durable class-based proponents of democratization.[2]

This book will explain how working-class movements weathered these authoritarian regimes. To do so, it will address six central questions: (1) what was the status of these labor movements on the eve of the military takeovers? (2) how were they deactivated thereafter? (3) how did they manage to survive under debilitating conditions? (4) how did they change as a result? (5) how did they confront their adversaries? and (6) how did they reconstitute themselves during and after the demise of these authoritarian regimes? To answer these questions, this study will emphasize three sets of variables: the economic and social structures enveloping workers; the institutional factors affecting trade union leverage and action; and the political strengths and weaknesses of labor's party allies.[3]

Capitalist Authoritarianism in South America and Southern Europe

The main focus in this book will be on the three 1970s–1980s dictatorships in the Southern Cone (Cono Sur) of South America: the military regimes in Uruguay (1973–84), Chile (1973–90), and Argentina (1976–83). These countries' experiences with labor-repressive governments exhibited many common features and patterns. One unifying characteristic was the atomizing, free-market labor policies of the despotisms.

For purposes of reaching more reliable comparative interpretations and generalizations, the extensive analysis of the Cono Sur's atomistic models will be contrasted briefly with four corporatist episodes. The most influential of these precursor cases—that of Brazil (1964–85)—will be examined the most thoroughly. To highlight Brazil's corporatist system, it will be compared with similar experiences in Portugal (1926–74), Spain (1939–75), and Greece (1967–74).[4]

Although separated by time and space, these seven capitalist dictatorships were related types. They all approximated the concept of "bureaucratic authoritarian" regimes. Portugal, Spain, Greece, Brazil, Uruguay, Chile, and Argentina, at the beginning of the twentieth-century despotic experiences examined in this book, exhibited reasonably congruent levels of socioeconomic development, as well as Western, Mediterranean, Catholic cultures.

All seven nations were situated on the semi-periphery of the world capitalist system. When the praetorians took them over, they were middle-level countries in the global hierarchy, falling somewhere between what used to be called the First World and the Third World. They pursued delayed, dependent capitalist development, relying heavily on foreign trade and investment. Urbanization and industrialization were well advanced.

All of these autocratic regimes took office when the local entrepreneurs seemed too weak to cope with challenges from below which threatened capital accumulation and economic growth. Most of the dictatorships arose out of the distributive struggle between capital and wages. Their seizure of power usually followed a period of redistribution to wage earners which was intended to expand the domestic market.

Before the dawn of the dictatorships, working-class militance had begun to frighten property owners, who therefore abandoned liberal democracy. Losing profits, power, and legitimacy, the economic elites were rescued by the military. The subsequent authoritarian governments applied coercion to maintain stability and investment, especially at the expense of workers. The new rulers turned back laborite movements that had already begun to assert themselves. Although benefiting capitalists, these regimes were relatively autonomous from them.[5]

These right-wing, military-based governments defended capitalism from populism, socialism, or communism by suppressing demands from the lower classes. They favored the private over the public sector, the wealthy over workers, capital accumulation over redistribution, hierarchy over equity, and order over social conflict. They also aligned themselves with the West in the Cold War. Although sometimes dominated by one person, these regimes were much more institutionalized and bureaucratized than are old-fashioned patrimonial, sultanic, "caudillo" dictatorships. Even while purging so-called defects in the prior political system, the new authoritarians vowed to lead the country onward to a sanitized form of democracy, which would exclude undesirable contenders and issues.[6]

After presenting a comparative analysis of labor movements before and during these dictatorships, this study will sketch the cases of Portugal, Spain, Greece, and Brazil as prologues and prototypes for the episodes in the Southern Cone. Portugal, Spain, and Brazil became influential archetypes of capitalist authoritarian regimes. The survey of these four experiences will establish patterns of state-labor relations that will reemerge or diverge in Uruguay, Chile, and Argentina.

These background cases will clarify what was predictable or novel in the Southern Cone in the 1970s and 1980s. Some features reappeared, such as the roles of the left, the Roman Catholic Church, and foreign actors. Other facets were surprisingly distinctive in the Cono Sur. These included the use of free-market strategies and the disdain for corporatist mechanisms. Most striking was the contrast in the situation that prevailed at the end of authoritarian persecution: whereas the labor movements in Southern Europe and Brazil had gained strength, those in Uruguay, Chile, and Argentina had grown weaker.

Capitalist Authoritarianism in the Southern Cone

The three Cono Sur dictatorships in the 1970s exhibited many common features and rich comparisons. All three were exclusionary, bureaucratic authoritarian capitalist regimes. Differences in the plight of their labor movements will stand out in high relief because several variables, such as the international context and the regional setting, can be held constant.

Prior to the dictatorships, three of the most developed, most industrialized, and most unionized countries in Latin America had produced three of the most significant labor movements. Before the radicalization of numerous Latin American workers in the 1960s and 1970s, most observers of the region stressed that structural limitations, institutional shortcomings, and political handicaps inclined trade unionists toward moderate strategies. Historically, Latin American trade unions were particularly constrained by their relatively small size and the minimal leverage they could exert in dependent, underdeveloped, highly agrarian societies with labor surpluses.

Despite nationalistic and socialistic rhetoric, most working-class movements in Latin America, so it seemed to scholars, dedicated themselves to practical and prudent bargaining and benefits. Although disadvantaged in absolute terms, the minority of laborers who were engaged in unionized employment in the industrial sector at least profited from privileges denied the poor in the urban shantytowns and rural shacks. For that reason, it was argued by analysts, most organized workers confined their activities within the boundaries of the existing economic, social, and political systems.

After an early radical period of emergence, most Latin American unionists relied heavily on social-political coalitions forged by populistic parties and leaders. These coalitions usually promoted import-substituting industrialization (ISI) and welfare reforms through the state. That strategy brought growth and marginal gains to organized laborers until it began running into bottlenecks and failed to move on to heavy industry.[7]

Between the 1960s and the 1970s, populistic modi vivendi between capital and labor based on ISI and the welfare state broke down. Instead of sharing gains under the auspices of reform governments, industrialists and workers increasingly clashed over scarce resources. Short of funds and overloaded with demands, the compromise state lost its capacity to mediate class conflicts. By the late 1960s, workers' organizations displayed rising activism against employers' hardening resistance.

The traditional scholarly picture of Latin American labor as essentially concerned with bread-and-butter issues was called into question by spiraling militance and even attacks on private property just prior to the coups d'état under consideration, especially in Chile and Argentina. The unraveling of populist alliances and programs, the outbreak of autonomous worker activism, and the upsurge of ultraleftist alternatives supplied justifications for new interpretations. Social scientists began emphasizing the taking of consciousness and the radicalization by the working class. Some authors wrote about an impending revolution in Brazil, the corrosion of the elitist two-party monopoly in Uruguay, the irreversible gains of the Marxists in Chile, and the shift toward socialism of Peronism in Argentina.[8]

High expectations for working-class advances were aroused by the emergence of the Frente Amplio in Uruguay in 1971, the election of Salvador Allende in Chile in 1970, and the return of Juan Perón in Argentina in 1973. But those hopes were all dashed by takeovers by despotic regimes. The authoritarian governments that began in Uruguay in 1973, in Chile in the same year, and in Argentina in 1976 targeted urban workers—and the workers' unions and political parties—as the principal victims of political repression, social demobilization, and capital reaccumulation.

All three dictatorships engaged in unprecedented persecution of their citizens. Brutality reached gruesome heights in Argentina and Chile. All three governments espoused the national security doctrine—a Cold War doctrine that defined the military's primary mission as the expunction of domestic leftists—and virulent anti-communism. The armed forces formed the foundation of these regimes, ruling in concert with technocrats, international capitalists, and national capitalists, especially those domestic entrepreneurs who were not devastated by the reduction of tariff protection.

Although these counterrevolutionary regimes did not emphasize deepening industrialization from consumer goods to capital goods, they all based their economic policies on repressing labor and its wages. They did so partly to facilitate capital accumulation in order to move beyond the stagnation of import-substituting industrialization. The regimes tried to spur economic growth by moving in the direction of free-market solutions and pledged to stay in office as long as it took to restructure their societies in a refurbished capitalist mold.

The inability of the potent labor movements in the Southern Cone to consummate their reform projects prior to the coups d'état or to rebuff reactionary assaults thereafter calls for a reevaluation of the political roles and prospects of urban workers. The stark contrast between the aggressive labor movements prior to the coups and the cowed ones thereafter was, of course, mainly due to the tremendous repression by the armed forces. At the same time, the inability of unionists to counterattack the Uruguayan, Chilean, and Argentine dictatorships gave new credence to older visions of the underlying debilities and caution of the working class.

Now that the despots have departed, it is possible to see what happened to the working class under the veil of authoritarianism. That legacy has shaped labor's role in the new democracies. Government persecution took advantage of the soft spots in these labor movements. The praetorians exacerbated problems that had existed before the coups. Because of repression, organized labor's general weakness increased. Therefore workers did not rise up enough to destabilize the dictatorships or the restored democracies thereafter. Now that capitalist authoritarianism has, for the moment, vanished from the hemisphere, it is time to reassess the situation of laborers from the commencement of those dictatorships in the 1970s to their departure in the 1980s.[9]

The Methodology Used in This Book

This analysis will focus primarily on organized industrial workers, mainly blue-collar manual laborers. They constituted a relatively well-off minority of the working class. Nevertheless, urban manufacturing wage earners who belonged to unions tied to progressive parties constituted the politicized core and vanguard of the labor movement in the cases examined in this book. Emphasizing these workers will help keep comparisons consistent across countries.

At the same time, other key wage earners and unionists—for example, in construction, mining, and services—will be taken into account when they played a major role. In most cases, workers in the informal sector and in agriculture will be given less attention, although sometimes the working class as a whole will be discussed. Middle-class white-collar employees will also be a secondary concern, but their significant participation in unions in some countries will be noted.[10]

The role of the labor movement will be explained mainly by looking at structural, institutional, and political factors affecting workers during the dictatorships. The influence of those factors during the periods before and after the authoritarian regimes will also be examined. The state played a major role in all three categories.

All three sets of factors interacted with each other, but they can be separated for analytical purposes. Different variables exerted more weight in some cases than in others. Although these structural, institutional, and political conditions will be examined briefly in the four background cases, they will be explored extensively in the three Southern Cone countries. The general impact of these variables on labor will be spelled out in chapters 2 and 3, which treat, respectively, the situations before and during capitalist authoritarianism.

To examine structural conditions, it will be necessary to place the labor movement within a general economic context reflecting each country's level of modernization, development strategy, pace of growth, and rate of inflation. Equally important were the sectoral distribution of output and employment, especially the size of industry, the composition of the workforce, and the balance between production for external consumption and production for internal consumption. For workers, levels of employment, wages, and income distribution were also fundamental.

At the same time, the behavior and achievements of labor were determined by the institutional setting. I will investigate the types and character —the location, size, membership, leadership, programs, and strategies—of local unions as well as of national federations and confederations. Their national and international allies will be assessed. It is also important to understand the legal framework in which unions operated and their degree of independence from government control.

Key political factors conditioning the labor movement were the national political system, the status of other political actors (such as the armed forces and the church), and workers' political attitudes and ideologies. In addition to touching on those issues, I will evaluate the political possibilities for the working class by concentrating on "labor parties," itself a relative term. It refers to significant political parties that, compared to their rivals, defined themselves as exceptionally devoted to the working class and were so categorized by other contenders for power.

To varying degrees, laborite parties featured leaders who claimed to speak for the proletariat. Their membership and electoral recruitment heavily targeted unions and workers. And their programs and propaganda emphasized the concerns of that social stratum. Moreover, many workers believed that these parties represented their interests, even though the country studies presented below will show that many other laborers did not share that view.

In democracies, all major parties appeal to some workers, but prolabor parties specialize in that audience. For example, the Chilean Christian Democrats were not a labor party even though they included some unions; their constituency was much more diverse and was highly middle class. Even the loose conceptualization of "labor parties" offered here obviously fit the Socialists and Communists in Chile and the Peronists in Argentina better than it did more multiclass entities in Uruguay.

Indeed, the differing characteristics, capabilities, and histories of these parties within particular national political systems constituted crucial variables in the country studies. Particularly salient were the relations between these parties and unions. Also important was the participation of these parties in governments prior to the military takeover. As will be discussed below, organized workers were most attracted to four types of political parties—communist parties, socialist parties, populist parties, and catch-all parties—only the first three of which could be classed as labor parties.[11]

Conclusion

This study will not ask why the working class failed to carry out a social revolution. Such a rare event was always unlikely in Chile and was never on the horizon in Argentina or Uruguay. Both the fearful perceptions of right-wingers and the hopeful scenarios of left-wingers were incorrect. Democratic countries with large middle classes and professional armed forces were not susceptible to an insurrection or fundamental transformation by leftists. Radicals and even reformers also fell short of their dreams in Portugal, Spain, Greece, and Brazil. Rather than criticize or prescribe working-class behavior, in this analysis I will try to explain why it was so difficult for labor unions and parties to have achieved more than they did—before, during, and after authoritarianism. Under the circumstances, their persistence and accomplishments were remarkable.

Labor Movements before
Capitalist Authoritarianism

The plight of labor during and after the dictatorships reflected its strengths and weaknesses in the previous democracies. This chapter will canvass the structural, institutional, and political handicaps that rendered organized workers unlikely to prevail in the years leading up to the coups and vulnerable to punishment thereafter. It will also reveal the ways in which labor politics set in motion the conflicts leading to the military takeovers.

Strengths of Labor Movements

Prior to the right-wing dictatorships, the most powerful labor movements would ideally have displayed some or all of the following traits. Under the best circumstances imaginable, they would have operated under favorable structural conditions: robust economic growth, a large and protected industrial sector, high wages, low unemployment, and a welfare state. They also would have enjoyed a positive institutional setting: a high union density (the percentage of the workforce unionized), strong and united enterprise unions, exceptional organization and solidarity at the national level of federations and confederations, independence from government control, effective collective bargaining, and empowering labor legislation.

In addition, the most powerful union movements would have benefited from close ties with effective and united labor parties, which would have provided the organizational and ideological capacity to mobilize the working class on both economic and political issues. Such parties were strongest where the system of political parties was based on the interests of social classes or groups (Spain, Chile, Argentina), weaker where clientelistic, catch-all parties predominated (Uruguay), and weakest of all where the central government overshadowed a feeble party system (Portugal, Brazil, Greece).

Labor parties were also better off where political participation was greater. The average turnout of eligible voters in presidential elections shortly before the coups was 88 percent in Argentina, 79 percent in Chile, and 72 percent in Uruguay and Brazil. The bigger turnouts usually represented greater electoral participation by workers. Also crucial to the leverage of the working class was the electoral share of the labor parties, which followed the same country ranking as electoral turnout—it was higher in Argentina and Chile than in Uruguay and Brazil.

Finally, pre-coup labor movements would be expected to exhibit the greatest vigor when their parties controlled the executive branch of government. If that control was of short duration, it could intensify class conflict, as on the eve of the military uprisings in Spain, Brazil, Chile, and Argentina. Presumably, labor movements would be less threatening to the status quo when out of power, as in Portugal, Greece, and Uruguay.

On the basis of qualitative and quantitative assessments widely shared by scholars, the conditions in our country cases can be ranked as relatively high, medium, or low in terms of being favorable for the labor movement in the twilight of democracy. The most propitious conditions existed when industry occupied a large portion of the workforce, general employment was high, a large percentage of the workforce was unionized, federations and confederations were healthy, union organizations were unified and independent of state control and had firm links to powerful political parties, and prolabor parties controlled the government. Table 2.1 rates these factors only as to their positive effects on working-class leverage. For example, although an all-encompassing national confederation existed in Greece, it is categorized as "low" because the confederation constrained rather than fortified the labor movement.

On the eve of authoritarian takeover, Argentina, Chile, Spain, and Uruguay, roughly in that order, clearly possessed the strongest labor movements. Much weaker labor movements existed in Greece, Brazil, and Portugal. When rated on most measures of industrialization, as well as on measures of the strengths of union and party institutions, the Southern Cone had a distinctive profile, similar to that of Spain but quite different from those of Brazil, Portugal, and Greece.[1]

TABLE 2.1
Ratings of Factors Affecting Strengths of Pre-Coup Labor Movements in Southern Europe, Brazil, and the Southern Cone

Factor	Portugal	Spain	Greece	Brazil	Uruguay	Chile	Argentina
Structural factors							
Industry strength	Low	Medium	Medium	Low	Medium	Medium	High
Employment[a]			High	Medium	Medium	High	High
Institutional factors							
Union density	Low	Medium	High	Low	High	High	High
Federations and Confederations	Low	High	Low	Low	Medium	Medium	High
Unity	Low	Low	Low	Low	Medium	Medium	High
Independence	Medium	High	Low	Low	High	Medium	High
Political factors							
Party ties	Low	High	Low	Low	Medium	High	High
Party strength	Low	High	Low	Low	Low	Medium	High
Role in Government	Low	High	Low	Medium	Low	High	High

[a] No reliable figures on pre-coup employment in Portugal and Spain could be found.

A similar conclusion can be derived for just the four South American cases by aggregating the variables in the previous table and drawing on the country literature in order to rank the situation of the Argentine, Brazilian, Chilean, and Uruguayan labor movements from best to worst (see table 2.2). The strongest labor movements thrived where economic conditions favored manufacturers and their workers, where unions were plentiful and powerful, where working-class parties were large and well organized, and where advocates for the proletariat occupied the government. According to these indicators as well as others, the working class faced a more hospitable environment in Argentina and Chile than in Uruguay or Brazil.

Constraints on Labor Movements

Structural Constraints

Most of the time, in most countries, economic factors are the most important determinants of the lot of labor. In the developing world, the rates of growth, inflation, and employment usually have a bigger impact on the standard of living of laborers than does the action of unions. Wages are mainly set by demand and supply in the labor market and by labor productivity. The normal factors giving unions important bargaining power—steady prosperity, full employment, government support, organizational

TABLE 2.2
Ratings of Brazil and the Southern Cone Countries with Regard to Factors Affecting
the Strength of Pre-Coup Labor Movements

Factor	Best ←			→ Worst
Structural conditions	Argentina	Chile	Uruguay	Brazil
Institutional features	Argentina	Chile	Uruguay	Brazil
Party assets	Argentina	Chile	Uruguay	Brazil
Roles in government	Chile	Argentina	Brazil	Uruguay

density and strength, and financial wherewithal—are often absent in poor countries. Although many studies show that unions probably do increase wages, the impact is debatable and is frequently not very great.

Economic factors affecting the working class are shaped by both the market and the state. Within given economic boundaries, different labor politics and ideologies—especially as expressed through sympathetic or unsympathetic governments—can produce divergent outcomes for workers. Labor organizations can of course accentuate or mitigate the impact of economic conditions, especially when they can influence the state's large role in shaping macroeconomic variables. Government intervention can distort market patterns; for example, the low wages in South America under military rule were clearly influenced by the policies of the dictatorships. The interaction of the state and the market is crucial to the economic obstacles or opportunities confronting workers.[2]

Almost regardless of regime type, macroeconomic conditions can be extremely harmful or helpful to workers. Examples of the centrality of economic trends can be seen under contrasting regimes in the Spanish and Chilean cases. In Spain, a depression debilitated labor under Francisco Franco in the 1940s, growth stimulated its strength—still under Franco—in the 1950s and 1960s, and stagflation undermined it under his successors in the 1970s and 1980s. Economically, workers did badly under dictatorship, then well under dictatorship, and finally poorly under democracy. At the same time, Franco's repression made their situation even worse in the 1940s and less positive than it might have been in the 1950s and 1960s. In Chile, labor fared very badly in economic terms under the despotism of Augusto Pinochet in 1973–77 and 1982–84 but relatively well under Pinochet in 1978–81 and 1985–90. They enjoyed even better circumstances under democracy in 1964–73 and 1990–95.

In the countries discussed here, as elsewhere, unions' fortunes usually followed the business cycle. Unions grew during prosperity and lost members during depression. By the same token, their bargaining efforts and strikes were more frequent and effective during booms than during crashes. They mainly pushed for wage increases, especially when workers were ravaged by inflation.

For unions, the cost of a strike rose during economic downturns characterized by high unemployment. Therefore, workers counted more on unions during good economic conditions but relied more heavily on government and politicians during bad economic times. In recessions, they switched from union mobilization to party activity, accompanied by political activism in public demonstrations. They lobbied for policies to counteract the business cycle.[3]

In developing countries, labor has repeatedly been asked to restrict its consumption in order to facilitate the capital accumulation necessary for national economic progress. When there have been severe resource scarcities and inequalities, conflict between wages and profits has been rife. Therefore union leaders have had to walk a fine line between satisfying the economic demands of the rank and file and satisfying the desires of the ruling elites in management, government, and the armed forces.[4]

From the 1930s to the 1960s, many Latin American labor movements flourished during the heyday of import-substituting industrialization, which was often accompanied by welfare reforms in the cities. As the working class expanded through urbanization and industrialization, so did parties appealing to labor. And the countries of the Southern Cone, especially Argentina, differed from most other Latin American countries in having relatively low levels of unemployment, which favored unionists. Given the historic vitality of industrialization, unions, and parties, the pre-coup labor movements in Argentina, Chile, and Uruguay were probably the strongest in Latin America.

By the second half of the twentieth century, however, import-substituting industrialization and populistic coalitions including industrialists, the middle class, and organized workers had lost momentum in the Cono Sur. A relatively easy stage, characterized by replacement of foreign consumer goods and placating of the urban middle and working classes, had given way to capital scarcity amidst multiplying contenders. Rural laborers and rural-urban migrants added their demands. Excessive pressures on slim resources caused inflation to skyrocket and growth to sputter. From 1945 to 1975, the three Southern Cone countries' share of the region's gross national product (GNP) fell. While all of Latin America's GNP grew an average of

6.2 percent per year, the Southern Cone only registered a growth rate of 3.5 percent.

Since industrialization did not keep pace with urbanization, manufacturing's share of the total workforce stagnated in the Southern Cone. In the years leading up to the coups, agricultural employment shrank, while the service sector ballooned. As in all industrialized countries, unskilled workers became increasingly marginalized. Although unions recognized that there was often a tradeoff between employment and wages, many witnessed a deterioration on both fronts.[5]

In all the countries in this study, the largest single segment of organized labor came from manufacturing, which spearheaded the union movement. Although the most militant workers typically belonged to industrial unions connected to reformist parties, they only accounted for a minority of trade unionists. In Latin America, they were encircled by vast numbers of nonindustrial unionists, unorganized urban workers, unemployed and semiemployed laborers, rural workers, and white-collar employees. The bulging service sector reduced the political weight of industrial workers.

Long before the coups in the Southern Cone, economies of scarcity—and factors such as relatively small manufacturing sectors and large, underutilized labor surpluses—limited the political strength of the proletariat in most of Latin America. The lack of full employment made it difficult for unions to extract higher wages by restricting the supply of labor. Although segmented labor markets and skill differentials still gave unions leverage, they were strongest among the skilled workers, who needed them the least, and weakest among the unskilled laborers, who needed them the most.[6]

Institutional Constraints

In developing countries, most unions flourish at the enterprise level rather than across entire industries in federations or in multi-industry national confederations. Union density is typically low. Trade unions often function as pressure groups vis-à-vis governments more than as bargaining agents vis-à-vis industries. Thus in these countries unions' dealings with political parties and the state are more important than they are in more industrialized Western labor relations systems.

Labor parties play a significant role in unions at all levels, including the shop floor, but particularly at the national level of federations and confederations. Action at all three strata is crucial. Collective bargaining in the plant deals with special local conditions and necessities without the restraints imposed by cooperation with other unions higher up the organizational ladder. Bargaining at the branch or sectoral level helps workers learn about each others' problems and transcend their fragmentation vis-à-vis an entire industry. Mobilization at the national level allows unions to lobby the government and tackle broader issues. However, the strength of national confederations is chiefly political and is sometimes merely symbolic, because most worker loyalties and finances go to local or sectoral unions.

In many developing countries, trade unions have at least nominally radical leadership. That opposition to the status quo has been common because of highly conflictual battles over sparse resources, extreme income inequalities, repressive capitalists and governments, and Marxian or populist-nationalist influences. Despite the appearance of radicalized leaders, however, the behavior of unionists has rarely been radical or revolutionary.

In less developed countries, the politicized labor movement commonly dwarfs other social organizations. It speaks for some nonunionized disadvantaged groups, offers an alternative vision of a national project, and uses its parties to try to influence the state. With very interventionist governments, the state is a crucial economic actor for unionists—the source of macroeconomic policies, the regulator of labor relations, a participant in collective bargaining, and a major employer. The government can also issue legislation on job security, wages, benefits, and working conditions, and can pressure companies to make concessions.[7]

Labor relations systems in Latin America have been distinctive for their high level of government intrusion, elaborate legal edifice, and decentralization of collective bargaining. Such systems have applied mainly to industrial workers in the private sector, although government unions have also been important. Also prevalent has been intense class, ideological, and political conflict amidst widespread poverty.

In Brazil and Chile, as well as Argentina, unions exercised representational monopolies, since all three labor systems derived from a corporatist rather than a pluralist model. Chilean unions were strongest at the enterprise level, Brazilian and Uruguayan unions at the federation level, and Argentine unions at both the federation and confederation levels. Brazil, Uruguay, and Argentina boasted industrywide collective bargaining, in contrast with the plant-level negotiating dominant in most of Latin America. In Chile as well as Uruguay and Argentina, collective bargaining was unusually frequent by comparison with the rest of the hemisphere, including Brazil, where unions were strong on paper but weak in practice.

As a result of institutional features, Brazil had an extremely pallid union system controlled by the state. Labor organizations possessed little power within the factory or the national arena. Uruguay boasted a solid system of unions, but the unions had no great influence among political parties. Chile maintained a democratic but institutionally weak union system, highly dependent on political parties for representation beyond the plant.

Whereas healthy labor parties compensated for frail unions in Chile, the opposite balance prevailed on the other side of the Andes. Argentina possessed a union system distant from the worker bases but with unusual clout in the national arena. Often outweighing political parties, the highest level of the Argentine trade union hierarchy crafted negotiations and pacts with the state and the armed forces.

Because of the necessity of bargaining with parties and the state, dualist labor movements developed prior to all the coups. Union bosses had to tend to the material needs of their followers and to the national needs of their parties. Especially in the Southern Cone and in Spain, the leaders of labor parties and unions won followings because of their ability simultaneously to pursue narrow, short-term concrete benefits and broad, long-term political projects.

The more incremental, moderate position was usually associated with the rank and file, and the more political, radical orientation with the leadership. These interlocking and conflicting clientelistic and ideological missions differentiated these movements, theoretically, both from economistic unionism purely committed to practical gains and from radical unionism totally dedicated to challenging the political order. The economistic model presumed overwhelmingly pragmatic leaders as well as followers, whereas the radical model required a highly politicized union base as well as leadership.[8]

Pre-coup labor systems in Southern Europe—with the partial exception of Spain—were also noteworthy for the feebleness of both base-level and upper-level unions. Therefore workers preferred the political marketplace to the economic one, emphasizing government legislation more than collective bargaining. They relied heavily on political parties to mediate with the interventionist state.[9]

In Latin America, the likelihood that labor unions and parties would achieve grandiose national transformations was reduced by deficiencies in the organization of those unions and parties, by schisms within these heterogeneous labor movements, and by government regulations on unions. Many of the individual trade unions remained tiny and anemic. They were divided among blue- and white-collar groups, urban and rural organizations, and competing political parties or factions. Many of them lacked muscular national federations and confederations to represent them to parties and the state. It thus proved difficult to consolidate the labor movement internally, to forge unified bonds with any single party, or to weave together coalitions between the proletariat and its potential allies in the white-collar sector, the urban shantytowns, and the countryside.

Labor laws made it attractive to unions to have political parties help them deal with the state. On a spectrum ranging from almost full state control over unions to virtual independence of unions, our South American cases would array themselves in the following order: Brazil, Chile, Argentina, Uruguay. Although labor legislation affected union behavior, legal theory and practice were not always congruent. For example, the law allowed for a national confederation in Brazil but not in Chile, yet such an organization had more success in the latter country. In all cases, the key to the impact of labor codes was their implementation by the government and their manipulation by labor unions and parties.[10]

The ways in which industrial laborers and their unions and parties operated in national politics prior to the military interruptions shaped their subsequent situations. In Uruguay workers expressed their grievances primarily by functioning as a pressure group on the government bureaucracy, in Chile they worked through national parties, and in Argentina they worked through powerful unions. In all three cases, as in most of the rest of the world, unions most often pursued incremental or defensive objectives rather than grand political projects, although the Chileans were more ambitious than the Argentines or Uruguayans.

Political Constraints

In all of the countries under discussion, the working class suffered from a number of problems in addition to inadequate economic leverage and insufficient social solidarity. Throughout most of their history, these labor movements also had to contend with obstinacy and oppression from intransigent employers and governments. The coups studied here constituted a quantum leap in the negative forces deployed against labor unions and their parties, but mistreatment and repression were scarcely novel experiences for urban workers. Over the years, industrial laborers had adjusted to these inhospitable environments in a variety of ways, principally by relying on trade unions and reformist political parties. However, those organizations proved no match for tanks.

Unions opted to act mainly in the economic or political markets by evaluating which methods entailed the lowest costs and the highest payoffs. That tradeoff depended on the relative resistance of employers and governments to union demands. It also reflected the relative strength of unions in the private and public spheres. In Latin America, the rigidity of the capitalists (who had far greater resources than the unionists) and the ample role of the state caused labor to emphasize political action. In many cases, workers found political factors easier to change than economic constraints. Compared to employers, governments were more likely to be generous, especially during periods of political uncertainty, when faced with the danger of being defeated in elections or being overthrown by a military coup.

Stronger politically than economically, most trade unions had more clout in the public arena than on the factory floor. Because labor unions and parties in Latin America rarely held political power, they often won concessions by threatening the president of the country with strikes and disruptions. To avoid destabilization, the administration might then grant favors to workers or persuade industrialists to meet some of labor's demands.

In South America at least, this style of "political bargaining" usually functioned best with an elected centrist administration. Under neutral democratic governments, labor sometimes held its fire to avoid worse alternatives. At other times, it mobilized to obtain concessions or to increase the chances of its allies replacing a government unable to maintain order. Middle-of-the-road governments could forestall challenges from the left by placating unionists or could avoid challenges from the right by suppressing unionists.

Playing on the government's fragility, this politicized approach by labor was a risky strategy of brinkmanship. With imperfect knowledge in a climate of uncertainty, labor leaders had to make intricate calculations about opportunity costs and future probabilities. Workers had to apply enough pressure to elicit benefits but not repression. They lost when the embattled president unleashed the military or succumbed to a coup d'état.[11]

This model of political bargaining encountered severe problems when avowedly prolabor or antilabor presidents took office. Under a government run by labor's own political partners, the politicized model would suggest a decline in union activism. It might be thought that workers would exercise restraint because that administration would meet their needs without being badgered and because disorder would endanger the administration's tenure. Instead, escalating working-class activities—as seen in Spain, Brazil, Chile, and Argentina—undermined those friendly governments, which the elites and armed forces were quite willing to scuttle.

Indeed, unions proved most likely to emphasize political action under prolabor governments. The potential costs imposed on laborers by those governments were either very low or unlikely to be exacted. Meanwhile, the possible benefits from laborite governments were very high and were likely to be delivered. Those benefits could include government promotion of high wages and fuller employment, redistribution of income downward, support for industrialization, the application of pressure to businesses to make them heed union demands, provision of social services, enhancement of union legal powers, and strengthening of labor parties. Given the rare occurrence and often short duration of prolabor governments, unions were tempted to maximize their mobilization and payoffs. The problem for labor was to calibrate its political activism so that friendly governments would not disintegrate into macroeconomic chaos—especially inflation—or fall victim to an election or a coup.

Under adversarial governments, especially right-wing authoritarian ones, political bargaining became ineffective most of the time. Unions faced a hostile regime prepared to respond to protests with troops. The costs of political activism were quite high and the benefits quite low. Worse, the government might impose the costs whether or not labor became active. Those potential costs included the implementation of antilabor economic policies to reduce wages and employment, the redistribution of income upward, discouragement of industrialization, support of obdurate employers, cuts in social services, attacks on worker organizations, restrictions on unions' legal rights, and attacks on labor's political allies.

Prior to authoritarian rule, workers relied heavily on prolabor parties. Nevertheless, large segments of the working class were neither represented nor controlled by those organizations, let alone dedicated to their broader programs. As chapters 5 through 7, on the Southern Cone, will demonstrate, scholars probing beneath labor's formal ties to parties discovered repeatedly that many workers lacked intense political commitments. Whatever their methodological virtues and defects, all studies of working-class political opinions and voting—whether scientific samples or smaller sets of interviews—found the largest and most enduring attachment to labor parties in Argentina and Chile rather than in Uruguay.

Of all the Southern Cone parties, the Peronists attracted the most solid backing from laborers and the largest electoral percentages. In contrast with Argentina and Chile, Uruguay showed hardly any correlation between social class and voting patterns. Nevertheless, scattered survey results tended to indicate that the workers possessed more faith in electoral, representative government in Uruguay and Chile than in unstable Argentina.

No electoral or attitude surveys in the Southern Cone turned up a majority of organized workers in favor of socialist or Marxist alternatives. Prior to the coups, the highest propensities toward these alternatives cropped up in Chile and Uruguay. There, studies revealed, respectively, 46 percent and 23 percent of urban workers in favor of socialist party coalitions. Not surprisingly, even laborers attached to the Marxist parties devoted much more energy to immediate necessities than to long-range utopias.

Some leftward movement in working-class electoral preferences transpired everywhere in the years immediately preceding the breakdowns of democracy. That shift could be seen in the Broad Front's draining of worker support away from the historic two parties in Uruguay in 1971, the rising percentage for the Popular Unity coalition (especially the Socialist Party) in Chile in 1973, and the emergence of the Peronist left in Argentina. This phenomenon also appeared in other countries prior to military takeovers—for example, it can be seen in the growth of the Popular Front in Spain, and the gains for the populists and Communists in Brazil.

In Europe as in Latin America, most workers have not pursued revolutionary objectives, even when their unions or parties issued inflammatory declarations. Although some European leftists have attracted higher percentages of working-class votes (e.g., 66–75%) than did their counterparts in South America, others have rarely garnered more than 50 percent of urban wage earners. In Western Europe, the level of unionization has tended to be higher than the level of total electoral support for labor parties. The reverse situation has typified Latin America, where labor has been stronger politically than institutionally or economically.

In most countries, labor parties have had trouble capturing anywhere near all the worker voters, or a majority of all voters. Working-class parties have always grappled with the dilemma of deciding whether to maintain the social and ideological purity of their dedication to the proletariat or to court other social groups to strive for electoral majorities. That dilemma has also bedeviled unions. They have wanted labor parties loyal to their interests but also capable of winning elections. If a single labor party has dominated, as in Argentina, that party has had to include nonlabor groups in order to take office; if a multiparty system has prevailed, as in Chile, the labor parties have had to form coalitions with nonlabor groups.[12]

In all seven of the countries I shall examine, political parties proved very important to unions. They supplied workers with union and party leaders, legal aid, legislative victories, influence with government agencies, media outlets, political education, and allies from other social sectors, such as professionals and students. An interdependent relationship developed, as these reformist parties also relied heavily on labor for their support, unity, and achievements. Indeed, union mobilization and cohesion often preceded advances by prolabor parties. In the Southern Cone, parties dominated the relationship in Chile, unions did so in Argentina, and neither side was dominant in Uruguay.

Four different types of parties most appealed to labor: communist parties, socialist parties, populist parties, and catch-all parties (see table 2.3).

In all of the countries discussed here, the Communists played a special role. They were fiercely ideological and dedicated to the proletariat. Often persecuted (particularly during the Cold War), they normally acquired greater strength within the unions than within the national electorate. Despite their revolutionary doctrine, they usually behaved in a moderate, gradualist fashion. The Communists participated in prolabor governments prior to the downfall of democracy in Spain and Chile but did so nowhere after the demise of despotism, except fleetingly in Portugal. Although they gained force during the dictatorship, they receded after democratization.

Socialist parties were major actors in Portugal, Spain, Greece, Uruguay, and Chile. The socialistic Party of Workers in Brazil could also be included in this category. The socialists and the populists were by far the most successful labor parties. The socialists were deeply involved with working-class organizations, to which they added middle-class elements. Prior to the right-wing military takeovers, the socialists were often highly ideological and even revolutionary. After the takeovers, however, they usually evolved in a social democratic direction. Although normally immobilized under the dictatorship, socialist parties experienced notable successes at creating labor governments both before and especially after military rule.

The most significant nonideological, multiclass parties for laborers were the populists. They gave labor special emphasis, participated actively in unions, and galvanized significant labor movements and governments. Their momentum often depended on charismatic leaders and redistributive programs. The best example was Peronism in Argentina, while personalistic vehicles in Brazil (such as the PTB) constituted pale imitations.

The organizations least intensively linked to labor were the nonideological, multiclass, centrist, catch-all parties. Not really "labor parties," they

TABLE 2.3
Characteristics of Parties Attracting Labor

Characteristics	Type of Party			
	Communist	Socialist	Populist	Catch-all
Class emphasis	Labor	Labor/Mixed	Labor/Mixed	Mixed
Union ties	Strong	Medium	Medium	Weak
Ideological emphasis	High	Medium	Low	Low
Electoral scope	Low	Medium	High	High
Success under democracy	Low	High	High	High
Success under dictatorship	High	Low	Low	Medium

maintained loose relationships with workers. They were usually not significantly involved with unions and only rallied laborers during election campaigns. They were equally devoted to other social sectors. These organizations did not put together powerful labor movements or governments. As we will see, these nonlabor parties were most important in Uruguay (e.g., the Colorados) and, to a lesser extent, Brazil (e.g., the Party of the Brazilian Democratic Movement) and Chile (e.g., the Christian Democrats).

In Uruguay and Chile, as often happens with labor movements in capitalist countries, union affiliations with parties were pluralistic and subject to keen competition. Only in Argentina did one party hegemonize unions, although identification with the party was more important than was the party itself. Unlike the Chilean Socialists and Communists, the Peronist party was more a creature of the labor movement than a mighty machine in its own right.

Among our South American cases, Chile boasted the most structured, programmatic, ideological labor parties dominating the worker movement. The Marxist orientation of the predominant Socialists (Partido Socialista [PS]) and Communists (Partido Communista [PC]) proved exceptionally successful at politicizing the workers, raising their class consciousness, and leading them in an offensive truly intended to restructure society. Most Argentine workers, like many of their counterparts in Brazil and elsewhere in Latin America, shunned Marxism to follow a populist movement electrified by magnetic leaders.

Although their links with labor remained thin, Uruguay's clientelistic, multiclass machine parties—the Reds and the Whites (Colorados and Blancos)—were deeply embedded in that polity and society. The new Broad Front—a collage of leftist mini-parties—claimed to speak for labor but actually attracted a diverse following. Uruguay also deviated from the other cases in that its coup was not preceded by a labor government, and this fact may have contributed to a lower level of human rights atrocities after the military takeover.

Both before and after the coups, all the labor parties, despite noteworthy achievements, suffered from limitations and shortcomings. In spite of dazzling gains, Uruguay's Broad Front entertained scant hope of breaking the stranglehold of the two traditional parties. The Popular Unity in Chile struggled to overcome a minority social base, acrimonious divisions within its own camp, and anti-communist enmity from its opponents at home and abroad. Peronism endured years of proscription and the loss of its founder. After smashing these potent but vulnerable movements, the armed forces accelerated economic trends that reduced the leverage of the working class, aggravated divisions within and restrictions upon trade unions, bludgeoned parties sympathetic to urban labor, and constricted the space available for worker activism of any kind.[13]

In the period leading up to the coups in the Southern Cone, the greatest radicalism among workers seemed to be associated not with the longstanding industrial unionists but rather with a minority of younger laborers. Newer to politicization, those Young Turks often worked in smaller industries or even outside the industrial sector. Sometimes they collaborated with student radicals. They prodded the traditional labor parties to be more daring. Some of these newcomers identified with fresher, more revolutionary political options, which borrowed luster from the Cuban Revolution.

Attempts by maximalist leftists to galvanize the working class, however, scored few successes anywhere. Among guerrilla groups, the Uruguayan Tupamaros, the Chilean Miristas, and the Argentine Montoneros attracted few recruits from organized labor. The same fate befell ultraleftists in Brazil and Southern Europe. They failed to mount political alternatives capable of challenging the labor parties for the adherence of the masses or the ruling groups for the control of the nation. Instead, they provided an excuse for reactionaries to crack down on all of the left and labor, and then suffered swift annihilation by the regular military and/or paramilitary antagonists.

Conditions on the Eve of the Coup

Until the 1970s, most of the literature on Latin American unionists painted a picture of handicapped working-class movements. To varying degrees, they were not fervently committed to or capable of fundamental socioeconomic changes advocated by powerful labor parties. If accurate, how can that portrait of relative weakness and reserve be reconciled with scores of accounts of mounting worker radicalism prior to the coups? What elicited such savage antilabor reactions from the armed forces acting on behalf of the frightened upper and middle classes? If, with the partial exception of Chile, labor unions and parties in South America presented no irresistible threat to the established order, why were they viewed as such dangerous enemies, who had to be curtailed?

Five explanations can be offered for this apparent contradiction between labor's behavior and its image, between its potential and the way it was treated. One reason for the overreaction to worker mobilization was that these were conservative societies that had slender resources and suffered from galloping inflation and industrial stagnation. Their precarious manufacturing elites depended heavily on the state, foreign capital, and low labor costs. Therefore, even relatively mild challenges from the organized working class and its political partners appeared inordinately threatening. The narrow margin for capital accumulation made nonrevolutionary pressures seem menacing. In the politics of scarcity, actors often behaved as though they were playing a zero-sum game.

A second reason for the disjuncture between labor's allegedly moderate inclinations and its militant reputation was that the mobilization, politicization, and radicalization of the worker movements were represented in an exaggerated fashion. This was done by panicky opponents who wanted to justify a blitz against popular forces. At the same time, idealistic proponents of labor movements were eager to embellish the strength of their parties and followers. Overheated rhetoric on both sides fanned misperceptions and confrontations.[14]

A third factor was the dread of communism, embodied in Latin America by the Cuban Revolution. Even though conditions in prerevolutionary Cuba bore little resemblance to those in South America, Fidel Castro's takeover inspired some imitators, leftward movement, and right-wing phobias. Castro's achievements made leftist organizations look more radical than they were and made the guardians of law and order paranoid. Among elites, fears spread that fire-breathing populists, anarchists, socialists, and communists might usher in a Soviet-style revolution.[15]

The fourth reason is that the crumbling of populist alliances, the deteriorating position of wage earners, and the rise of newly energized urban and rural worker groups did engender some extraordinary working-class radicalism prior to the coups. That is, the standard profile of Latin American labor as reasonably pragmatic and compromising, like industrial workers in

most societies, probably was still an accurate picture of a majority of unionists, but a militant minority of worker maximalists had emerged. The ruling elites reacted to that dangerous minority by punishing all labor unions
and parties.

A fifth and final explanation is that in Spain, Brazil, Chile, and Argentina, prolabor governments took power before the coups. Those administrations permitted and encouraged a very unusual level of worker
stridency. Sometimes labor actions went farther than the governments intended, conveying an image of spontaneous social combustion. And in the
eyes of the capitalists and the armed forces, some governments that were
not loyal to labor were nevertheless lax toward labor and therefore also
risky. Even in advanced industrial societies with more surplus to distribute,
such intense levels of labor militance, although nonrevolutionary, also
might have provoked crackdowns, if not such heavy-handed dictatorships.

The prolabor governments in South America went through four stages
typically associated with populist episodes in Latin America: (1) wage hikes
and other gains for labor; (2) spiraling inflation and labor-industrial conflict
as demand outran supply; (3) pressures from capitalists and the middle class
for stabilization, resulting in ineffectual government efforts at austerity; and
(4) a military coup d'état to impose economic and political order.[16]

The taking of office by a prolabor government in Spain, Brazil, Chile,
and Argentina created dilemmas as well as opportunities for trade unionists. On the one hand, South American unionists wanted to cooperate with
their elected representatives. On the other hand, they wanted to capitalize
on having their friends in power. Trying to extract maximal benefits with a
short time horizon, the workers clashed with the ruling labor parties. They
sometimes abandoned those organizations and even switched to rivals. This
behavior was visible in Chile under Allende and in Argentina under Juan
and Isabel Perón.

In other cases, the ruling labor party itself vacillated between serving the
government and serving its working-class constituency. The labor movement was torn between the need to deliver benefits to unionists and the need
to satisfy broader constituencies. It wrestled with agonizing tradeoffs between carrying out redistribution and managing macroeconomic stability.

The ascension to power of prolabor parties inspired the workers to take
their activism and demands to new heights. They were often undeterred by
government pleas for patience, austerity, and productivity. Union membership mushroomed. In Chile and Argentina, as well as, for instance, Brazil
and Spain, the presence of a laborite government—promising advances

while calling for sacrifices—led to accelerating divisions and politicization among the workers and their parties. Labor's struggle against its enemies in the higher social strata coincided with an internecine fight for control of the worker movement. That fratricidal battle intensified now that control of the movement offered exceptional opportunities under a government of labor's sympathizers.

The dual role of the labor parties—which provided both clientelistic services and ideological aspirations—proved more difficult to fulfil while in office. Both so-called "economistic" and "radical" groups challenged their governments, fostering the impression that the administration had lost control of its constituency. Of course, the capitalists opposed both sets of labor demands, especially those from the more radical groups.

The labor parties in power encountered disobedience and resistance primarily from economistic workers. These laborers demanded "bread-and-butter" benefits for themselves. After years of supporting politicians promising incremental gains, they wanted immediate material rewards rather than exhortations for continued dedication to long-range ideological goals.

The labor governments found it equally hard to discipline smaller clusters of radical workers. These groups supported promises of ultimate revolutionary change for the proletariat and believed that their parties were not pursuing ideological objectives avidly and rapidly enough. These increasingly maximalist elements wanted even less governmental attention to merely incremental improvements and more sweeping action to turn society on its head.

Under laborite governments, the ideological temper rose among labor's proponents as well as its opponents. Radical proposals and imagery emanated both from parties and from unions. Outbidding among some members of the governing coalition generated promises of revolutionary advances. Those pronouncements sometimes exceeded their capabilities or those of their followers, as seen in the fiery rhetoric of the Spanish and Chilean Socialists. Conservatives reacted to this discourse by warning that the left was about to take over by force. Although a canard, that charge was used by the military to justify intervention.

As political and social conflict escalated, it became increasingly unlikely that either workers or employers would trust the other group to sustain a compromise between wages and profits. Amidst such high uncertainty, both groups heavily discounted future opportunities. They concentrated on maximizing their gains and minimizing their losses in the short term. Therefore, workers became more insistent in their immediate demands, clamoring for wage hikes. Capitalists became more intractable, disinvesting as rapidly as possible. More members of both groups—especially the propertied class—became willing to dispense with democracy in order to impose their own maximalist preferences by force. In theory, such an outcome could have occurred either through a socialist or through a capitalist dictatorship; given the balance of forces, the latter was much more likely than the former.

From the point of view of the Southern Cone business elites, on the eve of the coups d'état labor unions and parties seemed to have broken the informal rules of the political game. Following the populistic simultaneous promotion of industry and welfare, it appeared that workers were no longer willing to accept compromise and stalemate with the middle and upper classes. In Uruguay, the labor movement distanced itself from the two-party system to promote class conflict and a new leftist political alternative. In Chile, laborers tried to transform capitalism into socialism. And in Argentina, the devotion of workers to Peronism and to increasingly leftist ideologies destabilized the economic as well as the political system.[17]

On the brink of the coups, the labor movements appeared more formidable and radical than they were. In fact, many unionists were already exhausted and dejected by the efforts and frustrations of trying to put through fundamental reforms. They had already lost a great deal of thrust, cohesion, and optimism, especially in Brazil, Uruguay, and Argentina. The military takeovers sealed the fate of these labor movements and choked off any rapid recuperation.

In Spain and Chile, the workers took the biggest fall because they had risen the farthest. Where labor and its party companions had been unusually integrated and radical, some had experienced and still had high hopes for a leap toward socialism. Only in Spain and—for a fleeting moment—in Chile did the workers marshal significant resistance to the military onslaught. And only in Spain did some units of the armed forces side with the left. The resistance was quickly snuffed out in Chile, while in Spain it paid a stupendous price to stave off defeat for three years. Elsewhere, the labor movements had no immediate recourse but submission to capitalist authoritarianism.

Labor Movements under Capitalist Authoritarianism

An examination of how workers fared under capitalist authoritarianism in the Southern Cone and in Brazil, Greece, Spain, and Portugal shows many commonalities and contrasts among the country cases. In this chapter, I explicate the different approaches of the dictatorships to labor and then survey how structural, institutional, and political constraints held laborers in check. Before those long-term measures took effect, however, working-class unions and parties were cowed primarily by thunderous violence.

Repression of Labor by the Authoritarian Regimes

Although the military takeovers had many causes, the governments they put in place all gave high priority to quashing worker organizations and unrest. Upon toppling the existing democratic governments, the dictators deployed more than enough firepower to quell the labor unions and parties. The armed forces accused many laborers and other citizens of being enemies who had backed the wrong side prior to the takeover. The victors carried out murders, arrests, kidnappings, tortures, beatings, dismissals, exiles, and other abuses on a massive scale, mainly against the working class.

One scholarly attempt to quantify the human rights violations by the armed forces in South America estimated the number of deaths and disappearances in Brazil as 100, in Uruguay as 36, in Chile as 4,000, and in Argentina as 10,000. The rough total numbers of political prisoners and exiles were, respectively, 25,000 and 10,000 in Brazil; 60,000 and 500,000 in

Uruguay; 60,000 and 40,000 in Chile; and 30,000 and 500,000 in Argentina. Relative to their population, Chile and Argentina ranked way ahead in per capita killings, while Uruguay took first place for prisoners and exiles, with Brazil lagging far behind in all categories.[1]

The varying ferocity of the repression reflected the relative strengths of the countries' labor movements. Both prior labor mobilization and subsequent state terror were greatest in Argentina and Chile and least in Brazil. Military violence was also comparatively mild against rickety working-class organizations in Portugal and Greece. Except for Brazil, where the labor government in power at the time of the coup had been a timid one, the armed forces engaged in more overkill where labor parties had actually held power: Spain, Chile, and Argentina.

After the initial blitzkrieg against the proletariat, the praetorians used more surgical strikes. They practiced selective repression to hold down the labor movement and selective institutional tinkering to let off steam or sow confusion. Coercion provides the fundamental explanation for the inability of the workers and their political allies—already hamstrung in many ways—to lash back. Within the confines of these police states, however, variations emerged which reflected national conditions and shaped future possibilities.

In Greece as well as South America, the military governments were motivated in part by the national security doctrine, which focused their attention on internal leftist "cancers"—mainly labor unions and parties—on the organic body politic. In all the countries, the anti-communist fervor of the armed forces directed the most lethal bombardment at the Marxist parties and unions. In the Southern Cone, this selectivity within the overall attack on working-class organizations proved most damaging in Chile, where the Communists and Socialists played a predominant role. The Chilean movement also suffered somewhat more than its regional counterparts because Pinochet's military regime delivered more severe and sudden political and economic shocks to the workers. Antilabor measures intensified gradually in the other South American cases.[2]

The Southern Cone dictatorships adopted broadly similar policies against labor unions and parties, although different emphases emerged. All of the militaries contained minority factions disposed toward populist approaches to workers, but those tendencies were quickly stamped out. None of the regimes followed the Brazilian and Southern European path of strictly enforcing corporatist controls, although some authoritarian groups in the Southern Cone suggested that model. Instead, the three regimes opted for a policy of devastation of labor, followed by the dismantling of

TABLE 3.1

Ratings of Brazil and the Southern Cone Countries with Regard to Factors Affecting the Strength of Post-Coup Labor Movements

Factor	Best ←—————————————————→ Worst			
Structural conditions	Brazil	Uruguay	Argentina	Chile
Institutional features	Brazil	Argentina	Uruguay	Chile
Political factors	Brazil	Uruguay	Argentina	Chile

working-class organizations, and accompanied by market discipline. In short, they atomized the labor movement.

In the Southern Cone, the military set out first to crush the most militant, radicalized, autonomous, leftist minorities among the workers. Then the armed forces tried to eviscerate, control, or co-opt the remainder of organized laborers. To oversimplify the patterns, we will see that the Uruguayan military closed down the entire representative system for parties and unions while maintaining some direct Ministry of Labor dealings with workers. The Chilean armed forces directed most of their ammunition against the leftist parties. And the Argentines primarily focused on the labor bureaucracy. These divergent approaches comported with the varying strengths and weaknesses of the labor movements prior to the coups.[3]

Differences in Constraints on Labor under Various Capitalist Authoritarian Regimes

The environment for the labor movement under the military in the three Southern Cone countries and Brazil can again be ranked from best to worst in terms of structural, institutional, and political factors (see table 3.1). Because its dictatorship promoted industrialization, maintained corporatist unions, and allowed limited political party and electoral activity, Brazil was best for organized workers after the coup, while it had previously been worst. By contrast, the Southern Cone despots—especially in Chile—presided over deindustrialization, dismantled unions, and banned most parties and elections. Thus they created much worse post-coup conditions for the working class. Those South American rankings can be disaggregated and the European cases can be included by looking at the key variables shown in table 3.2.

To an extent, these authoritarian experiences tended to produce the opposite of what had existed before. The dictatorships blamed the pre-coup conditions for the country's plight and therefore reversed those trends. If

TABLE 3.2
Factors Affecting the Evolution of Labor Movements under Authoritarianism in the Southern Cone, Brazil, and Southern Europe

Factor	In Countries with Containment Coups		
	Portugal	Greece	Brazil
Level of repression	Low	Low	Low
Structural conditions			
Changes in industrialization[a]	↑	↑	↑
Level of unemployment	Low	Low	Low
Institutional conditions			
Labor system	Corporatism	Corporatism	Corporatism
Union density	Low	Medium	Medium
Labor response	Infiltration	Infiltration	Infiltration
Political result	Radicalization	Radicalization	Radicalization

	In Countries with Rollback Coups			
	Spain	Uruguay	Chile	Argentina
Level of repression	High	Medium	High	High
Structural conditions				
Changes in Industrialization[a]	↑	↓	↓	↓
Level of unemployment	Low	High	High	Low
Institutional conditions				
Labor system	Corporatism	Atomization	Atomization	Atomization
Union density	High	Medium	Low	High
Labor response	Infiltration	Abstention	Abstention	Abstention
Political result	Moderation	Moderation	Moderation	Moderation

SOURCE: J. Samuel Valenzuela, "Labor Movements in Transitions to Democracy: A Framework for Analysis," *Comparative Politics* 21:4 (July 1989), 445–72. J. Samuel Valenzuela and Jeffrey Goodwin, "Labor Movements under Authoritarian Regimes," *Monographs on Europe* 5 (1983), 1–50.
  [a] An up arrow indicates increased industrialization, a down arrow indicates deindustrialization.

industry had been relatively small prior to the coup, the military-based government was more likely to promote industrialization, and vice versa. If the labor movement had been moderate, it tended to become more militant, and vice versa.

Beyond the pattern of reversals, there was a deeper logic that distinguished between the cases on two major characteristics, separating containment from rollback coups and, most significantly, differentiating industrializing corporatists from deindustrializing atomizers. On most of the dimensions shown in table 3.2, the four earlier experiences differed from the three Southern Cone episodes. Containment coups occurred to halt rather weak labor movements in Portugal, Brazil, and Greece. Those takeovers, as well as the one in Spain, came about in countries with low or medium levels of industrialization and union strength, in comparison with the Southern Cone. Therefore the police state imposed milder repression, except in Spain, where the powerful and highly ideological labor parties attracted a massive attack during and after the civil war.

All four of the earlier dictatorships—those of Portugal, Spain, Greece, and Brazil—enveloped labor in official corporatist organizations. That architecture facilitated the growth of the proletariat and of unions under state controls. However coercive and artificial they were, the compulsory syndicates for workers helped mediate between management and labor and thus contributed to industrial peace.

That institutional containment strategy fit with the regimes' economic strategy of raising the level of industrialization and employment. In turn, those institutions offered the outlawed labor parties official structures to infiltrate. As the working class grew in size, strength, and expectations, it became more militant—and in some cases more radical—than it had been before the coup. Spain was a partial exception because wholesale repression dampened the fighting spirit of labor much as in the Southern Cone.

Unlike the containment coups against feeble labor movements in Portugal, Brazil, and Greece, rollback or reactionary coups took place to incapacitate stronger labor movements in Spain, Uruguay, Chile, and Argentina. The Southern Cone governments meshed a policy to atomize and shrink the proletariat with an economic program that reduced industry and employment. Their free-market labor strategy to disassemble and disable unions matched their free-market economic strategy.

Neoliberal ideology eventually blended all these elements into a coherent and dynamic policy package. Unable to block industrial downsizing and restructuring, the working class became smaller and weaker, and its organizations did not infiltrate official institutions. Not surprisingly, the debilitated labor movements became less militant and more moderate than they had been before the coups in the Southern Cone.[4]

Structural Constraints on Labor

Following the political shock treatment of the coups and their aftermath, the Southern Cone regimes subjected the workers to the economic shock treatment of market-oriented policies. Although their economic programs varied, they all contained some ingredients that undercut labor, particularly trade unionists. Even without repression, these policies—complementing trends in the world economy—would have enfeebled any union movement. Coercion, of course, made these programs easier to implement, although not necessarily more successful. Even Chile, whose program was the most touted, suffered through deep recessions in the mid-1970s and the early 1980s.[5]

By repressing labor, all of these dictatorships held down real wages. That lid on working-class income helped to boost capital accumulation, to fund new growth, to raise productivity, and to improve competitiveness in the international market. Throughout the Southern Cone democracies, it had become difficult to generate capital both internally (because of labor demands) and externally (because of leftist-nationalist threats to foreign investors). Consequently, the military promoted capital growth by clamping down on labor domestically and by opening up the economy internationally.

The Southern Cone despots implemented these reforms in the context of an evolving new international division of labor. Globalization of capitalist relations of production, of transnational corporations, and of capital mobility drove developing countries to pursue export-oriented strategies based on cheap labor. Given the worldwide surplus of workers, poorer countries had little choice. Like their governments, national and local unions had scant hope of challenging the gargantuan forces of worldwide capitalism. To compete in the international market and to deal with the foreign debt, the Latin Americans implemented neoliberal policies. They cut back the state sector and exposed their economies to market forces.

In the 1970s and especially the 1980s, labor lost ground around the globe. Organized workers faced hard times in developed as well as underdeveloped countries, in democracies as well as dictatorships. The growing competitiveness associated with the globalization of the economy and international trade favored skilled rather than unskilled workers. Historically, unions had tried to create monopolistic control over the labor supply to extract concessions for workers, especially the unskilled. They had been most successful at doing this in tight labor markets, particularly for skilled laborers. From the 1970s to the 1990s, the growing underemployment and unemployment of workers, principally the unskilled, undercut the union movement in the United States as well as South America. Labor also was harmed by falling wages, increasing poverty, expansion of the service and informal sectors, government cutbacks, and—eventually—neoliberal, market-driven programs.[6]

Although the antilabor governments of President Ronald Reagan in the

United States and the military rulers in South America compounded those losses, the plight of unionists in those regions was not unique. Similar patterns appeared in Europe. The animosity of Reagan and the generals toward unions facilitated the restructuring of the U.S. and Southern Cone economies. These government leaders were trying to adapt to the new international trends and to transfer income away from unskilled workers without arousing massive protests. Unlike their Brazilian forebear, the three Southern Cone regimes in the 1970s jumped aboard a global bandwagon against Keynesian statism and in favor of market-oriented policies. Dedicated to the private sector, that school of thought came to be known as *neoconservatism* or, more commonly, *neoliberalism*.[7]

The position of organized labor under the authoritarian regimes was corroded by a number of economic phenomena, especially in the Cono Sur. Some of these factors were intentional, some unintentional. Some had a mixed impact, benefiting certain workers while disadvantaging others, particularly unionists. For example, a slowing of inflation helped some laborers cope with the cost of living, even though this slowdown was achieved at the expense of many unions.

To varying degrees, the despots undercut the labor movement by (1) suppressing inflation; (2) lowering wages; (3) encouraging flexibility and heterogeneity in the workforce; (4) redistributing income upward; (5) reducing social services; (6) changing sectoral distributions; (7) freeing trade; (8) increasing unemployment; (9) presiding over depression and debt crises; and (10) promoting recovery through neoliberal programs that emphasized pruning the state, privatizing public enterprises, and unshackling market forces. The impact of these economic factors can be seen in the chapters on specific countries and in the following discussion.[8]

In South America, the military initially gave highest economic priority to suppressing inflation. Crusades against triple-digit inflation dampened worker activism by defusing one of the longstanding detonators for protests. Those campaigns not only curbed inflation but also reduced internal demand and favored exports over imports. Anti-inflationary measures removed protections for unions and, at least temporarily, lowered real wages.

Through monetaristic stabilization policies, the dictatorships accelerated the redistribution of income from workers to capitalists, fortifying the upper class for future political combat. In the Southern Cone in the 1970s, Chile had the most success in bringing down inflation; Uruguay came in second, and Argentina third. By the end of the 1970s, a resurgence of inflation in Argentina and Brazil revived labor militance.

The deterioration in many laborers' standard of living, which was exacerbated by these belt-tightening policies, sapped their stamina and left them clinging to job security rather than clamoring for new gains. Workers were also afflicted by government austerity programs that reduced the role of the state in social welfare, leaving labor more dependent on employers. In the long run, however, some workers would recoup some of their losses through stabilization of the cost of living and through improved private social security systems.[9]

Within the boundaries set by economic factors, the military takeovers slashed the cost of labor by lowering wages. The installation of antilabor governments and the crippling of unions drove down pay for organized workers. Particularly devastating were the dictators' alterations in macroeconomic and wage adjustment policies. Some of these regimes decreed national pay scales, and lagged pay increases behind the rate of inflation.[10]

In general, in the 1970s and 1980s Latin American capitalists and governments pressured workers toward greater subservience to market discipline, encouraging flexibility and heterogeneity. These trends were more attributable to market forces than to government policies. Heightened competition, mobility, and use of labor-saving technologies led industrialists to demand more workforce flexibility. As in many other parts of the world, workers lost guarantees regarding types of work, methods, procedures, hours, treatment, location, environment, employment, and pay.

For many laborers, flexibilization translated into job insecurity, lower wages, reduced benefits, deregulation of the workplace, piecework, the farming out of parts of the production process, subcontracting, and greater reliance on part-time and contract work. With unions paralyzed, Southern Cone workers lacked defenses against flexibilization. Especially hurt were the less skilled, the group traditionally most in need of unions, while some skilled workers made gains.

The workforce in the Southern Cone became more heterogeneous in composition, occupation, compensation, and standard of living. Labor also became more diffuse because it was dispersed geographically. The Chilean and Argentine governments encouraged the relocation and expansion of manufacturing outside of the capital city. For example, they promoted industries in duty-free zones in the most distant provinces.

In the underdeveloped as well as the developed world, the individualization of wages and working conditions was anathema to the union movement and to worker solidarity. Flexibility and heterogeneity gutted organized labor. Particularly hurt were labor's abilities to influence national politics, to bargain collectively, and to mount strikes. As flexibilization spawned new forms of precarious employment, the state played less of an interventionist role in labor-industrial relations. Union activities became less politicized, less susceptible to party involvement, and less centralized. Bargaining at the level of federation or confederation gave way to myriad arrangements at the lower strata of diverse and rapidly changing enterprises.[11]

In the Southern Cone as elsewhere, neoliberal policies frequently generated growth but also redistributed income upward. Under all the military-based regimes, income distribution favored the rich at the expense of the poor. The big gains normally accrued to the wealthiest 20 percent of the population.[12]

The Southern Cone dictatorships pruned budgetary allocations to social services and handed some of those functions—most notably social security in Chile—to the private sector. Although a few of these reforms improved the situation of workers, others deprived them of safety nets. In either case, workers had to rely less on the state and more on employers. This reduced the ability of unionists to apply pressure to obtain political or economic benefits.

The crucial sectoral changes in the Southern Cone were the whittling down of industry and the growth of services and informal occupations, the latter free from government regulation. Deindustrialization, although significant, is tricky to analyze. The manufacturing sector tended to shrivel in the late 1970s, plummeted during the depression of the early 1980s, and then regained some ground in the late 1980s. The decline in industry under the Southern Cone dictatorships can look exaggerated if one focuses on the adjustment period in the 1970s or the recession at the beginning of the 1980s. Some of the deindustrialization was due more to the recession than to government policies, and some of it was not long-lasting, particularly in Uruguay.

To varying degrees, the Southern Cone dictatorships pared down the protected position of manufacturing and subjected many firms to international competition. These changes lowered wages and rates of employment. As a result, the industrial working class became smaller, poorer, more heterogeneous, more defenseless, and less strategic in the economy, especially in Chile. The accompanying growth of service occupations accentuated the isolation and vulnerability of laborers in manufacturing, mining, and construction. Sectors that were traditionally highly unionized, such as manufacturing and construction, weakened, while less unionized areas, such as commerce, grew. Some workers improved their individual situation, but the labor movement lost leverage.

Although deindustrialization undercut organized labor in both North and South America, perhaps more important in the long run was the restructuring of industry. Even when manufacturing did not dwindle much as a percentage of the gross domestic product (GDP), it often reduced its share of workers and their pay, lengthened its employees' work hours, and substituted automation. Factories became more mechanized, more efficient, more competitive, and more internationally oriented.

In previous decades, the growth of the industrial sector, the growth of employment in manufacturing, of unions, and of parties beholden to workers had all gone hand in hand. The reverse proved true during the downsizing and reorganizing of industry. Now labor parties could no longer count on capitalist expansion to automatically generate a more numerous, more homogeneous, more powerful working class for them to lead on to victory. Therefore, both labor unions and parties began reaching out to the service sector, the unemployed sector, and the informal sector.

The significance of these sectoral changes is highlighted by contrast with the cases outside the Southern Cone. While the Chilean, Argentine, and—to a much lesser extent—Uruguayan dictatorships presided over deindustrialization, Portugal, Spain, Brazil, and Greece promoted rapid industrialization. Thus, the size and leverage of their manufacturing workforce increased. In the industrializing countries, ironically, the expansion of the very groups who were exploited to finance the growth of manufacturing had by the time of the authoritarian regime's demise generated more assertive labor unions and parties.[13]

All these dictatorships trimmed the leverage of workers producing for domestic consumption and of workers in any dominant export industry. They did so by promoting, liberalizing, and diversifying foreign trade. These free-trade policies had the most impact in a monocultural export economy such as the one in Chile, where the reduction of copper from 77 percent to 50 percent of the value of all exports reduced the bargaining power of the miners, although they still exerted considerable leverage.

In all cases, the foreign sector accounted for a rising percentage of GNP. At least in the short run, opening up the economy hurt labor because international competition drove down the wages of many workers. At the same time, expanded trade reduced the need for high wages to generate domestic demand. Laborers became increasingly divided between those producing for external consumption and those producing for internal consump-

TABLE 3.3
*Rates of Open Urban Unemployment in Brazil, the Southern Cone,
and Latin America, 1970–1984 (in percent)*

	1970	1978	1979	1980	1981	1982	1983	1984
Brazil	6.5	6.8	6.4	6.2	7.9	6.3	6.7	7.5
Uruguay	7.5	10.1	8.3	7.4	6.7	11.9	15.5	14.5
Chile	4.1	13.3	13.4	11.7	9.0	20.0	19.0	18.5
Argentina	4.9	2.8	2.0	2.3	4.5	4.7	4.0	3.8
Latin America	6.9	7.2	7.3	6.9	7.2	8.9	10.4	10.9

SOURCE: Organización Internacional del Trabajo, Programa Regional del Empleo para América Latina y el Caribe, *La creación de empleo en periodos de crisis* (Santiago, 1985), 6–7.

tion, between those working for internationally competitive industries and those working for inefficient industries, and between those working in highly skilled occupations and those working in relatively unskilled occupations. These cleavages made union centralization and cohesion on economic issues more difficult.[14]

In the Southern Cone, record-breaking unemployment and underemployment further eroded the position of organized labor. This was especially true in Chile but also in Uruguay and Argentina. The diminution of the state and of the economic sectors most conducive to job creation— manufacturing and construction—contributed to unemployment. While Uruguay and especially Chile rose above the regional average for open unemployment, Brazil and especially Argentina stayed well below, although they exceeded their own averages. Brazil was still industrializing, and Argentina maintained a traditionally low level of unemployment.

The loss of jobs experienced in the Southern Cone reflected broader trends in Latin America in the "lost decade" of the 1980s. The international debt crisis and depression increased joblessness, precarious employment, the informal sector, income concentration, and poverty. The trough was reached during the crash of 1981–85 (see table 3.3), after which the situation improved slowly. By contrast with the bureaucratic authoritarian regimes in Uruguay and Chile, the industrializing corporatist dictatorships in the European cases of Portugal, Spain, and Greece kept employment high, as also occurred in Brazil.[15]

The oil crisis in 1973–74 was the first international jolt to hit all the countries studied here, except for petroleum-self-sufficient Argentina. When considering the subsequent years, it is necessary to make a distinction between the hardships imposed on workers by the neoliberal restructuring policies of the autocratic regimes in the Southern Cone and those caused by

TABLE 3.4
*Annual Rates of Growth of Gross National Product in Brazil, the Southern Cone,
and Latin America, 1981–1983 (in percent)*

	Manufacturing GNP	Construction GNP	Total GNP
Brazil	−4.5	−6.8	−5.8
Uruguay	−9.9	−11.8	−13.9
Chile	−6.1	−4.5	−9.9
Argentina	−4.5	−12.9	−9.0
Latin America	−3.1	−5.6	2.8

SOURCE: OIT, PREALC, *La creación*, 6.

TABLE 3.5
*Rates of Growth of Gross Domestic Product per Capita in Brazil, the Southern Cone,
and Latin America, 1960–1988 (in percent)*

	1960–70	1970–80	1980–85	1986–88
Brazil	3.1	6.1	−1.1	−0.5
Uruguay	0.5	2.7	−3.7	2.4
Chile	1.9	0.9	−2.0	4.8
Argentina	2.6	0.9	−3.6	−0.8
Latin America	2.8	3.4	−1.6	−0.4

SOURCE: Adapted from Miguel Urrutia, "Twenty-five Years of Economic Growth and Social Progress, 1960–1985" in Miguel Urrutia, *Long-Term Trends in Latin American Economic Development* (Washington, D.C., 1991), 23–80.

the international recession in the first half of the 1980s. The depression and debt crisis during 1981–85 made labor's situation much worse, as real wages and employment fell further (see tables 3.4–7). As a result of the early-1980s crash, union membership plummeted. Collective bargaining and striking, which had already been fairly ineffective, now became futile.[16]

During the economic downswing in 1982–84, political protests erupted against the Southern Cone governments, especially in Chile. In general, however, the depression, like the dictatorships, taught workers to rein in their expectations and activities. Workers concentrated on protecting their jobs and avoiding worse alternatives. In some cases, economic slumps helped elite-led democratization by stifling union demands.[17]

The recovery that began in the mid-1980s and lasted into the 1990s improved the economic situation of many Southern Cone workers. Especially in Chile and Uruguay, renewed growth finally brought laborers close to the standard of living they had possessed prior to bureaucratic authoritarianism. Although their employment rates and income improved, they remained inhibited by their memories of repression and depression. Some la-

TABLE 3.6
*Index of Real Industrial Wages in Brazil, the Southern Cone,
and Latin America, 1981–1986*

	1981	1982	1983	1984	1985	1986
Brazil	108.5	121.6	173.6	105.1	112.6	131.9
Uruguay	106.7	103.5	82.1	80.2	97.6	103.3
Chile	111.6	108.5	96.3	95.5	90.4	92.1
Argentina	89.7	80.3	103.9	126.3	102.9	107.8
Latin America	101.3	99.4	99.7	92.9	92.2	96.3

SOURCE: PREALC, as reported by Ian Roxborough, "Organized Labor: A Major Victim of the Debt
Crisis," in Barbara Stallings and Robert Kaufman, *Debt and Democracy in Latin America* (Boulder, Colo.,
1989), 91–108.
NOTE: 1980 = 100.

TABLE 3.7
*Urban Unemployment Rates in Brazil, the Southern Cone,
and Latin America, 1984–1986 (in percent)*

	1984	1985	1986
Brazil	7.5	5.3	3.6
Uruguay	14.5	13.1	10.7
Chile	18.5	17.0	13.1
Argentina	3.8	6.1	5.2
Latin America	10.9	11.3	10.6

SOURCE: PREALC, as reported by Roxborough, "Organized Labor," 91–108.

borers also behaved with restraint out of hopes that neoliberal policies,
however unwelcome, would at least bring about growth and stability.[18]

By the time of the recovery, neoliberalism had triumphed nearly everywhere. Workers had no coherent and viable alternative. The entire package
of market-oriented reforms made the state—and thus political parties—less
relevant to laborers. Instead of bargaining with and relying upon the central government, they had to put more emphasis on their relations with
their employers. As a result, unions became less political and less leftist.
Their protests against neoliberal policies fell on deaf ears. By contrast, some
unions—notably in Chile and Argentina and particularly in the new export
sectors—came to support market-friendly economics.

During recovery, the state continued to prune its activities and to shed
enterprises. Privatization was a double-edged sword for labor. The process
undercut employment and unions in parts of the public sector, erasing
some traditional protections and benefits, especially in declining industries.
However, privatization gave some workers higher wages and even participation in management, mostly in divested industries that were expanding.

Whether it hurt or helped workers, privatization usually undermined unions.

All the labor parties had to come to terms with the juggernaut of neo-liberalism. Following the acceptance of many neoliberal precepts by those parties, groups to their right and left had few counterproposals, and labor had nowhere else to go. Their conversion to neoliberalism showed again that economic conditions, more than parties or ideologies, usually determined the policies toward labor and the lot of labor.[19]

Throughout the tenure of the authoritarian regimes, workers adopted numerous survival strategies to cope with the economic impacts described above. More family members (especially women) worked in paid employment, toiled longer hours, took on more than one job, did piecework at home, entered the informal sector, reduced their standard of living, pooled resources with other community members, and even emigrated, most frequently from Portugal, Spain, Greece, and Uruguay. All of these adaptations reduced the likelihood that laborers would spend much time on unions, strikes, parties, or politics.

Institutional Constraints on Labor

The authoritarian regimes fettered the labor movements with new restrictions on unions, union leaders, federations, confederations, collective bargaining, and labor laws. These blows descended most heavily on industrial, blue-collar, larger, and Marxist unions. Although generally negative, some of these institutional innovations also provided opportunities which were seized by organized labor.

The dictatorships' fundamental policies toward unions were divided between corporatism and atomization. The first strategy relied on social control and inclusion, while the second emphasized social expulsion and exclusion. Corporatism fit better with industrialization, atomization with deindustrialization. Some of the dictatorships cobbled together elements from both systems, encapsulating some unions and ejecting others. For example, Greece was a mixed case, where most unions were paternalized but some were atomized.[20]

Corporatism prevailed in the Portuguese, Spanish, Greek, and Brazilian dictatorships. The corporatists included workers in government-controlled syndical organizations with compliant leaders. The syndicates were hierarchical, unitary, compulsory confederations. Legally they had the right to engage in centralized collective bargaining at the national level, but in actuality they were usually impotent supplicants at the feet of the state. In practice, rights were almost as restricted in corporatist systems as under the atomizers. Rather than vehicles for working-class representation, the syndicates were devices for social control.

In cases such as that of Brazil, where the dictatorship appropriated and tightened preexisting corporatist organizations, the state had more success at encompassing worker participation in the official structures. In cases such as that of Spain, where the government imposed totally new state-sponsored labor institutions, such institutions became something of an empty shell. In both instances, however, the fact that few effective benefits were derived through the autocratic channels prompted laborers to maintain or create outlaw organizations of their own. Faced with the official institutions, opponents were torn between delegitimation through abstention, and subversion through infiltration. Although some of the workers who took part in the corporatist unions became supportive of that system, other participants converted those organizations into bastions of the opposition labor movement.[21]

Atomization rather than corporatism predominated in Uruguay, Chile, and Argentina, although the Argentine dictatorship vacillated. The atomizers chopped and diced the labor movement: they outlawed union political activity; banned confederations and federations; ousted truculent labor leaders; confiscated union resources; pushed the decentralized union movement down to the plant level; removed most of workers' rights to organize, meet, bargain, or strike; confined labor-management negotiations to local issues in which employers had the upper hand; and abandoned workers to the ebb and flow of the marketplace. They divided unions from each other and from their base. Chronologically, this depoliticized, economistic, free-market model came to prevail over the corporatist approach as neoliberal ideas circled the globe.

Unlike corporatism, the atomizing variant of capitalist authoritarianism involved few gestures intended to enfold labor in state structures. Because of their enmity toward the workers, as well as the workers' own recalcitrance, the Southern Cone regimes made only minimal efforts to tame labor through co-optation, least of all in Chile. When these governments extended small incentives for cooperation, they usually went to white-collar, non-Marxist, and smaller unions, some of which reciprocated with support. Under atomization and marketization, the opposition had to struggle to build back up from the plant level to recreate the national labor movement.

In the Southern Cone, the military made few efforts to give birth to surrogate unions by fiat or inducements, and those initiatives foundered. These regimes also failed to fabricate new federations and confederations. Workers' loyalties to past organizations and leaders proved to be deeply ingrained. Most of the attempts by the armed forces to encourage progovernment unions fell flat because the regime feared the politicization even of friendly forces. It refused to give them significant rights, benefits, or positive policies. Consequently, these dictatorships came into conflict with most of organized labor.[22]

All the dictators grappled with a dilemma with regard to both labor unions and parties: how to eliminate those organizations' ability to represent and mobilize but retain or replace their capacity to mediate and manage their followers. Because constant coercion and vigilance were costly ways to control workers, the authoritarians tried to devise a new system—including fresh unions, leaders, and laws—for managing relations between labor and industry. That reorganization, however, required the activation of enough labor leaders to make the system operate. To exert authority, those leaders also needed some credibility with the rank and file, and thus their demands inevitably regenerated conflict with the dictatorships.

When the authoritarian regimes allowed some amicable unions space to operate, those organizations, in order to represent their members and not lose them to opposition unionists, had to criticize some government policies. Thus, quisling unions frequently gravitated toward opposition unions, which seized the space ceded by the government to mobilize labor unity against the regime. What the police state could not figure out was how to get regulation without representation, how to get the unions to cooperate with the military as well as the rank and file, and how to get valid but supine interlocutors.

Uncertainty about authentic leaders for workers created problems not only for the opposition but also for the government. Without elections, it was hard to establish who spoke for organized labor, especially at the national level of federations and confederations, as well as among political parties. When the dictatorships allowed a few union elections because they needed effective intermediaries, they were usually dismayed because the winners normally came from the opposition.

Although the Southern Cone dictatorships put into office or encouraged new union leaders, many older union representatives survived, and many newer leaders proved equally unbending in their defense of workers' interests. Even union spokespersons who were opposed to socialism or populism had to advocate the practical needs of their membership. The ejection of many leftist unionists from their posts and jobs did increase the strength of more conservative labor leaders, but that realignment was sometimes superficial and temporary.

The Southern Cone regimes could get rid of politicians but not the working class. Therefore they soon sought new institutional arrangements for the permanent containment of workers without the need for constant surveillance. Before the tyrants introduced new legislation, unions suffered from a loss of their previous legal rights, which became simply inoperable and unenforceable. Then new laws criminalized social and political activism by the working class. These schemes to restructure labor policies, organizations, and systems, however, proved less successful than crude repression.

Typically, the Southern Cone dictator's legislation mandated that unions and their leaders and funds, as well as the wages and working conditions they obtained, be subject to government approval. Most of these codes also discouraged organization and bargaining above the plant level, hampered unionization by public employees, reduced privileges and protections for union leaders, disallowed the closed shop, legalized lockouts, and restricted strikes. They also banned political activities.

In the Southern Cone, most attempts to make unions more cooperative and force them to obey more constricting laws experienced only limited success. It proved very difficult to really recast a deep-seated labor movement. Pinochet's new code for labor-industrial relations was the most ambitious and durable; unlike his Uruguayan and Argentine counterparts, he had ten years to hammer home his new institutionality. Although the Southern Cone dictatorships proved skillful at destruction, it was mainly the workers themselves who reconstructed the labor movement from the rubble.

Some government proposals for the permanent shackling of labor backfired. Although most workers rejected legislation designed to hobble unions, they took advantage of the new laws to reorganize and reassert themselves. The issuance of a fresh labor code gave workers not only something more to complain about but also a new channel for those complaints. Unionists tried to stretch the boundaries of that legislation as far as possible. Paradoxically, the revival of the labor movement flowed from the issuance of regulations intended to keep it comatose. Thus the rulers had to pay the costs of either suppression or institutionalization.[23]

After the coups, the workers found it extremely difficult to bargain with either their employers or their new rulers. Mobilization against military-based governments was very rare because it was very risky. Union activism usually only sprang up when national economic or political crises opened a space for disruptions. Even then, it was very hard for labor agitation to shorten the tyrant's tenure.

Under capitalist authoritarianism, unions could select their options from a spectrum ranging from lowest cost to highest cost: from hibernation, through cooperation with the regime, negotiation with the dictatorship, pressure through the state's own institutions, and conflict with employers, to frontal clashes with the government. Avoiding the regime and/or supplicating it were sometimes the only avenues open to trade unions when both the political and economic playing fields had been closed. Dialoguing or negotiating with the dictatorial government entailed low costs but also was unlikely to achieve benefits. Moreover, an accommodationist strategy could cost union bosses support from union members. During dictatorships, unions' behavior and fortunes were determined not only by state policies but also by the business cycle and by relations with employers. Given the inherent disadvantages of unionists vis-à-vis management, antilabor militaristic governments devastated workers.

Following the implantation of all the dictatorships, the labor movements typically went through five stages: (1) hibernation, in which unions retreated in order to survive the most lethal blows; (2) regrouping, in which unions began to recompose and to test the limits of permissiveness, either through conciliation with the regime or, more commonly, through probes such as conversations, slowdowns, meetings, and manifestoes; (3) resistance and confrontation, in which unions remobilized, first to press workers' needs per se and then to challenge the dictatorship itself, both through the regime's own institutions and through illegal channels; (4) cooperation and concertation, in which worker organizations ceded the leadership of democratization to the reborn parties and restrained their members so as to reach understandings with capitalists and other right-wing groups to facilitate a smooth transition; and (5) relegalization, normalization, and frustration, in which unions recaptured their civil rights but expressed exasperation at their inability to extract many bread-and-butter benefits from the restored democracy. As a result, they frequently engaged in fruitless strikes and protests.

Denied most opportunities for expression, labor unions and parties did not succeed in ambushing, derailing, or capsizing these authoritarian regimes. Although labor resisted the coup in Uruguay with a general strike and the coup in Chile with scattered armed groups, efforts to rally the rank and file against the military's seizure of power proved limited, futile, and short-lived. Unions quickly retreated into silence and watchful waiting. Although severely hampered, labor gradually devised creative ways to survive, to parry some of the worst abuses of these governments, to carve out niches for activity, to reassemble its ranks, and to prepare for future democratization.

In the absence of overt labor party activities, workers came increasingly to rely not only on their own organizations but also on surrogate allies, such as human rights groups and intellectuals. Most important were international labor entities and the Roman Catholic Church. In the 1970s and 1980s, the international labor organization that had the most Latin American affiliates was the ORIT (the Interamerican Regional Organization of Labor), a subsidiary of the ICFTU (the International Confederation of Free Trade Unions). Although the AFL-CIO (American Federation of Labor–Congress of Industrial Organizations) had long dominated ORIT, social democrats had taken charge by the start of the 1980s. At the same time, the AFL-CIO became more active in promoting union rights and democracy under conservative as well as communist dictatorships, especially in Chile, Uruguay, and Argentina. Much smaller followings were claimed by the Social Christian or Christian Democrat CLAT (the Latin American Workers Central, a branch of the WCL—the World Confederation of Labor) and the Communist CPUSTAL (the Permanent Congress of Union Unity of the Workers of Latin America, an offshoot of the WFTU—the World Federation of Trade Unions).

Also helpful were the United Nations (UN), the International Labor Organization (ILO), and the Organization of American States (OAS). The UN's International Labor Organization pressed governments to respect union rights in accord with treaty obligations. Since the dictatorships wanted to remain in good standing with the ILO, they sometimes responded positively to its criticisms and tried to send sympathetic unionists to its international meetings. That ploy gave those delegations opportunities to negotiate with their oppressors for more favorable labor policies. Unions also used foreign recognition to establish their legitimacy vis-à-vis the government and vis-à-vis other claimants to union leadership.[24]

Another key external ally was the AFL-CIO in the United States and its international arm, the AIFLD (the American Institute for Free Labor Development). The North Americans were more welcome now in Latin America than they had been in the intense Cold War years of the 1960s and 1970s, when they had primarily campaigned against leftists. Now they issued declarations calling on the military governments to respect union rights, threatened boycotts of products from countries under military rule, provided financial and advisory assistance to beleaguered unions, and challenged the dictators with on-site visits.

At the same time, the human rights campaigns promoted by the United States and other foreign entities aided unionists and their parties. Although helpful, this foreign assistance was also divisive, especially so long as the Cold War inspired U.S. unions to oppose their Marxian counterparts in Latin America. In all of the cases discussed in this book, the Cold War delayed democratization by giving the dictatorships a patina of legitimacy as bulwarks against communism and by tainting the labor movements as potentially revolutionary or subservient to Moscow. Because the United States constituted the most powerful external actor in all the countries considered here, its anti-communism made democratization more difficult.

Prior to the coups, Brazilian unions were independent of any international organization, Uruguay's national confederation (the National Convention of Workers [CNT]) was unattached but close to the CPUSTAL, Chile's umbrella organization (the Unified Workers' Central [CUT]) was also officially unaffiliated but friendly to the CPUSTAL, and Argentina's General Confederation of Labor (CGT) belonged to the ORIT. After the military takeovers, unions in Chile most benefited from foreign connections, partly because the highly circumscribed labor parties there had the highest international visibility. Although the Argentine Peronists had little experience with international ties, they quickly turned those linkages to their advantage. By contrast, the Uruguayan CNT benefited little from allies overseas, and the Brazilian federations were not allowed by their government to join internationals.[25]

Especially in Catholic countries, the reformist turn of the Roman Catholic Church from the 1960s onward was a boon for unionists and democrats. Although the church played a positive role in the waning years of the dictatorships in Portugal and Spain, only in Brazil and Chile did the clergy supply significant backing to unionists. In those latter two countries, the church issued declarations, sheltered dissidents, provided legal assistance, and offered social services. However, its invaluable role as a surrogate could only go so far before labor unions and parties had to resume their traditional functions.[26]

Paradoxically, by denouncing almost all social activism as political subversion, the dictatorships rendered virtually all union activity automatically "political." This paradox came about even though the unions primarily stressed moderate, material objectives rather than social or ideological conquests—mainly because they had little choice. More than seeking improvements in wages and working conditions, unions had to concentrate on job security in the face of declining incomes, rising unemployment, and government animosity. Nevertheless, labor could not pursue its instrumental needs without mounting an inherently political challenge to the regime. Therefore the workers gradually escalated from requests for small concessions to calls for systemic changes. Consequently, almost every incremental gain became another small victory against the entire system of oppression.

In all seven of the countries discussed here, especially those with corporatist systems, the opposition debated whether to work with the regime's institutions or to deny them legitimacy. This split reflected debates over strategies and tactics, often following party lines, not a division among types of unions or industries. Normally the result was that some opposition members opted to subvert while others chose to boycott. The Communists usually led the attempt at participation.

The liberation of political spaces by civil society lay the groundwork for formal democratization under the leadership of the political parties. In virtually all cases, laborers mobilized against the dictatorship as it neared the end of its tenure. They often rose up in the wake of an economic or political crisis, in harmony with international pressure, in reaction to new labor regulations by the regime, in response to divisions within the authoritarian coalition, in the throes of liberalization, and in solidarity with other democratic forces. Labor's courage emboldened other democratic sectors, including students, intellectuals, artists, and entertainers. Attempts to salvage a weakening authoritarian regime by instituting restricted liberalization failed, partly because of the resistance of organized workers.

As we shall see in most of our examples, social mobilization initially was a response to, more than a cause of, regime liberalization. Thereafter, social pressure and regime response interacted in complex but discernible patterns. Social turmoil usually preceded political activation by the opposition parties.

That "resurrection of civil society" elicited either a crackdown or an opening-up by the tyrants. An opening was usually the outcome, even if it followed a momentary backlash. With the original emergency sparking the coup long gone, repression became harder to justify, and so the openings normally expanded. In all of our cases, unions progressed from near muteness under the triumphant dictatorships to mobilization as the regimes lost power, to relative restraint during the delicate stages of redemocratization, and finally to renewed assertiveness under the restored democracies.

The character of the reinvigorated labor movement was shaped by the socioeconomic changes under the dictatorship and by the unions' political inheritance from the periods before and during the regime. The strongholds of the aroused workers were often the same areas in which they had predominated prior to the coup. Those bastions of laborism—such as the Barcelona workers in Spain or the copper miners in Chile—possessed strategic and symbolic significance for the rest of the working class.

Labor activation helped to undermine the regime by raising the cost of repression, casting doubt on the tyranny's legitimacy and efficacy, pushing liberalization to move on to democratization, and inciting foreign criticism of the regime. Thereafter, labor restraint showed that authoritarian controls were not necessary to maintain order. By displaying a capacity to represent and regulate workers, the unions established credibility with their membership and with other actors with whom they would have to negotiate.[27]

In the Southern Cone, the global recession and debt debacle in the early 1980s reignited trade union protests against government policies. That working-class resistance to further immiseration undercut the dictatorships. Thus, crises in the world economy and their domestic ramifications contributed to both the inauguration and the subsequent atrophy of these regimes.

As protests became more frequent, unions recreated their outlawed national confederations. They tried to speak for other social movements as well, including the unemployed, the self-employed, the underemployed, and the unorganized poor. Since their traditional base had been narrowed, the unions reached out to a wider gamut of the lower classes, especially in Chile, where they most needed allies. Street demonstrations by the underprivileged shook the regime and heartened its opponents.

The dictators counterattacked with dragnets, dispatching the most contumacious leaders to jail or exile. However, government whip-cracking often escalated the number of strikes and marches, thus furthering unity within the labor movement. Vanguards used strikes to make workers more militant and political. The cacophony also stemmed from competition among unions as they regained freedom.

After years of enforced silence, workers in South America—especially Brazil—called general strikes as the dictatorships faltered (and even more so after the tyrants withdrew). (See table 3.8.) As defiance of the authorities spread, unions debated whether to emphasize mobilization or concertation, confrontation or consensus. Those choices were not mutually exclusive, and many unionists employed a mix of strategies and tactics. While

TABLE 3.8
The Number of General Strikes in Brazil and the Southern Cone, 1973–1986

	Brazil	Uruguay	Chile	Argentina
1973	0	1	1	0
1974	0	0	0	0
1975	0	0	0	1
1976	0	0	0	1
1977	0	0	0	0
1978	0	0	0	0
1979	0	0	0	1
1980	0	0	0	0
1981	0	0	0	1
1982	0	0	0	1
1983	2	0	1	1
1984	5	0	1	1
1985	15	2	0	2
1986	25	2	1	4

SOURCE: Edward C. Epstein, "Conclusion: The Question of Labor Autonomy," in Edward C. Epstein, *Labor Autonomy and the State in Latin America* (Boston, 1989), 275–90.

some laborers argued that agitation would accelerate redemocratization, others feared that mass upheaval would delay or even derail the restoration of civilian rule. Some contended that assertiveness during the transition would stake out a bigger role for unions after democratization. Others worried that if the working class made too many demands it might remain marginalized. The labor parties also recommended prudence. Leery of conflict, many unionists came to rely on concertation, especially as the final stages of redemocratization loomed ahead.

The advocates of concertation and consensus-building proposed three modes of operation. First, they urged compromise and coalescence among all the parties and social groups who were in favor of democratization. Second, they promoted dialogue and deals between socioeconomic adversaries, especially business and trade unions. It was a preemptive attempt to reconcile economic inequality under capitalism with political equality under democracy by negotiating understandings and concessions between management and labor. Third, they pressed for negotiations between the dictatorship and the opposition.

All three modes of operation could lead to formal pacts, but they more frequently led to informal or tacit agreements, or to dead ends. In most cases, concertation made redemocratization easier, mainly by reassuring business and military elites that the new regime would not harm their interests. After the experience of right-wing authoritarianism, union leaders believed that it was essential to reach compromises with other social sectors, but they were not in a good position to bargain or to coordinate their followers.[28]

Most top union leaders also favored concertation because it increased their power as spokespersons for the labor movement. Endorsing national pacts augmented the clout of the big confederations not only vis-à-vis the state and business but also vis-à-vis individual unions and unionists. Labor leaders were struggling for control of the movement as well as for national economic and political objectives.[29]

Most leaders of labor unions and parties came to believe that they could bring about redemocratization and thus the restoration of their rights and benefits only by joining a broad, multiparty, multiclass coalition to ease out and replace the military regime. Opposition parties formed alliances first among unionists because cooperation within and among factories was crucial for working-class advances. Those alliances paved the way for the parties to weave coalitions at the national political level. Ironically, by crippling the ability of labor organizations to function on their own, the dictators left the unions relying on political parties as partners. Thus they recreated the very political fusion that the coups had been designed to eliminate.[30]

Political Constraints on Labor

It is very difficult to know the attitudes of workers toward communism, socialism, populism, liberalism, or democracy during the oppressive years of the dictatorships. Most laborers probably remained loyal to their traditional parties and unions, as they did before and after authoritarianism. However, that does not necessarily mean that they supported the beliefs—whether revolutionary, reformist, or conservative—of their leaders. In all of the countries under discussion, the few polls done among workers under despotism—as well as before and after—found them to be more moderate than might have been expected on the basis of their exploitation or the pronouncements of their leaders.

Under withering repression, working-class movements showed little capacity to strike back at the dictatorships. Among the four South American cases, it was in Argentina and Chile that labor unions became more effective than labor parties at resisting these regimes and their assaults, especially in the early stages of remobilization. The unions proved most crucial to the survival of their parties where those bonds had been strongest before the coups.

By contrast, political parties experienced the most success at confronting the dictatorships in Brazil and Uruguay. In those countries, repression was more nuanced, free-market policies were less intense, labor movements were less formidable, and the major parties were nonideological and of the catch-all variety. In sum, parties became more effective at acquiring room for maneuver where they were much less tied to labor and to programs for structural change. Those parties were more tolerable to the military and its conservative supporters.

Labor's party allies usually operated most effectively in the spaces granted to them by the ruling elites. Parties seldom created political space, they filled it; they rarely displayed any ability to force political openings themselves. In the Southern Cone, the parties least capable of counterattacking the military regimes were the parties most mutilated — the Marxists — whereas the Christian Democrats, the Colorados, and the Peronists were allowed more leeway to engage in guarded political activity. Among types of parties available to laborers, persecution was harshest against communist parties, less oppressive against socialist parties, still less brutal against populist parties, and least harsh against catch-all parties. All of the dictatorships crushed any attempts at armed struggle.[31]

Although the coups terminated the labor parties' abilities to deliver many clientelistic benefits to their followers, those vehicles still provided some services. Most significantly, they (1) preserved their identity and their key leaders, often in exile or underground; (2) mounted an international campaign to condemn and isolate the dictatorship and to furnish aid to its adversaries; (3) maintained some contact with their social bases; (4) supplied allies (such as students and intellectuals) and assistance (such as legal advice) to workers; (5) exerted influence through nonparty channels, such as unions, universities, think tanks, human rights advocates, churches, clandestine media, and international organizations; (6) provided the outlines of shadow governments and alternative programs, thus implying the illegitimacy and transience of the dictatorship; and (7) underwent profound soul-searching and self-reappraisal that proved salutary for eventual reactivation.

Although often criticized and denigrated in contrast with older, more organized, and better-funded entities in Europe, the parties in the Southern Cone displayed remarkable adaptability and tenacity. Their endurance bespoke their immersion in a working-class subculture that nurtured these political attachments in the home and factory. Most Southern Cone unionists held fast to their party affiliations, despite losses. The new regimes offered them few attractive alternatives, while their historical memories and consciousness still drew them to their parties.

At the same time, party ties that had proved beneficial under democratic systems now became a liability for unions linked to the political enemies of the dictatorship. Therefore, party influence withered somewhat and for the most part was confined to hard-core loyalists. That shrinkage could be seen in the decline of the left and the takeover of some Marxist unions by Christian Democrats in Chile. It was also evident in the contraction of support for the Peronists in Argentina.[32]

While in exile, labor party leaders drummed up international pressure on the dictatorships, and sent assistance and beamed broadcasts to loyalists back home. They also developed new coalitions with their compatriots exiled from other parties. At the same time, they drew lessons from party models and political systems in their host countries, especially from social democratic colleagues in Western Europe. Tension developed between the external and the internal leadership, with the latter proving more pragmatic and effective over time. The domestic forces gradually took charge, especially as redemocratization drew near.[33]

In all seven of the cases under discussion, the opposition parties wrestled with the dilemma that clandestinity provided security but minimized mass mobilization. Conversely, open agitation on the dictator's own turf generated challenges to the regime but facilitated detection and destruction. The more the opposition expanded, the more vulnerable it was to state terror. In most cases, the Communists proved most capable and most agile at operating in the two modes—aboveground and underground—simultaneously. Other segments of the opposition frequently failed on both counts. The majority of the opposition did not dare go public until the worst years of oppression were over and liberalization had begun.

One result of the banishment of regular politics was the "Argentinization" of the labor movements. In Chile and, to a lesser extent, Uruguay, unions had funneled their demands through political parties during democracy. But now the parties had to pipe their propositions through the increasingly autonomous unions. Like other civic organizations, the trade unions came to play roles previously monopolized by the parties. They served as representative mechanisms, as opposition spokespersons, and as providers of policy alternatives.

In many cases, persecution eventually increased workers' reliance on unions, solidarity between union leaders and followers, unity among unions, and identification of unionists with their martyred party sympathizers. When the unions recouped enough to campaign for incremental worker rights and benefits, they naturally created space for the simultaneous demand for redemocratization. They blazed a trail for the reassertion of the parties that were allied with them.[34]

By closing down the opposition parties' public arenas, the despots did not eliminate those parties. The dictators did, however, cause most of them to shrink, to fracture, to freeze their leadership and ideas, and to stay on the defensive for several years. As a result, more militant or radical labor parties grew up in Portugal, Greece, and Brazil. But in Spain, Uruguay, Chile, and Argentina, the labor parties became more moderate.

By clamping down on the parties, the dictatorships minimized these opposition groups' ability not only to represent their constituents but also to effectuate social control. Because the parties were bound and gagged, social movements temporarily took their place. The first mass protests against the dictatorships were often eruptions in working-class factories and neighborhoods, with little party control.

As the parties gradually took charge of those outbursts, they made mobilization not only more effective politically but also more moderate and institutionalized. They gave the regime a counterpart with which to negotiate during liberalization and with which to manage an orderly extrication. Thus, in certain respects, political parties were simultaneously the most dangerous nemeses of the dictatorship and indispensable institutions for its exit.

The strength of parties under the dictatorship was difficult to measure, and appearances were deceptive. The Communist Party often became the strongest party within the labor movement because of its discipline, dedication, and external support. In Portugal and Spain, it surpassed the anarchists as the most important group of revolutionary workers opposing the despot; the Communists braved torture, exile, and death in the front lines of working-class opposition movements. Following the Popular Front strategy in the mid-1930s, de-Stalinization in the 1950s, and *perestroika* in the 1980s, most of the Communist parties became increasingly gradualist (with the partial exception of the Chileans). Under the dictatorships, Communist parties were the opposition parties most prone to infiltrate the official syndical organizations.

However, the PC's strength was often exaggerated, not only by the party but also by dictators trying to claim legitimacy in the name of anti-communism. For ideological and international reasons, the Communists found it very hard to form effective multiparty alliances with other adversaries of the tyrannies. Especially during the Cold War, they were usually shunned by the other opposition parties. The PC's effectiveness was also diminished by its need to dance to changing tunes from Moscow and to purge disloyal members. Moreover, the skills—such as secrecy and obedience—suitable for combating the dictatorships were not necessarily the same ones—such as charisma and multiclass appeal—for besting political opponents in democracies.

In the absence of elections, parties' apparent shares of popular support under the dictatorship were not a good guide to postauthoritarian politics. In Portugal, Spain, and Chile, the Socialists looked very debilitated and drained under the yoke of authoritarianism, but they had a remarkable capacity to rebound after democracy was restored. The same was true for the Broad Front in Uruguay and the Peronists in Argentina. And the catch-all parties bided their time, only to reemerge during redemocratization with few changes in their makeup or scope.[35]

Eventually, the dictatorship unintentionally promoted greater cooperation among the parties as well as the unions. It gave them a common enemy. The opposition struggled to forge unity among party factions, among parties, among social movements, and among parties and movements. Divisions always remained, especially where the Communists were strong. Nevertheless, the regime's antagonists ultimately pulled together—at least informally, at least partially, and at least enough to replace the dictatorship with democracy.

Corporatist Precursors to the Southern Cone Regimes:

Southern Europe and Brazil, 1920s–1980s

The earlier capitalist authoritarian regimes in Portugal, Spain, Greece, and Brazil exhibited many traits in common with those of the Southern Cone. In broad strokes, those commonalities included subordination to the great powers of international capitalism, middling levels of modernization on the world scale, and Mediterranean culture. The Southern European and Brazilian dictatorships also differed significantly from those in Uruguay, Chile, and Argentina. A key distinctive feature was the construction of corporatist institutions for laborers during industrialization. Although occurring in different times and places, these corporatist examples provide valuable grist for a comparative analysis of the origins and types of modern antilabor dictatorships, patterns of working-class resistance, and modalities of redemocratization.

The four non–Southern Cone cases shared a common trajectory: (1) an upsurge of labor unrest and leftist political ferment on the eve of the dictatorship; (2) the installation of an antilabor, militaristic government that facilitated capital accumulation by repressing unions and wages; (3) support from capitalists for the authoritarian regime as it promoted industrialization and economic growth; and (4) liberalization and democratization in the wake of the 1973–74 global oil crisis.[1]

Like those in the Southern Cone, the Southern European and Brazilian cases of "reactionary despotism" occurred in late-developing, dependent capitalist economies with glaring social inequalities. Although underdeveloped by Western European standards, Portugal, Spain, Greece, and Brazil ranked well above the Third World on most socioeconomic indicators. At the time of their democratic breakdowns, their level of modernization resembled that seen in the Southern Cone on the brink of the military takeovers there.

On the verge of the military usurpations in Southern Europe and Brazil, unions and parties representing labor—although neither very dense nor unified—were mobilizing and becoming radicalized. The armed forces saw working-class aggressiveness as a threat not only to the economic and social order but also to their own privileged position. One of the main reasons they seized power was to break and muzzle labor and the left. By stressing anti-communism, the tyrants forged collegial relations with the United States during the Cold War.

In the aftermath of the international petroleum shock of 1973–74, the transitions back to democracy unfolded during a crisis of stagflation, which weakened both the dictatorships and the workers' movements. That economic downturn accentuated social unrest, especially among the working class, though the unrest was less marked in Greece. Mounting labor agitation took on increasingly political, rather than just economic, objectives. In Portugal, Greece, and Brazil, labor unions and parties became more militant and leftist than they had been before the dictatorships. In Spain, where they had been more radical before the dictatorship, the horrifying legacy of the civil war and the high level of modernization made them more moderate.[2]

When the dictatorships in Portugal, Spain, and Greece began, those countries possessed a small but growing industrial structure and proletariat. The despotisms contained the working class with corporatist institutions and with high rates of employment, partly due to emigration. Labor grew in size thanks to industrialization.

Then quite unexpectedly, between 1974 and 1977, all three nations jettisoned their dictatorships. They swiftly established stable parliamentary systems and soon elected Socialist governments with working-class support. Meanwhile, the Communists faded from a prominent position in the resistance to a more marginal existence in the restored democracies. All three countries had to erect democracies amidst economic difficulties.[3]

The Southern European Socialist parties were essentially new, born or reborn during the struggle against the dictatorships. The largest of the parties that attracted workers, they gained electorally from widespread desires for social reform as part of democratization. Their meteoric rise also resulted from the magnetic appeal of their leaders.

Once in office, these Socialists shifted abruptly from Marxism to social democracy. These laborite parties tolerated socioeconomic inequalities in exchange for participation in electoral politics, government, and the welfare state. The continuing globalization of international capitalism soon convinced them, like their counterparts in the Southern Cone, to accept some key elements of the neoliberal canon. Their endorsement of market-oriented development programs undercut the right as well as labor.[4]

The Earlier Precursors: The Military Regimes in Iberia

Latin America's mother countries created archetypes of capitalist authoritarian regimes which impressed their offspring in the New World. These two Iberian prototypes—first as dictatorships and then as new democracies—influenced each other as well as their former colonies in America. This impact could be seen in many areas, including Brazil's admiration for the corporatist features of the Portuguese New State, Augusto Pinochet's emulation of Francisco Franco, and the moderation that socialist and populist parties practiced in order to facilitate redemocratization.[5]

In the interwar years before the military takeovers, neither industry nor unions were highly developed in Portugal or Spain. Anarchists, Socialists, and Communists dominated the increasingly ideological labor movements. The Socialists provided the strongest party for the proletariat. In both countries, workers became clamorous during the lead-up to the coup. In Portugal this agitation occurred under a government lenient toward laborers, while in Spain it took place under an administration tied to organized labor.

In both cases, the working-class radicalization exceeded the wishes of the parties in office, as also occurred in South America decades later. Ideological divisions hampered labor's struggle for power under the democracies and for survival under the subsequent dictatorships. The military cracked down much harder on workers in Spain because of the workers' militant parties and ideologies, their tenure in government, their revolutionary potential, and, above all, the civil war.

During the Iberian dictatorships, the official union organization was a corporatist hierarchy primarily intended for containment rather than representation of workers. That labor system followed the outlines previously laid down in Benito Mussolini's Fascist Italy. The compulsory labor institution succeeded in replacing truculent leaders with pliable bureaucrats and in co-opting many unionists. It tried to meet the regime's contradictory needs for a working-class organization that was both representative and submissive.

The state controlled unions' leadership, funds, and behavior, as well as wage agreements. It prohibited union autonomy, as well as most strikes, and political activities. The illegal labor parties operated outside as well as inside the corporatist system.

Although often feeble, frightened, and frustrated, working-class organizations provided the core of the democratic opposition. As major victims of the police state, Spanish and Portuguese unionists built up resistance slowly. But after many years of government terror and labor surrender, the movements recovered from the 1950s onward. That recuperation was assisted by a reformed Roman Catholic Church and by Western governments and international organizations, although the Cold War restrained the West.

Unions began to reassert themselves by stressing narrow issues concerning workers' rights and wages. They became even more vocal in response to modest reforms of the labor code by the dictatorships, utilizing those openings while also condemning them as insufficient. Only near the end of the tyranny did unions rally around broader political demands.

Under authoritarianism, the political adversaries of the Iberian military regimes made little progress. The anarchists vanished, the Socialists hibernated, and the Communists persevered. The opposition movements in both countries traversed the trajectory of defeat and withdrawal, exile and regrouping, dashed hopes for Allied intervention after World War II, futile armed resistance, gradual rebuilding inside the country, expansion during regime liberalization, vain attempts to topple the tyranny through mass civil disobedience, and full reemergence after other forces terminated the dictatorship.

Throughout their struggle, the opposition parties agonized over the dilemma that clandestinity or exile provided security but impotence, while open agitation produced advances but vulnerability. Not surprisingly, most of the dictators' enemies opted for safety. Although the mainstream parties had little impact, exile politics kept dim hopes flickering.

Meanwhile, the Iberian Communists operated with relative success both underground and aboveground. They displaced the anarchists as the most important group of revolutionary workers. After a period in defiance and isolation, the Communist Party (PC) reconstructed its labor base primarily by infiltrating the official organizations. It increasingly monopolized overt confrontation with the regime.

The PC became much more powerful within the labor movement than it had been prior to the military takeover. The Cold War inflated the party's role as the most significant opposition organization, blocked efforts at unity against the dictatorship, and gave the despot legitimacy in some eyes as a bulwark against Marxism. The Cold War handicapped the opposition and bolstered the regime, as it did later in South America.

In the 1960s, both the Communists and the Socialists became less Marxist and more reformist. De-Stalinization and Eurocommunism softened the Communist position. However, the Portuguese PC maintained a more radical posture than did its Spanish namesake. As in South America, movements farther to the left failed to attract many workers. At the same time, the moderation of Western European socialists and social democrats reshaped the Iberian Socialists. In both Portugal and Spain, the previously dormant Socialist Party (PS) underwent a resurrection in the 1960s and 1970s. Both Socialist parties were dominated by personalistic leaders who pulled them to the right and aligned them with European social democrats.

This shift away from the left, however, did not engender much cooperation between the two antagonistic labor parties. In neither country did the Communists and Socialists succeed in pushing the regime to democratization. They did, however, manage to drive democratization in a more inclusionary and reformist direction once it was uncorked from above. The PC and the PS had laid the groundwork for the lower classes to insist on participation.

The authoritarian regimes in Portugal and Spain proved to be extremely long-lasting and personalized. Once the tyrant died, however, liberalization could not save the political system. Industrialization and urbanization had generated a larger and more powerful working class. It had also spawned a more diversified, specialized, and articulated civil society. The new social groups were primed for democratization, at odds with the anachronistic, closed regime, and difficult to police. The dictatorship unraveled quickly as it became clear that most citizens would not settle for anything less than a representative democracy along Western European lines.

Between the dictator's death and the end of authoritarianism, laborers vented their pent-up anger. Their belligerence made it more likely that democratization would come about and that it might include their organizations, parties, and demands. Then they lowered the volume during the most delicate period of the transition so as not to derail the process. After the restoration of democracy, labor intensified its activity—partly out of dismay that its issues and role had been shunted aside, and partly in reaction to economic decline.

At the end of the regime the Communists, as the most vigorous and visible opponents of the autocracies, initially constituted the strongest party, especially among laborers. They were soon eclipsed electorally, however, by centrist Socialist parties, whose slumber during the dictatorship disguised enormous capacity for renaissance thereafter. Following the transition to democracy, the PC stagnated electorally but retained a hard core of voters and a solid base within the unions.

As democratization stabilized, the Socialists succeeded the first postauthoritarian administrations. In both countries, the PS was the largest national party, held power for an extended period of time, and consolidated the democracy in a social-democratic mold. The Socialists also presided over austere neoliberal programs that were required in order for the newly democratized nations to join and compete in the Western world. As in postauthoritarian South America later, the center of the political spectrum came to dominate.

The Iberian Socialists reflected the classic dilemma of democratic socialist parties. They tried to hang on to working-class support while broadening their appeal among the middle classes to obtain an electoral majority, and they increasingly resembled "catch-all" parties that were less clearly defined by social class and ideology. Their rightward drift left more conservative parties with no sharply contrasting economic programs, and labor with few champions for its claims to social justice. In Portugal as well as Spain, the right became fragmented, confused, and ineffective, while labor became domesticated and discontented.[6]

There was historical justice in the replacement of the dictatorships by their left-wing enemies. However, economic modernization, the transformation of the international environment, years of relentless repression, and political learning by the chastened leftists eliminated any chance of radical socialist outcomes. Although the despots were superseded by democracies, their objectives of moderating the opposition and preserving capitalism were realized and outlived the regimes.

Portugal, 1926–1974

Following the installation of the First Republic (1910–26), Portuguese organized labor made unprecedented organizational gains, which included the right to form national federations and to strike. As in our other democracies in the penumbra of dissolution, labor agitation and violence skyrocketed. Facing working-class assertiveness, capitalists reacted against the democratic experiment. Military officers shared their revulsion at radical ideologies and at government laxity toward labor turmoil. The Roman Catholic Church was appalled by anticlericalism and social disorder. Even the Republic's erstwhile supporters in the middle and working classes criticized its ineptitude, deficit spending, soaring inflation, and social commotion. When the government fell, it had few defenders.[7]

Following the coup in 1926, the right-wing military junta turned to economics professor Antonio de Oliveira Salazar to stabilize government finances and the nation's economy. After consolidating his New State (Estado Novo) in 1933, Salazar ruled until his death in 1968. Thereafter Marcelo Caetano succeeded him until the authoritarian regime's demise in 1974.[8]

The Portuguese opposition evolved through the following stages: (1) a flurry of armed retaliation followed by recoil into clandestinity, 1926–31; (2) defeat, division, and demoralization, 1931–41; (3) a rebirth of resistance and of the Portuguese Communist Party (PCP), 1941–49, accompanied by disappointment that the victors in World War II did nothing to bring down Salazar; (4) renewed retreat and fragmentation exacerbated by the Cold War, 1949–57; (5) a resurgent but ineffectual offensive by the growing working class and other nonconformists, 1957–62; and (6) quiescence and reorganization of the government's adversaries until the reformist military coup, 1962–74.[9]

As in our other corporatist cases, after the unions had been decapitated the Portuguese regime tried to make labor encapsulated, dependent, coopted, and impotent. Following the banishment of free trade unions in 1933, anarchists and Communists sought in vain to maintain clandestine unions. As the anarchists withered away, the Communists eventually decided to burrow into the official unions. As in Spain, this proved a more successful approach.

In 1933 Salazar's National Labour Statute replaced the former trade unions with obligatory, vertical associations intended to harness workers. The code restricted most unions to the local level, required leaders to be approved by the government, regulated and censored meetings and publications, banned strikes and lockouts, discouraged horizontal organizations, forbade membership in international labor organizations, and proscribed political activities. Under this legislation, the state intervened to stage union elections, to set wages, to adjudicate disputes (normally in favor of employers), and to maintain generally peaceful industrial relations. Nevertheless, legal unions and their membership were allowed to grow within the official system.[10]

At the end of the 1960s, Salazar's successor, Caetano, tried to pacify labor, the left, moderates, and international public opinion through piecemeal liberalization. As in all the other cases under discussion, even mild or cosmetic reform of the labor system from the top down sparked working-class mobilization. Instead of mollifying labor, liberalization motivated workers to accelerate their demands and strikes.[11]

In Portugal as in Greece and Argentina, an external military adventure torpedoed the dictatorship. In 1974, the armed forces deposed Caetano principally to halt the colonial wars in Africa, but they also favored democracy and social reform. Labor played no direct role in the overthrow of the dictatorship, but immediately thereafter workers pushed the army's "revolution" to the left.

More than in the other cases discussed here, the governments that succeeded capitalist authoritarianism in Portugal implemented much of the workers' agenda. Shortly after the initial coup, the provisional administrations issued a spate of prolabor legislation. The new rulers demolished the corporatist union structure, promoted and protected unionization, recognized the right to bargain collectively and strike, reduced the work week, and increased wages. The Constitution of 1976 guaranteed labor's rights to work, to organization, to health care, to education, to housing, and to social security.

Although the workers' revolution did not prevail, the proletariat made enormous gains under the new democracy. By the end of the 1970s, however, organized labor was still hobbled by the small size of the industrial workforce and of unions, by workers' heterogeneity, and by dependence on fairly autonomous political parties. At the same time, many Portuguese had a greater desire for economic growth and modernization than for redistribution.[12]

In the wake of the 1974 coup, leftist parties—especially the rival Communists and Socialists—rushed to fill the political vacuum. The PCP served briefly in the government. When radicalization began outstripping the reformist intentions of most of the military, more conservative segments of the armed forces halted that trend in late 1975. As in the other transitions we are considering, the Communists were most effective when championing workers' nonpartisan opposition to the authoritarian regime, but less so when voters began to choose among leftist party alternatives. Into the early 1980s the PCP remained the strongest party among labor unions, but it lost out to the PS in national elections.[13]

Like Felipe González in Spain, the moderate Mário Soares dominated the Socialists in Portugal. In 1976 the Socialists began their ascent in Portugal's first parliamentary elections in half a century. After winning a plurality of the popular vote, the PS followed in the footsteps of its European brethren. The party ruled over a period of social democratic reform and prolabor policies lasting until the mid-1980s. However, the Socialist governments disappointed labor and the left on many measures because they had to implement austerity to restore macroeconomic stability and to compete in the Western world.[14]

Spain, 1939–1975

Spain provided a paradigmatic case for the more developed countries of Spanish America, particularly Chile, to a greater extent than Portugal did for Brazil. On the eve of Salvador Allende's ouster in 1973, Chile's Popular Unity warned of a repetition of the Spanish Civil War (1936–39). After taking power, Augusto Pinochet displayed his admiration for Francisco Franco. And during redemocratization, the Chilean opposition—especially the renovated Socialists—looked to the moderate Spanish example. Despite commonalities with South America and Portugal, Spain's experience was also distinctive, mainly because of the catastrophic civil war.

As in Brazil, Chile, and Argentina, a prolabor government preceded the military takeover in Spain. The multiparty Popular Front's electoral victory in 1936 inspired massive worker activism, including strikes, demonstrations, and property takeovers, sometimes in excess of the government's desires. That effervescence motivated many business elites, landowners, church officials, and military officers to back the uprising by General Francisco Franco in 1936. Although labor was less radical than it appeared before and after the civil war, its revolutionary image and potential aroused right-wing phobias and ferocity. The quarrelsome, fissiparous, and outgunned coalition of Socialists, Communists, Republicans, and anarchists finally fell to Franco's forces in 1939.[15]

The working class bore the brunt of repression under General Franco. Many officials of outlawed working-class unions and parties fled into exile. Many who remained faced jail or execution. As in Chile, the military tried many leftists retroactively for having been politically incorrect before the inauguration of the authoritarian regime.[16]

As in Portugal and Brazil, the economic modernization that resulted from squeezing the income of wage earners to fund capital acquisition eventually increased the size and strength of the working class so that it could demand a fairer share. In contrast with the dictators in the Southern Cone, the Portuguese and Spanish autocrats partly pacified workers with job security. The Spanish workers also acquired social security and other minimal welfare services. By the 1950s, Franco had locked laborers into an "implicit social contract" wherein he gave them stable employment in an expanding economy but restrained their wages and activism. Toward the end of the dictatorship, industrialization and urbanization had raised worker capabilities and demands to heights not seen since the 1930s.[17]

During his first five years, Franco pulverized the pre-existing institutions of the working class. He immediately decreed a new labor code, drafted in 1938. The government enrolled workers and employers in hierarchical public institutions, soon named the Spanish Syndical Organization (OSE). The state also outlawed strikes and most collective bargaining, used compulsory arbitration to mediate relations between workers and employers (usually in favor of the latter), monitored working conditions, and set wages.

An arm of the government, the vertical syndicates were supervised by the Ministry of Labor. Franco's official party, the Falange, selected the leaders of the OSE, which attempted to both control and represent labor. In addition, these surrogate unions furnished many workers with education, vacations, recreation facilities, cooperatives, insurance, pensions, medical care, and housing.

Although the OSE never backed strikes and allegedly enjoyed little worker support, it did provide channels and legal services that enabled individual workers with grievances to present them to the Ministry of Labor. As in the case of Brazil, these paternalistic, clientelistic mediations with the state may have served the regime's purpose of mitigating class conflict. As in some other cases, these official bodies apparently failed to co-opt most organized laborers, although more union leaders may have cooperated than critics believed.[18]

After enforced submission in the 1940s, workers began reasserting themselves in the 1950s, as they prepared to become the leading social force bucking Franco. As in the Southern Cone, their actions were a response to the introduction of a new labor code, one element in a general liberalization. The government had launched the new charter partly in reaction to criticisms from foreign labor organizations at a time when Spain wanted to insert itself into the Western economic universe. The Collective Bargaining Law of 1958 allowed some negotiating over wages and working conditions, mainly through local OSE committees in individual plants, although it still prohibited strikes.

As in our other cases, the authoritarian regime failed to resolve the dilemma of labor interlocutors. Spanish workers took maximal advantage of any small opportunities opened up by the regime, while still criticizing the system as inadequate and undemocratic. Although the corporatist hierarchy continued to control labor issues nationally, its adversaries—especially the Communists—took charge at the local level. Franco's opponents used the limited collective bargaining opportunities in the plants to generate demands and conflicts that fostered political activation.[19]

The combination of a political legacy and socioeconomic change provided impetus for the new unionism. Working-class militancy reemerged chiefly in areas that had been hotbeds for unions and the left in the 1930s. By the 1960s, industrialization was also highest in those regions. Those historic bastions of laborism became a strategic and symbolic beacon for the rest of the working class, much as they did in the Southern Cone.[20]

Under the new labor code, the legal unions still failed to deliver much for the workers. Consequently, as in Brazil in the 1970s, independent organizations sprang up on the factory floor. These informal committees spawned Workers' Commissions (Comisiones Obreras [CCOO]) that brought together local laborers and their leaders from different firms in similar industries, and from legal as well as illegal workers' groups.

After arising outside the official syndicates in the late 1950s, the Workers' Commissions began infiltrating the OSE in the 1960s, and winning elections. The CCOO evolved from ad hoc local gatherings to become national organizations in the 1960s and ultimately a full-fledged labor confederation in the 1970s, the largest single amalgamation of unions. As under some other authoritarian regimes, opposition parties formed alliances within the labor movement first. These coalitions succeeded partly because cooperation within individual factories, among similar factories, and within the Workers' Commissions was so indispensable for the laborers. In its spontaneity and leftism in its early years, the CCOO resembled the Brazilian Party of Workers (PT), but the prevalence of the Communists gave it a more traditional labor confederation cast.[21]

The great debate within the left and labor in Franco's Spain—as later in Pinochet's Chile—had been whether democratization would come about through rupture or through reform. Following Franco's death in 1975, worker protests escalated. By 1976, however, the Communists and the Workers' Commissions had scuttled their idea of bringing down the authoritarian regime through mass upheaval. They joined the Socialists and other opposition groups in negotiating democratization with the government.

As elsewhere, the working class and the left pulled their punches because of the fear that democratization might revert to authoritarianism. Thus labor had much more success at facilitating political democratization than at pursuing socioeconomic reforms. Through its caution, the Spanish workers' movement earned a great deal of the credit for the tranquil restoration of democracy. Thereafter, its steadfast support for democracy and its vow to defend that political system also served as a deterrent to would-be coup makers.[22]

The working class facilitated democratization by accentuating the crisis of the dictatorship, by discouraging an ultraconservative transition that would have preserved the essence of despotism, and by denying reactionaries any excuse or opportunity to turn the clock back. Trade unionists in Spain went through a pattern of political mobilization and restraint similar to the pattern subsequently seen in the Southern Cone. They picked up the tempo in the ebbing years of the dictatorship, then muffled their voices during the delicate moments of the transition, and finally revived under the new democracy.[23]

Formal democratization had been preceded by the conquest of political spaces by civil society, including intellectuals, artists, entertainers, professionals, and above all, the working class. Labor disputes had emboldened other democratic sectors, especially students. Once the lower and middle classes had affirmed their nonconformity with the ossified political system, the long-stifled opposition parties picked up the banner.

The two most important opposition parties were the Spanish Communist Party (PCE) and the Spanish Workers Socialist Party (PSOE). The former grew larger under the dictatorship, while the latter shrank but then revived to recapture the leadership of the left. As in Chile, the Communists closed ranks while the Socialists fragmented. Both parties received help from abroad, the Communists from the Soviet Union and Eastern Europe, the Socialists from Western European Socialists and the Socialist International. As in the Southern Cone, the outlawed parties worked through social organizations, especially the labor movement. Thanks to deep roots and family socialization, the parties survived underground and in exile, keeping many of their cadres alive and useful.

Unlike the leaders of the Communists, the leaders of the Socialists resided in exile for most of the Franco era. The PSOE, like the Chilean Socialist Party, was sundered by factionalism, which rendered it ineffective during many years of struggle against the dictatorship. However, those same internal disputes eventually generated seminal renovation of the party's leadership and doctrines. Like their counterparts in Chile, the "renovators" tried to make the party more modern, moderate, and unquestionably democratic, without completely renouncing its worker roots, class struggle, or Marxist inspiration.[24]

Like their counterparts in the Southern Cone, the enemies of Franco did not overthrow the dictator, but they did lay the groundwork for a democratic future. Redemocratization took place through a brief transition from Francoism to parliamentarism (1975–77), followed by a longer transition to consolidation (1977–82). That process culminated in 1982 with the Socialist takeover, led by Felipe González.[25]

In composition, character, and outlook, the labor movement that took part in democratization was different from the one that had been aroused by the Popular Front and then pummeled by Franco. Much of the past radicalism was suppressed, first by repression in the 1940s and then by socioeconomic modernization from the 1950s to the 1970s. Most laborers were strongly committed to democratization and moderation. During the transition, however, unions complained about the slow pace of change, about subordination to political parties, about the emphasis on social pacts with business and the state, about insufficient reform of the labor laws, and about the paucity of economic gains by workers. Apprehensive about the return of authoritarianism, unionists watched their own agenda being shoved into the background by politicians crafting a new democracy. In that system, labor soon became even weaker, not stronger.[26]

In Spain as in South America, the new democracy only granted minor concessions to the working class. The political elites hoped that these gains would be sufficient when contrasted with the hideous conditions under authoritarianism. They were more concerned with placating the right than the left, realizing that rightists posed the greatest threat to democratization. The administrations that guided the transition from 1977 to 1982 encouraged strong parties and weak unions.[27]

At the time of the transition, the OSE disappeared. It was replaced by independent unions, primarily led by either the Communist or Socialist national confederations. As in the other countries under discussion, many workers who backed the Communists in the union halls preferred other parties, in this case the Socialists, in the voting booths.

The state legalized unions and their activities in 1977 and spelled out their rights in the 1978 Constitution. However, it postponed a new labor charter until the end of the decade. In Spain as in Brazil, Uruguay, Chile, and Argentina, the trade unions did not immediately get the full bill of rights for which they had been asking under the dictatorship. Also as in Brazil, some of the corporatist features of the authoritarian system became more attractive to workers under democracy when contrasted with the risks of free-market unionism.[28]

As the new Spanish democracy took shape under the transitional, center-right presidency of Adolfo Suárez in 1976, representation of the workers in negotiations passed from unions to the opposition parties. Working-class material needs had to wait, since the first postauthoritarian government was led — as in Argentina, Uruguay, and Brazil — by groups unattached to organized labor. As in Portugal, Brazil, and Chile, when the authoritarian veil was lifted, uncertain and untested parties scrambled for followers and niches.

The right suffered the most acute disorganization and exhibited fewer continuities than did the formerly persecuted organizations. To press for inclusion, the Communists and Socialists had to reassert and to prove their claim to speak for the working class. In response to the economic crisis and labor unrest, the new government and the opposition parties composed the Pact of Moncloa in 1977 to stabilize wages and prices. The Moncloa deal and subsequent accords between right and left, capitalists and workers, made Spain the epitome of redemocratization achieved through concertation negotiated by elites.

In the 1977 and 1979 national elections, the PCE and PSOE ran best in urban and working-class areas, especially where they had been strong prior to Franco's reign. Indeed, electoral continuities were so striking from the 1930s to the 1970s that it appeared that voting patterns had been frozen. Although workers gave almost three-fourths of their votes to leftist parties with revolutionary heritages and vocabularies, polls did not reveal that laborers had any noticeable preference for radical solutions. They voiced the same restraint expressed by the Pact of Moncloa and the more moderate Socialists.[29]

Although the PCE embraced moderation and consensus, its support slipped away as the transition unfolded. During democratization, the PSOE owed its phenomenal growth not only to union loyalties but also to historical memories, family networks, and regional strongholds. It also benefited from international connections, the influx of a new generation, personalistic appeals, and an increasingly temperate program, thus combining older and newer assets.

The contradiction between the moderate attitudes of many workers and the radical pronouncements of some Socialist politicians which was seen at the start of democratization was reversed in 1982. After taking power, the PSOE swung to the right of its rank and file. Like most labor parties in other capitalist democracies, the Socialists downplayed some worker demands in order to broaden their electoral base, especially with the middle class.

The ruling Socialists embarked on neoliberal restructuring in the 1980s to curtail inflation and expand investment. Those belt-tightening, market-friendly policies proved almost as damaging to the standard of living of workers as had some periods of right-wing repression. In a reversal from Franco, workers now had more rights but less job security. The Socialists' labor allies complained vociferously about widespread unemployment, insufficient wages, and neglect of social needs. Nevertheless, the government stayed on course because of the need to cooperate and compete with international capital, especially as Western European integration gathered momentum.[30]

Although labor unions and parties were far better off after Franco's regime, they did not scale the heights they had dreamed of reaching once that yoke was removed. Following militant activism against the dictatorship, labor organization and agitation soared in the late 1970s and then declined steeply in the 1980s. The Socialists held power but lost their sense of mission. In the process of democratization, in the Iberian peninsula as well as the Southern Cone, the legacy of authoritarianism was not completely erased. The dictatorship's fundamental achievements of taming the labor movement, stamping out Marxism, and obliterating any alternative to market capitalism remained in place.[31]

The Later Precursors: The Military Regimes in Greece and Brazil

In the 1960s, two more dictatorships foreshadowed what was to come in the Southern Cone. Taking power during the Cold War, the authoritarian governments in Greece and Brazil trumpeted their anti-communism and received support from the United States. The military in both Greece and Brazil repressed labor and workers' wages to stabilize the economy and to accelerate capitalist growth. They relied on market-oriented models, more so in Greece than in Brazil, but maintained a significant role for the state. The expansion of industry improved the size and employment of the workforce in manufacturing, but widened income inequalities. As a result, worker expectations and demands had escalated by the end of the authoritarian episodes.

Even before their dictatorships, both countries had long had weak trade unions subject to state controls. Before the coups as well as after them, the governments exerted extraordinary supervision over unions' existence, leaders, funds, behavior, strikes, and wage agreements. For workers, lobbying the government was often more important than negotiating with employers.

Unusual labor growth and assertiveness—sometimes bursting out of official channels—preceded both military uprisings. However, neither takeover was a reaction to any awesome threat to the status quo, so the armed forces applied relatively mild repression. During the subsequent economic growth, more union leaders were favorable toward the undemocratic government in Greece and Brazil than in the other countries under discussion, despite labor's fundamental opposition to the regime.

Thereafter, democratization brought Greek and Brazilian unions invaluable rights and operating room. But it did not usher in the fundamental transformations in the industrial-labor relations system which many unionists had hoped for. Labor remained tethered and monitored by the state. Although sturdier than before the coups, the labor movements were still divided organizationally and ideologically.

Along with fragile economies and unions, Greece as well as Brazil had long hosted flimsy political parties. Those organizations existed in a political system where the military exerted great sway, whether in power or behind the scenes. Before the coups, both nations had possessed limited parliamentary democracies wherein the armed forces retained vetoes over participation and policy.

Most Greek and Brazilian political parties eluded sharp definition by social class or ideology. Rightist parties lost ground to centrists and leftists during the lead-up to the coups. Just as labor and its parties developed later in Brazil than in the Southern Cone, so they developed later in Greece than in the rest of Western Europe. The only well-organized working-class party was the outlawed Communists. They fared better within the unions than with the national electorate. Whereas the democratic breakdown in Brazil occurred during a prolabor government, disintegration in Greece took place during a centrist administration that was merely lax toward labor.

Both militaries had imbibed the national security doctrine from France and the United States and defined labor, leftists, and reformers as subversives to be combated by the armed forces. Both dictatorships claimed to be eliminating communism, but they were mainly suppressing populism. Neither takeover encountered any significant resistance in the first several years, since neither labor nor the left was strong enough to mount a challenge. Minor attempts at armed resistance came to naught. During the struggle against the dictatorship, new socialistic laborite parties arose. They filled a longstanding vacuum between the establishment and the Communists.

Both Greece and Brazil underwent democratization from the top down. Union and party opponents of the dictators scored few successes, especially in Greece. However, Brazilian laborers exerted relentless pressure in the waning years of the autocracy, helping to push liberalization to move on to democratization. Although capitalists benefited from both dictatorships, many of them became willing to disengage from those regimes. The elites engineered liberalization, but it failed to satisfy the masses or fortify the despots. Guided from above, both transitions evolved smoothly and initially handed power over to conservative successor governments.

After redemocratization, most political parties attracting workers still offered multiclass, personalistic, patron-client machines without crystallized ideologies or social bases. But now traditional party appeals were challenged by new prolabor parties and charismatic leaders. When both authoritarian regimes concluded their terms, labor unions and their party allies were stronger than they had been when the armed forces had seized power.

Greece, 1967–1974

From the 1930s to the 1960s, the Greek state controlled trade unions. Above the local chapters and national federations stood the unitary General Confederation of Greek Workers (GSEE). It was dominated by leaders loyal to the current government, just as supporters of the colonels would take charge after the coup d'état.   Unions and their national organizations expanded in the years leading up to the military intervention. Activist unions arose inside and outside the GSEE, and strikes proliferated.[32]

A constrained parliamentary democracy heeded the wishes of right-wing military officers. Before the colonels toppled the government, no large party represented the non-communist left. The organization with the strongest bond to the working class was the small Communist Party (KKE), outlawed from 1947 until 1974.[33]

George Papadopoulos, a colonel in the Greek army, seized power in April 1967. The armed forces stepped in to make sure that the rising reformist forces of the center, the left, and labor did not change the existing distribution of political power, particularly the military's tutelary role. The soldiers launched a preemptive strike to foreclose the possibility of centrist, populist, and leftist gains in the upcoming elections.[34]

Somewhat like the Uruguayan dictatorship, the Greek regime never succeeded in achieving legitimation, institutionalization, or consolidation. The military government enjoyed less popular support and controlled society less than did the comparable administrations in Portugal, Spain, or Brazil. Since there was no leftist menace, however, there was no initial resistance to the coup d'état.[35]

In Greece as in Portugal, Spain, and Brazil, the dictators' encouragement of industrialization fueled the growth of the urban working class. Although full employment was maintained, the junta slashed the bargaining power of labor organizations and converted them into even more supine state agencies. The ruling colonels immediately banned many trade unions—especially leftist and Communist units—and all unauthorized meetings, publications, and strikes. They arrested, tortured, and sent to concentration camps hundreds of union leaders. As in Brazil, the armed forces discharged scores of union officials and substituted government loyalists. In 1969 they installed sycophants to replace the already conservative officers of the national labor confederation.

Between 1968 and 1971, decrees changed a few of the laws for labor-industrial relations, further emasculating unions. That legislation clamped more severe restrictions on the right to unionize or strike, especially for workers connected with the public sector. Consequently, no major strikes took place under the junta.[36]

Neither unions nor parties mustered any widespread opposition to the regime. Martial law stamped out virtually all political activity. The junta proscribed all parties, disallowed free elections, and incarcerated or banished the top politicians of the center and the left. Attempts at opposition unity foundered, often because of ideological differences.

In exile, Andreas Papandreou, the populist son of the previous democratic prime minister, launched the Panhellenic Liberation Movement (PAK) in 1968. It was the forerunner of the Panhellenic Socialist Movement (PASOK). Its campaign against the colonels had little impact in Greece. Nevertheless, as in Brazil, a new, more leftist party appealing to workers had emerged out of the struggle against the authoritarian regime.[37]

As in the other countries under discussion, attempted legalization and liberalization of the regime failed to alter the antipathy of the citizenry or to preserve the government. The colonels tried in vain to institutionalize their rule in the Constitution of 1973. Like the Argentine junta's Falklands /

Malvinas Islands invasion, the 1973 Cyprus conflict was an act of desperation. That clash did not generate lasting popular support for the regime but
rather brought it to its knees, especially after the army's defeat by Turkey in
Cyprus.[38]

Redemocratization resulted not from mass mobilization but rather from
carefully choreographed changes among the ruling elites. Neither labor nor
other interest groups played a prominent role, although student protests
jolted the regime. After the disgraced colonels stepped down in 1974, a conservative civilian administration presided over democratization, as in Spain,
Brazil, and Uruguay.

The new trade union law of 1976 restored the basic features of the status
quo ante. That code made Greek unions legally free and independent, but
it kept them bound, as they had been throughout most of the twentieth
century, by state paternalism and regulation. Through the Ministry of Labor, the government retained great sway over union leadership, finances,
collective bargaining, strikes, and wage agreements; this was similar to
what occurred later in Brazil. Most unions remained frail, fragmented, and
ineffectual, highly dependent on the state and political parties.

After the dictatorship, the political party panorama displayed some continuities with the previous array but showed some very significant alterations. After military rule, the traditional right declined, the old center
evaporated, and the new left ballooned. In 1974, the new government legalized all parties, including the Communists. The most important innovation was the rise of PASOK to capture the center of the spectrum and pull
it to the left. Although shrinking, the rightist parties maintained promi-
nence. In Greece as in Brazil, most political parties remained feeble, clientelistic organizations, without strong class or ideological identifications, except for the Communists.

True to the pattern in the other countries we are studying, the Communist Party emerged from the transition back to democracy as a solid, com-
pact organization without much capacity for growth. The KKE established
a foothold in parliament, attracting about the same percentage of votes as
before the coup. Probably a majority of unionists aligned themselves with
the Communists, while the second-largest number followed PASOK.[39]

With a populist, nationalist appeal, the Panhellenic Socialist Movement
under the magnetic Papandreou attracted an eclectic following. Like the
Portuguese PS, it was dominated by the middle class, had important but
moderate ties to labor, appealed to the underprivileged in general, and became a catch-all party. The new party's Marxist rhetoric sounded more rad-

ical than its social democratic behavior actually was. Experiencing a mete-oric rise like its brethren in Portugal and Spain, the Greek Socialist party vaulted from its foundation in 1974 to take power in 1981. Once in office, it became significantly more moderate.[40]

Regardless of ideological labels, Greece replicated the Spanish and Ar-gentine pattern, in that a laborite party took over after the first postauthor-itarian government. As in Portugal, Spain, Uruguay, Chile, Argentina, and—to a lesser extent—Brazil, parties in the center or center-left of the spectrum came to dominate the restored democracy, often with the support of organized workers. In Greece as well as Brazil, the forces of labor and the left emerged from capitalist authoritarianism with greater vigor and vitality than they had enjoyed when it began.

Brazil, 1964–1985

Of the two precursors in the 1960s, Brazil was by far the more successful and had more influence over similar political processes among its neigh-bors. Indeed, it boasted the paradigmatic "bureaucratic authoritarian" regime, wherein the institutional rule of the armed forces and civilian tech-nocrats demobilized the working class in order to hasten economic growth. Because of the long shadow it cast over the Southern Cone, we will give the Brazilian case more attention than the other precursors.[41]

Despite similarities, fundamental differences separated Brazil from the Cono Sur. The contrasts between the preauthoritarian and the postauthori-tarian labor situation were greater in Brazil. Prior to the coup d'état, work-ing-class institutions exhibited greater weakness in Brazil than in the South-ern Cone, so there was enormous room for improvement. Because worker mobilization was not so menacing in Brazil, repression was less ruthless.

The proletariat in Brazil, unlike that in the Southern Cone, grew under the dictatorship. Partly because the Brazilian military took office in a more rural country, it emphasized building up industries rather than opening them up to foreign competition. As in Southern Europe, the armed forces chained unions but also allowed them to carry out some functions and to grow.

In a country where existing political parties had little relevance before or after the coup, workers found space to launch new party initiatives during redemocratization. At the same time, other channels remained more im-portant than party connections, both before and after redemocratization. Those channels included personalistic leaders, regional elites, and the state.

In sum, in a country still industrializing, employing a corporatist system of state-labor relations, and hosting puerile political parties, labor's experience under authoritarianism reflected those structural, institutional, and political differences with the Southern Cone.[42]

From the 1930s to the 1960s, Brazilian labor benefited from import-substituting industrialization, but that drive had lost momentum by the eve of the coup. Less than 10 percent of the economically active population worked in the industrial sector. As in the Southern Cone, worker demands outpaced economic growth. Although real wages rose in the 1950s, triple-digit inflation had eroded those gains by 1964. Spurred by populist policies, the rising cost of living caused an increasing number of strikes. However, the surfeit of underemployed and underpaid workers always blunted labor action.[43]

The Brazilian labor movement also suffered from its small size, the frailness of labor organizations, its leadership's lack of independent muscle, and control by the state. Less than 10 percent of those employed belonged to trade unions. The most important, albeit anemic, organizations were municipal-level unions and their federations.

Laborers remained very disunited and primarily identified with five separate national federations. Although by the early 1960s the newly formed General Command of Workers (CGT) claimed to speak for organized workers as a whole, it remained an illegal organization with minimal grassroots vitality. The Brazilian Communist Party (PCB) and, to a lesser extent, the populist Brazilian Labor Party (PTB) led the CGT.

Before the coup, Brazilian labor had approximated the South American model of "political bargaining." For the most part, unions engaged in mediation with the state rather than collective bargaining with industries. They represented the "political unionism" typical of populism, in a case where unions were exceptionally flaccid and paternalized by the central government.

Traditionally, most Brazilian unions, despite some resistance, had reconciled themselves to operating within the corporatist legal system, codified in 1943. The president, the Ministry of Labor, the labor courts, the social security system, and the unions themselves policed the workers. The government collected union dues, oversaw elections, approved or removed all union officials, forbade most collective bargaining and strikes, and set minimum wages.

In 1963-64, the administration of João Goulart flirted with turning the corporatist apparatus into a mechanism mainly for state support of labor rather than containment, for representation rather than domination. Some official union leaders lost control, as many worker groups threatened to break out of their halter. Labor demands began embracing more national leftist causes in addition to bread-and-butter issues.[44]

In such a statist labor-industrial relations system, political parties could provide workers with indispensable allies from other social sectors and influence over government policies. But no powerful, national, well-structured, programmatic, mass-based labor machine appeared. Enduring repeated persecution, the Brazilian Communist Party developed strength in the unions but not in the electorate—a situation akin to what occurred in Portugal, Spain, Greece, and Uruguay. The PCB, which was illegal from 1947 to 1985, took a moderate stance in favor of gradual reforms. Whereas the PCB was small but durable, the other parties were large but diaphanous. The Brazilian Labor Party of Goulart and the vehicles of other populists offered only patchwork, regionalized, personalistic, opportunistic, and evanescent instruments.

Little pre-coup evidence existed of the extent of working-class attachment to party democracy in general or to any party or ideology in particular. The few electoral and attitudinal studies suggested that Brazilian workers spread their loyalties widely among the available political options. Nevertheless, the industrial proletariat displayed a tendency to vote for populists, especially the growing PTB. Scholars discovered few workers who openly favored drastic socioeconomic transformations. This prudence was common even among industrial laborers affiliated with the Communists.

Perhaps this seeming lack of enthusiasm for class or party struggle was not surprising. It was probably due to blue-collar workers' disadvantages in democratic competition, the defects of the parties claiming to speak for them, the shortcomings of their unions, and their longstanding dependence on the state. Equally inhibiting may have been their realization of marginal gains relative to the unorganized urban and rural masses, who were far more deprived. However moderate the majority of workers, many analysts and elites believed that a growing number of laborers entertained increasingly radical aspirations in the years leading up to the coup.[45]

During 1961–64, Goulart's government energized the labor movement. Goulart inspired fresh politicization, raised expectations, and aggravated divisions over goals and methods. However, having a prolabor president did not produce an integrated union-party coalition with any coherent or radical political project. Although labor's animation and radicalization reached intoxicating heights, the government tried to pipe most of that activism into populist alliances and policies.

The mounting number of union members, strikes, protests, marches, and demands under Goulart revealed the president's and the PTB's lack of control over labor. The biennial total number of strikes soared from 132 in 1959–60 to 192 in 1961–62, and to 215 in 1963–64. As in Uruguay, Chile, and Argentina, a militant minority of laborites exaggerated their own strength or had their strength exaggerated by their enemies. Reflecting upper- and middle-class hysteria, the armed forces seized power in 1964. They vowed to stamp out populism and communism, primarily meaning labor mobilization.[46]

The Brazilian military regime went through four phases: (1) economic stabilization and consolidation of authority, in 1964–67; (2) high rates of economic growth (the "Brazilian Miracle") and violations of human rights, in 1968–73; (3) economic deceleration and political decompression-liberalization, in 1974–80; and (4) economic crisis and extrication, in 1981–85. Although methodically repressive and brutal, the Brazilian armed forces did not carry out the multifarious and macabre types of atrocities committed in Spain, Argentina, and Chile. As in Portugal, their victims were not as formidable or as numerous. When likened to Chile's Augusto Pinochet, Brazil's last military president, João Figueiredo, snapped back, "One can not compare a surgeon with a butcher."[47]

Unlike the authoritarian regimes of the Cono Sur, Brazil's military rulers were not enamored of free-market models. They retained a greater role for the state and stimulated the growth of the modern industrial sector. Their model of state capitalism still encouraged import substitution as well as export promotion for manufacturing. Although the strategy for growth was different than in the Southern Cone, there was a fundamental similarity that required suppression of labor: there was a reliance on low wages to curb inflation, to increase investment, to attract foreign capital, to raise productivity, and to boost nontraditional exports.

The military government primarily determined wages by establishing minimum rates with periodic adjustments. This policy rendered most collective bargaining pointless. The regime held down wage increases to combat inflation, especially during the stabilization campaign from 1964 to 1967. The real minimum wage index, with July 1940 = 100, declined from 112 in 1961 to 92 in 1963. From there it fell steadily until bottoming out at 54 in 1974, and then climbing to a peak of 66 in 1982; thereafter it eroded to 50 in 1986. During the 1968–73 economic "miracle," GDP grew an average of

10 percent per year, real wages rose above the minimum scale, and inflation dropped from 27 percent to 17 percent.[48]

Between 1960 and 1980, a high level of economic growth and population growth in the cities restructured the economy. The proportion of the population living in rural areas dropped from 55 percent to 32 percent. While the proportion of the economically active population engaged in the primary sector plummeted from 54 percent to 30 percent, those in the secondary sector rose from 13 percent to 24 percent, and those in the tertiary sector from 33 percent to 46 percent. Between 1960 and 1980, employment in manufacturing and construction climbed from 3 million to 11 million, from 9 percent of the economically active population to 16 percent. The size and leverage of the working class increased particularly in the most sophisticated manufacturing branches. In industries such as metalworking, enhanced skill levels tightened the labor market, earned higher wages, and made collective bargaining more plausible.[49]

Despite growth, in the late 1970s the proletariat was still relatively small, young, and compacted regionally. Nearly half of all industrial workers were younger than thirty and lived in the state of São Paulo. A very high proportion of laborers in the cities still lacked steady jobs, marketable skills, literacy, professional organization, or political mobilization.

The growth of the informal sector and of new social movements for the unorganized masses also challenged Brazilian unions. Far more than in the Southern Cone, parties appealing to the working class would have to reach out from the narrow industrial base to enroll other followers. Those recruits were located in the middle sectors, the shantytowns, the countryside, and the nonunion social movements.

In contrast with the Southern Cone, Brazil's model of economic growth did not foster unemployment. Nevertheless, the presence of excess workers and vast underemployment, especially in the mushrooming tertiary and informal sectors and among unskilled laborers, still hindered the labor movement. While growth elevated productive employment and brought absolute gains to most workers, it also increased income inequality. From 1960 to 1980, the proportion of national income going to the poorest 50 percent of the population declined from 18 percent to 14 percent, while that accruing to the richest 10 percent rose from 40 percent to 48 percent and that accruing to the richest 1 percent rose from 12 percent to 18 percent. Within the working class, the gap between skilled and unskilled workers widened.[50]

In the second half of the 1970s, rising labor militance followed a period of prosperity. This mobilization coincided with a slowdown of economic growth and an upturn in inflation. Then conditions grew much worse during the economic crisis of 1981–83, as production, wages, and employment fell. That recession curtailed labor activism. Another reason that strike activity declined between 1980 and 1983 was a 1979 law giving a majority of workers annual wage increases 10 percent above inflation.

By 1984–85, renewed labor activity was occurring in reaction to the whipsaw of unemployment and inflation. Union protests spilled over from the last days of authoritarianism into the first days of democracy. Fortunately, the democratic forces took office after the worst of the recession was over. However, stagflation persisted and left scant resources for social reforms.[51]

Because trade unions had to resolve most issues with the government rather than with private businesses, the presence of an antilabor administration devastated Brazilian workers. Immediately following the coup, the government intervened in approximately five hundred labor unions and federations. It ejected leftist union leaders, cinched the bureaucratic strait jacket on workers' organizations, and banished their political parties. The authorities principally attacked large federations and big unions rather than the small, local, less political organizations.

Instead of having to gag most workers as in Chile, the Brazilian military only found it necessary to neuter the relatively small radical segments. Although the 1964 coup hit suddenly and encountered virtually no resistance, extraordinarily heavy-handed treatment of labor came gradually. The harshest repression really took hold in 1968 and lasted—not coincidentally—through the economic boom until 1973.[52]

The new Brazilian rulers were more successful than the later military dictators in the Southern Cone in replacing obstreperous working-class leaders with compliant servants of the regime. The armed services jailed and tortured recalcitrant union bosses. As in past raids on labor, the government mainly aimed to drive out the Communists. Their party and union leaders went to prison or went underground. The armed forces intervened in most of the major unions and placed them under the command of government loyalists, the so-called *pelegos*, while excluding former PCB or PTB union leaders from holding office.

Brazil also differed from the Southern Cone in the fact that great continuity prevailed in labor organizational structures. Rather than devising a new legal harness for trade unions, the dictatorship rigorously enforced the existing corporatist restraints. After the coup, unions became even more subservient state welfare agencies with little role in bargaining, mobilization, or politicization. Normally run by progovernment bureaucrats, they obtained guaranteed organizational and financial stability in return for submission to the state.

Within the legal system, the military regime allowed union expansion to keep pace with the growth of population, in sharp contrast with the dictatorships of the Southern Cone. Almost one-third of the industrial workforce belonged to unions by the mid-1970s. Trade union membership quintupled between 1964 and 1980. By the end of military rule in 1985, some 9 million out of 40 million workers belonged to approximately four thousand unions.

The government controlled not only union leadership but also funds for unemployment or strikes. Normally illegal, strikes became very rare from the mid-1960s to the mid-1970s. The number of strikes fell from 192 in 1963–64 to 25 in 1965 and to 0 in 1971. Work disruptions became increasingly risky because the government had rescinded laws protecting job security.

Significant resistance to military rule took shape slowly. While Goulart surrendered without a fight, the CGT reacted to the coup with a call for a general strike that went unheeded. The lack of any widespread working-class activation until the late 1970s was due to several factors: the absence of powerful, unified, class-conscious labor parties; multiple divisions within a pallid and cautious labor movement; government controls over trade unions; and of course, the police state.[53]

Whereas survival of the labor movement would later be the crucial question in the Southern Cone countries, the movement's transformation was paramount in Brazil. Following a brief outburst of strikes in 1968, the dictatorship silenced labor for a decade. By fastening leg irons on legal unions, the military unintentionally encouraged the growth of more genuine organizing from the grassroots. As in the Southern Cone, the hostility of the state generated closer relations between union leaders and the rank and file.

In the late 1970s, worker mobilization became more possible because of the growth of the industrial proletariat—especially in São Paulo—and because of liberalization by the regime. During the political permissiveness under Goulart, militant labor leaders had tried to radicalize the movement by seizing control of top positions within the state corporatist structure. During the gradual political reopening beginning in 1974, dissatisfied unionists tried to radicalize the movement from the bottom up. As in Portugal and Spain, they agitated both against and through the state system. In the second half of the 1970s, they operated with greater independence from both the state and parties, much like their Southern Cone counterparts.

Even though the Brazilian government did not totally prohibit political parties, the two toothless legal parties offered little to organized labor. Therefore, as in our other cases, nonparty instruments assumed importance to workers. The Roman Catholic Church provided crucial financial, organizational, and moral support to union rebels in the 1970s. Clerics condemned violations of labor's legal and human rights. Priests helped foster the "new unionism" and the Party of Workers (PT). Since the labor code required government approval for affiliations with international organizations, most Brazilian unions did not belong to foreign groups. Nevertheless, European and U.S. sympathizers applauded the union dissidents and assailed government oppression.[54]

As in other authoritarian experiences, trade unions were torn between cooperating with or confronting the government, which shrewdly played them off against each other. Whereas in Chile highly ideological unions proved extremely difficult to wean over to the dictatorship, many Brazilian workers tried to compromise with the regime. Even laborers who were diehard opponents of the autocracy agonized over whether to remain aloof from or to bore into the official labor system.

In the second half of the 1970s, Brazilian labor clustered in two main camps. The largest labor group remained the orthodox unions under Communist and pelego leadership. Known as "Syndical Unity," they defended the existing institutions while admitting the need for piecemeal reforms. Many of these traditionalists argued that labor would benefit more if the government would manage the corporatist system properly—if the state would exercise generous paternalism toward workers.

These orthodox unionists opposed the desire of rebels to install a system of independent trade unions. They feared that without state protection they would be in a poor position to bargain face-to-face with industrialists. To retain credibility with the rank and file, however, the traditionalists had to support some demands of the dissidents, especially demands regarding wages. Although the insurgents registered gains, the Communists still controlled about 15 percent of the unions and the pelegos around 66 percent in 1984.[55]

The opponents of the traditionalists had sprung from diverse roots. In the mid-1970s, radical Catholics and non-communist leftists formed the "union opposition" to challenge the official organizations by launching parallel "factory commissions." By 1977, that rebellion surfaced from underground and evolved into the "new unionism." Like the Workers' Commissions in Spain, it operated both outside and, increasingly, inside the official organizations. These challengers called for a restructuring of the existing labor system. They tried to make the unions more autonomous from the state, more representative in their leadership, more responsive to their members, more militant in their demands, and more effective in their collective bargaining.

Metalworkers in the São Paulo automobile factories, which were closely tied to foreign capital, spearheaded the new unionists. They relied on their charismatic leader, Luis Inácio da Silva ("Lula"). Like their counterparts in Argentina (notably in Córdoba), these Brazilian metalworkers constituted a novel challenge. Their strategic employment, technical skills, geographic concentration, and lack of loyalty to old parties and corporatist agencies made them unusual. In the mid-1970s, they exacted some local concessions through small-scale strikes, stoppages, and slowdowns.

That activity by the new unionists led to a larger campaign for retroactive wage increases in 1978–80. The rebellious laborers disobeyed legal restrictions on strikes. Those massive walkouts did not achieve many of their concrete objectives, but they did resurrect labor politics. Because the government usually remained intractable, that worker campaign, blending demands for economic and political change, linked up with the broader national drive for democratization. From the late 1970s onward, unions and parties gained ground simultaneously.[56]

During democratization, unions divided over the utility of alliances, although virtually all sided with the opponents of the government. Most new unionists disdained close collaboration with other foes of the regime, fearing dilution of their movement's class and ideological content. They also spurned any concertation with capitalists or rightists. Their independent stance was symbolized by their new Party of Workers and contrasted with the more cooperative strategy pursued by most trade unions in the Southern Cone. Despite their wariness, the new unionists did coordinate many tactics with other democratic forces.

Other Brazilian laborers expressed more enthusiasm about closing ranks with other opponents of the regime. They allied themselves with the official opposition party (the Party of the Brazilian Democratic Movement [PMDB]) and the broader campaign for democratization. Just as weak unionists had joined multiclass alliances before the 1964 coup, so most components of a handicapped labor movement enrolled in heterogeneous compacts in opposition to the military dictatorship. Many unions stitched together a multiclass front with the proponents of redemocratization in the 1980s, culminating in the military's departure in 1985. Like its counterparts in the Southern Cone, the Brazilian labor movement also reached out beyond the unions to tap other members of the working class. It became a banner and a megaphone for myriad subaltern groups.[57]

Attempts to found a single national confederation floundered. In 1983, the new unionists and their Party of Workers established the Central Unica dos Trabalhadores (the Unified Workers' Central [CUT]). The traditionalists, the Party of the Brazilian Democratic Movement, and the Communist Party countered in the same year with the larger and more moderate Coordenação Nacional da Classe Trabalhadora (the National Coordinator of the Working Class [CONCLAT]). In 1986, the CONCLAT became the Central General dos Trabalhadores (the General Labor Center [CGT]). In contrast with the CUT, the CGT remained more loyal to the corporatist order.

Under the restored democracy, the CUT outstripped the CGT in size as well as combativeness. By 1991, the former claimed 1,679 unions and 15,097,183 members, while the latter spoke for 972 unions and 8,055,877 members. Despite continuing divisions, trade unions during the struggle for democracy had made progress in five areas where they had historically been weak: base organization, breadth of coverage, interunion linkages, collective bargaining, and political mobilization.[58]

One factor that had restrained labor unions' and parties' resistance to military rule was that many workers apparently accepted the regime, at least during periods of prosperity. According to some survey research, a plurality of workers in 1972–73 preferred the dictatorship to the last democratic government. For them, the economic crisis, runaway inflation, escalating strikes, and social tumult under Goulart had been disconcerting, while Goulart's redistributive measures had been minuscule. They blamed a radicalized minority of politicians and union leaders for the ferment that had brought down democracy.

Of those Brazilian workers questioned in the early 1970s, a vast majority expressed no interest in national politics. Numerous workers placed little value on elections and parties, which, like the unions, had little power under the military. If accurate and representative, these interviews may have reflected objective conditions at the time. During the miracle years from 1968 to 1973, most workers' jobs and incomes improved, even though workers fell farther behind the wealthy in relative income shares. Although living in dire poverty in the cities, migrants from rural areas experienced gains over what they had known in the countryside. At the same time, decades of corporatist control had conditioned many workers to expect authoritarian treatment.[59]

Even within the boundaries imposed by authoritarianism, however, other laborers appreciated that unions and parties provided some of their few channels for expression. In 1965–68 and in 1972–75 (before and after the boom years), a series of interviews with Brazilian textile workers found that they valued unions, especially as welfare agencies to provide medical care and other assistance. They realized that unions provided benefits for them by putting political pressure on the state, and therefore felt that party activities were useful.

These more politicized interviewees also perceived the post-1964 state and the capitalists as their adversaries. Most of them saw the official government party—the National Renovating Alliance (ARENA)—as the instrument of oppressors, just as they had characterized the Democratic National Union (UDN, a conservative party) as an enemy prior to 1964. And the vast majority voted for the MDB (Brazilian Democratic Movement) in the government's managed elections after the coup, just as they had voted for the PTB in the free elections before. At least to that limited extent, many workers identified with their unions and their party choices. Differences among workers in attitudes toward the dictatorship were reflected in the later splits between traditional and new unionists.[60]

Workers' connections with progressive parties had been tenuous prior to the coup, after which populist vehicles disappeared and the Communists retreated into clandestinity. Until the late 1970s, the regime only allowed two official political parties: the progovernment National Renovating Alliance and the antigovernment Brazilian Democratic Movement. They bid for votes in semicompetitive elections rigged in the government's favor.

After the economic downturn, workers increasingly backed opposition parties—for example, in the 1974 elections. Thereafter, political decompression by the regime and greater activity by the parties helped the labor movement to reassert itself, even though direct ties between unions and parties remained thin and problematic. As in the Southern Cone, political parties acquired rising importance for workers as redemocratization drew near.

In the late 1970s, Lula and other new labor leaders remained suspicious of the old opposition parties. Although many of the new unionists backed the MDB (later, PMDB) in the 1970s as the only vehicle available, they became disillusioned with its moderation. The new laborites promoted greater autonomy of the workers movement in order to avoid populist or corporatist traps. Therefore they, along with some intellectuals and members of the clergy, launched their own small but innovative Party of Workers (PT) in 1979, after the regime legalized the existence of a multiparty system.

As evidenced by the socialistic PT, more workers radicalized their party orientation under authoritarianism in Brazil than in the Southern Cone. Labor's neophyte party became more classist and leftist than any significant contender had been before the coup d'état. The PT strode forth as a fresh organization representing a working class larger and more assertive than in the past.

In Brazil, the unions dominated the labor party more than in most of the other cases discussed here. Like labor parties during redemocratization in the Southern Cone, the PT increasingly emphasized its antiauthoritarian character and promoted participatory democracy within its own ranks. It also tried to reach beyond trade unions to encompass the unorganized poor.

In the early 1980s, the PT remained more important symbolically than numerically. It still did not mount a formidable leftist threat to the military and the capitalists. In the 1982 national elections, it received only 3 percent of the votes, and over 70 percent of its share of the votes came from São Paulo. Although most of its ballots derived from the poorer areas of São Paulo, it lost most of the working-class vote to the centrist PMDB.

The PT appeared to be repeating the earlier experience of the Communist Party, performing much better in the union halls than in the electoral arena. By projecting an increasingly temperate, inclusive image, however, the Party of Workers grew spectacularly. It scored much better in the 1985 mayoral elections and then in the 1989 presidential contest, when Lula finished a close second.

During the waning years of the dictatorship, many laborers outside the PT, including those still beholden to the Communist Party, continued to vote for the PMDB. The PCB itself remained outlawed and lost some strength in the labor movement to newcomers such as the PT. Retaining the same cautious orientation that had characterized them prior to 1964, the Communists normally argued for working-class moderation so as not to derail democratization.

In the early 1980s, other worker votes and sympathies were scattered among a variety of minor parties. One lively contender was the populist Democratic Labor Party (PDT) in Rio de Janeiro. Although the politicization of skilled, organized workers was increasing, their electoral alternatives remained mainly weak patron-client parties.[61]

Little hard evidence of precise working-class political preferences existed.

At a national conference of labor unions in 1981, a poll found that 59 percent of the workers there belonged to political parties: of those, 54 percent adhered to the PT, 35 percent to the PMDB, 6 percent to other tiny opposition parties, and only 1 percent to the government party (the Social Democratic Party, PDS, previously known as ARENA). Among the 41 percent without party affiliations, 44 percent preferred the PMDB, 31 percent the PT. If reliable, such findings indicated that the workers clearly aligned themselves in opposition to the government, but thereafter dispersed among party options.[62]

As the autocratic regime prepared to step aside in the early 1980s, Brazilian working-class organizations held out more promise than ever before. During the last decade of the dictatorship, Brazil stood out in contrast with the Southern Cone because of the relatively wide latitude permitted to labor union and party activity under military rule. That political relaxation occurred not because the labor movement there was more powerful but rather because historically it had been weaker. Those Brazilian organizations did not yet equal their Southern Cone counterparts in their potential to extract significant concessions for the workers from the established order.

The Brazilian authoritarians tolerated more liberalization because labor unions and parties had never constituted a fundamental threat. Many unions remained under firm corporatist controls. The debilities of the parties reminded observers of the deficiencies of the pre-coup political system. Although bucking the will of the majority of Brazilian voters, the military regime still commanded vast support, especially in the rural areas. And conceivably it could have reversed the opening orchestrated from the top if labor and the left had become too assertive.[63]

In Brazil as in the Southern Cone, labor mobilization cooled down as the transition to democracy came to a conclusion. Most opposition parties did not encourage labor volubility as the return to democracy approached. They did not want social strife to upset the political timetable. Therefore, most workers subordinated their socioeconomic grievances to the interclass crusade for civilian rule. At the same time, many in the PT insisted on the autonomy of the workers' movement and its right to make specifically working-class demands.

As under the dictatorships of Southern Europe and the Southern Cone, labor followed a pattern of upsurge as the dictatorship liberalized, acquiescence to party leadership and calls for restraint during redemocratization, and intensified activism as the new administration settled in. From 1980 to

1984, the volume of strike activity in Brazil declined as measured by the average size (e.g., the number of participants) and length of strikes, as well as their frequency. However, the total number of strikes soared from 293 in 1983 and 434 in 1984 to 712 in 1985 and 1,148 in 1986. In those same years, the number of national strikes rose from two to five, then to fifteen, and finally to twenty-five. General strikes jolted the nation in 1983 and 1986. As civilian rule took over in 1985, workers pressed their economic issues harder, and the volume of strike activity multiplied.[64]

After twenty-one years in power, the authoritarian regime finally gave way to the "New Republic." Through indirect elections, President José Sarney restored civilian rule in March 1985. His government was a creation of the moderate opposition, especially the PMDB, and of soft-liners who had previously supported the dictatorship. It was not a product of the leftists or the PT.[65]

In Brazil as in the Southern Cone, the labor party had to switch agilely from defining the main conflict as regime versus opposition (authoritarians versus democrats) to defining the conflict as bourgeoisie versus proletariat. The PT had to change from cooperating with other democratic parties to competing with them. That shift was especially important since the PMDB advanced from the largest party in the opposition to the largest party in the government.

After the dictatorship ended, unions had to rely on political parties to try to change the content and implementation of labor laws. However, the national leaders of the political opposition to the dictatorship, of the transition toward democracy, and of the first civilian government focused mainly on changes in political institutions, not on significant social reforms. Although the administration made some timid changes in labor relations, it did not approach the sweeping alterations previously favored by the PT. Eventually the new 1988 constitution included some mild liberalization of the corporatist system and some new rights for trade unions. As in the Southern Cone, the return to democracy gave workers crucial new freedoms but maintained most of the legal and social subordination that affected them and their unions.

The new unionists in Brazil immediately assumed a more independent, militant, and confrontational stance toward the first civilian administration than did the labor movements in the Southern Cone. Along with the CUT, the PT severely criticized the new government, which the CGT supported. The dissident unionists pushed for a shorter work week and higher wages, but unbridled inflation undercut most of their efforts. Unchained, labor agitation soared far above the crests reached under military rule, but without endangering the new regime.[66]

Unlike its counterparts in the Southern Cone, the Brazilian labor movement emerged from the authoritarian period much stronger than it had been prior to the military takeover and during the first decade of the dictatorship. It boasted strikingly different social composition, demands, and strategies. It was based in more modern industrial sectors, it challenged key features of the corporatist system, and it operated as a more vital actor in national politics.

Despite remarkable achievements, however, Brazil's heterogeneous labor unions and sympathetic parties still had not scaled the heights reached previously by the labor movements in the Southern Cone, especially in Argentina and Chile. Many Brazilian business executives realized that labor still posed no grave threat and was far from having revolutionary possibilities. The political potential of Brazilian workers seemed unlikely to be realized until their parties and party system became more robust.

Among numerous alternatives by the end of the 1980s, laborers focused their hopes on various centrist, populist, and socialist options. They converged briefly behind Lula's near-win in 1989. He made the strongest showing by a worker candidate for president in Latin American history. Despite expectations that his popularity would rise, Lula came in a distant second in the 1994 presidential election.

Although those electoral efforts fell short, they indicated that labor unions and parties were playing a much bigger role than ever before in Brazil. They were making more gains than their counterparts in the Southern Cone. Still, the Brazilian labor movement also had to operate within limits acceptable to the adversaries who had contained it for so long.[67]

FIVE

Uruguay, 1973–1984

The Uruguayan authoritarian regime, our first case in the Southern Cone, inaugurated the switch from corporatization to atomization of the working class. Like the military in Argentina, the Uruguayan armed forces initially concentrated on destroying leftist guerrillas and then turned their guns on workers. In relative terms the Uruguayan dictatorship was not extremely violent, partly because the labor movement it confronted was not very formidable. Indeed, the military government always seemed anomalous in a country with such a low level of leftist threat and such a vibrant democratic history.

Since the early decades of the twentieth century, the Uruguayan labor movement had exhibited a mix of distinctive features. It had developed within an unusually stable democracy rooted in a large middle class. Although reliant on the state and on political parties, Uruguayan labor unions retained their autonomy from both. Workers needed political allies not only on the left but also within the two dominant centrist parties. So long as the left was not a serious contender for the presidency, laborers split their allegiance between the leftist parties in union elections and the catch-all parties in national elections.

Although officially Marxist and classist, the labor movement did not solidly back Marxist parties and relied heavily on unionists from the middle sectors. It had to balance blue-collar and white-collar constituents in its heterogeneous social base. Although benefiting from being concentrated in the capital city, Montevideo, Uruguay's labor unions and parties wielded less strength than did their counterparts in Chile and Argentina.

From the 1930s through the 1950s, the centrist Colorado (Red) Party, with the acquiescence of the rival Blancos (Whites, also called the National Party), had negotiated a classic populist compromise among factory owners, the middle class, and workers in the cities. That arrangement simultaneously promoted import-substituting industrialization and the welfare state. The politicians forged this ISI coalition without the inclusion of a labor party. Because urban labor was satisfied with this "compromise state," it backed the two historic parties—especially the Colorados—in national elections and did not insist on a laborite alternative. The traditional "politicos" in Congress served as ombudsmen between unionists and government bureaucrats but seldom as national labor spokespersons.

After economic stagnation destroyed that tacit policy coalition, class conflict escalated in the 1960s. The upper stratum saw this breakdown of the longstanding ISI coalition around the welfare state as a leftist challenge. Labor-management clashes occurred more often. As industrialists increasingly favored the repression of unions, laborers looked to direct dealings with the state and to alliances with middle-class unionists to fend off worsening conditions. At the same time, more and more workers abandoned the multiclass, catch-all parties to side with the Marxist Frente Amplio (FA; Broad Front). That movement to the left coincided with gains by the left wings of the Colorados and the Blancos, a change in the behavior of the Blancos, who now offered a more reformist alternative to the increasingly conservative Colorados, and the emergence of urban guerrillas known as the Tupamaros.

By the 1960s, Uruguayan labor had assumed a dual role. On the one hand, it operated as a standard pressure group within the political system, defending union rights and demands. On the other hand, it increasingly aligned with leftist parties as an opposition movement against the political and economic status quo. The instrumental short-term orientation was strongest among the rank and file, the more radical long-term outlook among the leadership. In the 1970s, the military would repress both roles, especially the expression of an alternative ideological project.[1]

In Uruguay, unlike our other South American cases, laborite politicians never took power. Nevertheless, the armed forces fiercely assailed the labor movement from 1973 to 1984. After a decade of punishment, labor unions and parties did not disappear. They did, however, learn to restrain their behavior to reach a new accommodation within the limits of a middle-class, capitalist democracy.

Uruguayan labor's longstanding characteristics helped explain both its defeat under the armed forces and its resurrection during redemocratization. Before, during, and after the military takeover, unionists were weak because of the decline of real wages, the relatively small size of the industrial workforce, and the shortcomings of prolabor parties. The dictatorship accentuated those debilities. Nevertheless, the labor movement's independence, its tenacity, and its party allies helped it emerge from the authoritarian period with most of its components intact. Following the military's exit, labor looked as though it had reverted to its traditional role as a rather weak player in a capitalist democracy, albeit now more closely tied to the increasingly moderate Frente Amplio.[2]

Before the Coup

Structural Constraints on Labor

Uruguay's industrial worker organizations never exercised great power. In the years leading up to the coup, the service sector and the middle class overshadowed the proletariat, which was diminishing in size. By 1973, workers and employees in manufacturing accounted for 21 percent of the economically active population. Industrial laborers were scattered in tiny factories; over 90 percent of the manufacturing firms employed fewer than twenty workers apiece.[3]

As import-substituting industrialization stagnated beginning in the 1950s, conflict intensified over a shrinking surplus. The GNP declined by 12 percent between 1954 and 1972. Per capita income and wages contracted, while inflation soared. Unemployment had reached 9 percent by the time of the military takeover.

By the 1960s, economic decline had resulted in rising labor militance and elite quests for new growth policies. Even before the coup, labor had resisted government attempts in 1968–73 to place more emphasis on comparative advantage, to reduce protection for domestic-oriented industry, to cut back on employment in such manufacturing and in the public sector, and to drive down wages. For example, governments began awarding wage readjustments that were less than increases in the cost of living. However, no severe alterations in the economy were carried out until authoritarianism replaced democracy.[4]

Institutional Constraints on Labor

In the 1960s, union membership expanded, especially among white-collar employees. The public and private white-collar sectors in Uruguay were more widely unionized and more aligned with blue-collar organizations than were the corresponding groups in Chile and Argentina. Still, only 30 percent of Uruguay's economically active population belonged to trade unions. Most unions remained small and lacked any strong central bureaucracy, source of funds, or social service agencies. They normally pursued highly defensive and economistic demands. Uruguayan unions promoted explicitly political causes much less often than did their Chilean and Argentine counterparts.

As in most of the countries under discussion, unions in Uruguay functioned at three levels: in the firm, in federations of like occupations, and in national confederations. Some 90 percent of the unions had signed on with the National Convention of Workers (CNT) by the time of its consolidation under Communist leadership in 1966. It boasted some seventy associated unions and two hundred thousand members. However, the CNT remained a young and unimposing peak organization, with no international affiliation.

Neither a professional union bureaucracy nor political parties provided the primary conduit for working-class grievances. Instead, workers, like other pressure groups, primarily negotiated directly with the clientelistic state. As elsewhere in Latin America, unions in Uruguay experienced little success bargaining on their own, face-to-face with enterprises. They most commonly attempted to persuade the state to mediate their conflicts with management.

Given the efficacy of those institutionalized networks for resolving most conflicts, no labor code existed. Labor's basic rights to organize and strike were guaranteed in the Constitution, in conventions with the International Labor Organization, and in a series of separate laws. Unions operated with great freedom from government control. The need for state intervention in relations between labor and industry, however, made democratic politics crucial to unionists. A procapitalist authoritarian regime would leave labor virtually helpless in confrontations with management.

Despite its established position as an independent interest group in the political arena, labor became disenchanted with the existing system as its economic situation deteriorated in the 1950s and 1960s. In addition to voicing economic concerns, unions looked more often to leftist parties. Unionists began calling for broader sociopolitical transformations, such as land reform and worker participation in management. The number of strikes per year, and their length, spiraled upward between the mid-1950s and the early 1970s; the number of strikes per year rose from 121 in 1957–58 to 405 in

1963–64 and to 552 in 1969–70; in the year before the coup, 26 general strikes convulsed the nation.

In Uruguay as in Chile, by the end of the 1960s the moderate Communist leadership of the labor movement increasingly faced challenges from the left. A minority of unionists praised the Cuban Revolution, criticized the incremental approach of the PCU (Communist Party of Uruguay), called for greater CNT commitment to political struggle, and emphasized social mobilization in preference to electoral tactics. This radical tendency emanated from some white-collar as well as blue-collar groups. By the start of the 1970s, the CNT was calling for "national liberation" to create "a society without exploited or exploiters." On the eve of the coup, the radical language and image of the labor movement far exceeded its potential.

Although increasingly politicized, this dualist unionism still stressed instrumental objectives over political ones. It posed no uncontainable threat to the hegemony of the venerable party elites, let alone the bourgeoisie. Nevertheless, conservatives in Uruguay, like those in Argentina, overreacted to this union activism, which was linked in their minds with Marxism, the Tupamaros, and Cuban-style revolutions.

At the beginning of the 1970s, the government responded with increasing repression. It imposed restrictions on civil liberties in the name of national security, mainly to clamp down on subversion by guerrillas and activism by labor. In the five years prior to the coup, the state became less conciliatory and more authoritarian, not only with leftist insurgents but also with organized workers. Those right-wing trends intensified under the Colorado government of Juan María Bordaberry, elected president in 1971.[5]

Political Constraints on Labor

Most Uruguayan unions always claimed to be independent not only of the state but also of party direction. Labor leaders were more oriented toward union concerns per se and less oriented toward party positions than was the case in Chile or Argentina. Not only were clearcut labor parties much weaker in Uruguay than in Chile or Argentina, so too was any linkage between social class and party preference.

The bifurcation between the way workers voted in their unions and the way they voted in national elections allowed the labor movement to sustain an anti–status quo position within the union halls but participate in and reinforce the status quo in national politics. Until the 1960s, this schizophrenia worked satisfactorily for laborers. They were well organized as an interest group, they benefited from the ISI compromise, and they received welfare rewards from the state.

The political system was based more on clientelism than on class cleavages. Nevertheless, some class differences showed up in a few opinion polls in the late 1960s and early 1970s, which revealed the strongest support for continuation of party democracy among the middle and working classes. Surveys in the 1960s also uncovered a slight tendency for the middle- and lower-income groups to prefer the Colorados.

Neither of the two traditional parties had ever tried to establish a special, formal bond with trade unions, through either party or governmental institutions. The Colorados were the largest of the two patron-client parties and were historically the most successful at appealing to urban workers. Although rooted in the countryside, the Blancos resembled the Colorados in their catch-all social makeup. Votes for leftist factions within the two traditional parties in 1971, however, indicated rising discontent with the seeming vacuousness of politics as usual.

On the eve of the 1971 election, a Gallup poll revealed the Frente Amplio, despite its Marxian appeals, attracting a very mixed constituency. It apparently resonated better with the middle than the working class, especially among youth. The Frente's social base may have reflected its strength with middle-class trade unions.

The Front grew out of social movements, especially the unions. Its platform echoed the radically reformist program of the CNT. The unification of the labor movement and of the leftist parties was synergistic. The FA, which became an official entity in February 1971, constituted the first successful effort to unite the Uruguayan left. The Front represented more than twenty small political organizations, the most important being the Communists, the Socialists, and the Christian Democrats, along with some dissidents from the two mainstream parties. Even as the Broad Front surged forward in 1971, however, many workers still preferred the two traditional parties, which had a much greater chance to control the government.[6]

Within the labor movement, the Communists prevailed. They boasted that 75 percent of their members belonged to the proletariat; of that percentage, most were in trade unions. The PCU controlled approximately 80 percent of the leadership positions in the CNT. The Uruguayan Communists sustained a more moderate, gradualist program and strategy than did their Chilean namesakes. In the 1962 congressional elections, the leftist parties—mainly the Communists—captured only 6 percent of the national votes, and in 1966 only 7 percent. Even in the extremely unlikely case that all those ballots came from the working class, a majority of workers and union members were obviously not voting for the leftist parties.[7]

In the second half of the 1960s, the left and labor came together to challenge the deteriorating status quo. Between 1966 and 1971 in Montevideo, the Communists, Socialists, and Christian Democrats rose from an aggregate 16 percent to 30 percent of the electorate, while the Colorados declined from 51 percent to 30 percent. In the 1971 elections, the Frente claimed to have obtained its highest electoral percentages in the working-class neighborhoods of Montevideo. Its emergence turned Uruguay into a two-and-one-half party system. Despite this leftward slide, the two historic parties only declined nationally from 89 percent of the total votes to 81 percent, while the Front climbed from 10 percent to 18 percent (contrasted with a pre-coup peak of 44 percent for the Popular Unity in Chile and 63 percent for the Peronists in Argentina).[8]

Both in its composition and in its program, the Frente Amplio was much more moderate and diverse than was Chile's Popular Unity, whose presidential victory helped inspire the unification of the Frente. Because a majority of Uruguay's population belonged to the middle strata, the left tried to appeal to those sectors as well as to the proletariat in order to forge a class alliance against the oligarchy and imperialists. In Congress, it resisted the growing imposition of internal security measures, which were applied against not only Tupamaros but also trade unions and leaders of the Frente.[9]

The ultraleftist Tupamaro guerrillas in Uruguay, like the Miristas in Chile and the Montoneros in Argentina, failed to attract significant labor backing. As in Argentina, the government's vendetta against the guerrillas provided an excuse to repress labor activities. The military had essentially defeated the Tupamaros before its final assumption of power. Thus the level of threat—perceived or real—that labor and the left posed to the established order was much less in Uruguay than in Argentina or Chile at the time of the coup.

Conditions on the Eve of the Coup

Unlike Brazil, Chile, and Argentina, Uruguay did not have a prolabor government on the eve of the coup. Therefore, labor unions and parties never became as active as in the other cases. Repressive legislation and treatment for the working class had taken shape well before the military takeover, to a greater extent than occurred even in Argentina. Harsh re-

sponses to labor unrest began before the rise of the Tupamaros and continued after their demise. Although the death of democracy in Uruguay had
many causes, a key reason for the armed intervention was the intensifying
mobilization and protests by workers and their political allies.[10]

The coup took place against a labor movement that was already debilitated and depressed. It was increasingly alienated from the traditional parties but only partially attached to the Frente, itself a collection of Lilliputian
organizations. Many in the working class did not vehemently oppose the
coup—in part because they were already dispirited, and in part because the
armed forces had issued some early hints of populist inclinations, although
these were quickly discarded.[11]

After the Coup

After gradually usurping power in order to combat the guerrillas and
other loosely defined leftists, the Uruguayan military took over fully on
June 27, 1973, behind the facade of President Bordaberry. The armed forces
closed down Congress and other democratic institutions. Soon Uruguay
hosted more political prisoners per capita than any other country in the
world. Many of those incarcerated were unionists. Although the dictatorship in Uruguay caused fewer deaths than the military governments in
Chile or Argentina, it was just as determined to dismantle social movements, especially trade unions. The repression weighed heaviest on the re-
maining Tupamaros and the CNT at first, and then bore down on the
Communists from 1976 on.[12]

Structural Constraints on Labor

Unlike the dictatorship in Brazil, the authoritarian regimes in Uruguay,
Chile, and Argentina tried to reorient industry rather than deepen it from
light to heavy manufacturing. The Uruguayan generals favored manufacturing for export more than for domestic substitution or production of capital goods. After two decades of economic crisis, one of their motivations
for coercing labor was to encourage capital reaccumulation, greater competitiveness, and renewed growth. In a survey of three hundred industrialists in 1976, a majority named "control of labor unrest" as the most important accomplishment of the armed forces.[13]

The military's most urgent task was stabilization. While the government
unshackled prices, it compressed wages and salaries. As the Uruguayan

writer Eduardo Galeano quipped, "In Uruguay, people were in prison so that the prices could be free."[14] Austerity measures and wage controls lowered the rate of inflation from 104 percent in 1973 to 45 percent in 1977, and slashed the real income of workers by 29 percent. The decline of real wages accelerated under the military government: from a base of 100 in 1957, the index dropped to 70 in 1972, 46 in 1980, and 35 in 1984. Between 1968 and 1986, real wages in Montevideo tumbled by 50 percent.

As a result, the share of national income accruing to employers increased by 27 percent and that going to wage earners plummeted by 34 percent. Whereas wages as a percentage of national income accounted for an average of 40 percent during 1968–73, they fell to 35 percent during 1974–78 and 27 percent during 1979–82. Between 1973 and 1979, the income share of the richest 10 percent of families ballooned from 28 percent to 41 percent, while that of the top 5 percent catapulted from 18 percent to 31 percent. During those same years, the share of the other 90 percent fell from 72 percent to 59 percent. Between 1973 and 1983, the portion of family income in Montevideo accruing to the wealthiest decile of the population rose from 28 percent to 36 percent, while that going to the bottom three deciles slipped from 12 percent to 7 percent. Between 1976 and 1984, the number and percentage of families defined as indigent in Montevideo grew annually. This regressive redistribution helped to divide the middle from the working class, but it primarily increased the domination of the upper tier over all those beneath.

The government compounded this deprivation of workers by cutting back welfare programs and terminating employer contributions to social security and fringe benefits. The relative share of the national budget going to social services declined in the late 1970s. To further lighten the burden on business, regressive indirect taxes rose.[15]

Uruguay proved less avid than Chile or Argentina in its adherence to free-market economics. Like the military takeover, structural changes in Uruguay took place gradually. A distinction must be made between the impact of the authoritarian regime and the impact of the recession in the early 1980s; the latter was even more devastating to industrial workers than the former. Deindustrialization did not form part of the military's program in the 1970s, although manufacturing lost ground in the 1980s. In Uruguay, the main economic policy that debilitated industrial labor was the slashing of its real wages and the redistribution of its income to the upper strata, not the reduction of its size.

In Uruguay, unlike Chile and Argentina, manufacturing did not shrink under the military in the 1970s. Between 1973 and 1980, manufacturing growth at 6 percent per year far outpaced agriculture and services. Whereas industry contributed 19 percent of the gross domestic product during 1968–73, it provided 28 percent during 1974–80. That spurt was led by new industries producing for export, which accounted for one-third of the growth in manufacturing. Some older industries oriented toward the domestic market also did well and retained some of their customs protection, while others failed to adjust to tariff reductions and competition.

Between the eve of the military takeover and the late 1970s, the percentage of the economically active population employed in manufacturing changed little, dipping from 21 percent to 19 percent. While the number of blue-collar industrial workers fell, the number of white-collar employees increased. Only favoring piecemeal liberalization, the dictatorship refrained from going very far with erasing protectionism, trimming the central government, or contributing to the growth of unemployment.[16]

Beginning in 1973, rising prices for petroleum imports and falling prices for Uruguay's traditional exports prompted the government to encourage nontraditional exports. Foreign trade rose from 31 percent of GDP (in 1970–72) to 41 percent (in 1976–77). The value of Uruguayan exports skyrocketed almost 100 percent between 1973 and 1977. During 1974–80, total Uruguayan exports grew at an average annual rate of 19 percent.

As a result of sales abroad, most Uruguayan manufacturers remained more satisfied with the dictatorship's market-oriented economic policies than did their counterparts in Chile and Argentina. They welcomed the tailspin in real wages and the climate of industrial peace. They also appreciated, after years of stagnation, real growth of the GDP averaging over 4 percent per year between 1974 and 1980.

In Uruguay as in Chile, the economic crisis in 1981–83 brought civil society, the labor movement, and social protests back to life. After a decade of imposed quiescence, workers reassembled a national labor confederation in 1983 and began protesting their deteriorating standard of living. During the economic collapse, many business leaders turned against government policies, but not necessarily against the authoritarian regime.[17]

The GDP declined by 10 percent in 1982, 5 percent in 1983, and 2 percent in 1984, until recovery commenced in 1985. Unemployment in Montevideo went from 12 percent of the economically active population in 1963 to 8 percent during 1974–79 and then to 13 percent during the 1981–82 international recession, peaking at 16 percent in 1983 and thereafter winding back down to 12 percent in 1985. Real wages plummeted by 28 percent in 1982–83.[18]

After growing as a share of GDP between 1973 and 1980, manufacturing fell from 28 percent to 23 percent between 1980 and 1982. Between 1978 and 1984, the ranks of workers employed in manufacturing thinned both absolutely and relatively. Their number sank from 168,000 to 121,000. The percentage of the economically active population in manufacturing declined from 21 percent (in 1963) to 19 percent (in 1975) to 18 percent (in 1985). In those same years, the share of the workforce in agriculture dropped from 18 percent to 15 percent. In Montevideo, the percentage of the economically active population employed in industry fell from 31 percent in 1970–74 to 23 percent in 1983–87, while the service sector rose from 35 percent to 42 percent. Fewer people produced goods, more produced services.

Labor-saving technological changes, dispersion of workers in smaller shops, and growth of the informal sector also reduced the size of the workforce that had been the mainstay of industrial unionism. Workers in manufacturing suffered from increasing mechanization, as factories tried to become more competitive internationally. Out of the economically active population in Montevideo, the percentage of self-employed workers rose from 16 percent in 1975 to 22 percent in 1985, swelling the informal sector.[19]

All of the crisis trends mentioned above reduced the fortitude and feistiness of the working class, which had already been sapped by the repression of its organizations and wages in the 1970s. Public opinion polls in 1984 found that unemployment and low salaries were cited as the most important national problems by 26 percent and 17 percent of respondents, respectively. Again in 1987, polls showed Montevideo residents overwhelmingly citing low employment as the first national problem and low income as the second.[20]

Workers responded to worsening conditions with increased hours, multiple employment, piecework, an increase in the number of women working outside the home, self-employment in the burgeoning informal sector, and emigration. Consequently the manufacturing workforce became younger, more female, more compartmentalized in small enterprises, less stable, and harder to organize. These family survival strategies reduced not only workers' quality of life but also their capacity and the time they had available for collective action. These burdens hurt the middle as well as the working classes. During the period of redemocratization through 1984, labor continued to face depressed economic conditions. Thereafter, recovery gave the new democratic government breathing room.[21]

Institutional Constraints on Labor

As in Chile and Argentina, the military atomized the labor movement in Uruguay. The generals wreaked havoc on organized labor by removing its top leadership, shearing off its more radical sectors, and abolishing its rights to bargain or even exist. They disallowed any legal actions by unions until the introduction of new labor legislation in 1981–82. In the first hours after the coup, the regime dissolved the CNT, seized its assets, and arrested its key leaders, as part of a general assault on labor and the left. A state of siege now governed the working class. Lacking strong party or bureaucratic mechanisms, the unionists, after resisting with a fifteen-day general strike, caved in within a month after the 1973 coup.[22]

As in the rest of the Southern Cone, the military in Uruguay found it easier to hush labor than to reinvent it. Attempts to concoct surrogate unions and union leaders were fiascoes. Immediately after the coup, the minister of labor called for some workers to renew their union affiliations. He expected fresh organizations and leaders to arise in place of the previously predominantly Communist apparatus. When 90 percent of the workers reaffiliated with their old organizations, the regime canceled all such democratic union processes.

Another effort by the government to replace the CNT with an official General Confederation of Uruguayan Workers also encountered rejection by laborers and by the International Labor Organization. From underground and exile, the CNT persistently called for the unity of all social and political forces to bring down the dictatorship. In 1977, the Ministry of Labor lamented that its attempt "to create a new generation of union leaders . . . and a new trade union mentality has failed."[23]

In contrast to the dictators of Chile and Argentina, Uruguay's rulers offered labor a few more inducements along with constraints. They halted the CNT general strike against the coup not only with mass arrests but also with small salary increases. Even more than before the military takeover, the Ministry of Labor became active in addressing complaints about wages and working conditions; the number of cases handled by that office quintupled between 1973 and 1980. Despite the near-total illegality of labor organizations, parties, and activities, the regime soon quietly allowed a few noncommunist unions to reorganize and bargain locally, with increasing leeway by the end of the 1970s.[24]

The 1981–82 laws regarding "professional associations" primarily ratified existing government policy toward unions. They discouraged organization beyond the plant level, required government recognition of unions, restricted the rights of public employees, banned former activists from leadership posts, and forbade political activities. The government designed this legislation—like Chile's Labor Plan—to shift from coercion to containment of unions. But—as also occurred in Chile—these laws failed to achieve some of their basic purposes. This legislation gave unions space to reorganize and reassert themselves to a far greater extent than the dictatorship had intended. This attempt to regulate unions from the top down reawakened autonomous activities.[25]

In Uruguay, unlike Chile, neither the Roman Catholic Church nor international organizations contributed much help to labor. Exiled CNT leaders did get assistance from the ILO and other international labor organizations to denounce violations of human rights and imprisonment of trade unionists. Government conventions that were signed with the ILO restrained repressive legislation. Instead of making much progress with stand-ins for the political parties, however, unions had to await the revitalization of the party organizations.[26]

As in Chile, repression succeeded in deactivating labor from 1973 to 1980. Then the Uruguayan union movement rebounded because of three principal events: the beginning of redemocratization promoted by the political parties after the 1980 plebiscite, the regime's attempt to create a new institutional structure for labor-industrial relations in 1981–82, and the economic crisis of 1981–83. The pattern was almost the same as in Chile except that in Uruguay party reactivation preceded labor resurrection. The political opening began not because of social pressure on the regime but because of the government's own decision to hold a referendum that turned into a surprising defeat. Social mobilization responded to, rather than caused, the initial liberalization.[27]

Beginning in 1982, labor reconstituted itself by forming unions at the enterprise level, as authorized by the 1981 legislation. Then labor leaders moved beyond that restrictive law to revivify the traditional union structures. Without legal authority, they created the Interunion Plenary of Workers (PIT) in 1983. Since the Communists were banned, imprisoned, or exiled, younger non-communist union leaders constructed the PIT. Between 1973 and 1983, the national confederation's leadership evolved from a group in which Communists were in the majority to one in which they were a minority. It acknowledged its historical continuity by adding a suffix (National Convention of Workers [CNT]) to its name, becoming the PIT-CNT in 1984. That dual name also signaled a struggle within the confeder-

ation between newer leaders and older-line Communists, as the latter returned to legality.

Although born of new organizational efforts under the dictatorship, the
PIT-CNT, in its basic structure and ideology, looked much the same as the
labor movement had appeared before the coup. That confederation startled
the despots with the first big political demonstration against the regime on
May 1, 1983. There the PIT demanded the full restoration of democracy and
of union rights, expansion of production and employment, recuperation of
wages, and freedom for political prisoners, encapsulated in the slogan "Lib-
erty, Work, Salary, Amnesty."[28]

The unions applied mass pressure on the dictatorship, while the parties
negotiated with the regime at an elite level. The unions and all the major
parties, including the Colorados, together organized large rallies in favor of
full-fledged redemocratization. As the general representative of workers,
the PIT-CNT also symbolized the broader aspirations of poor Uruguayans,
far beyond the confines of organized labor. Largely on its own, in January
1984 the confederation successfully organized the first general strike since
1973, calling for material improvements for all workers and redemocratization for all citizens.

The unions also became a channel for political parties, especially persecuted leftists. Demonstrations by unionists bolstered the claim of their
main ally, the Frente Amplio, to be included in the return to democracy. As
in Chile and elsewhere, the unions soon ceded the political high ground to
their party compatriots. Most important was the reemergence of the Front,
which had helped to create the PIT and which had become more closely
linked to the labor movement.[29]

Political Constraints on Labor

At the time of the coup, the Frente Amplio and part of the National
Party called, in vain, for resistance. They backed the CNT's demands for an
immediate restoration of liberties. The military, however, dispersed their
demonstrations and jailed their leaders.

The dictatorship also ordered the Colorados, Blancos, and Christian Democrats to suspend all activities, but without declaring the parties illegal.
Although many Colorado leaders and a few Blancos backed the military
regime, the traditional parties officially went into a holding pattern until
1980. The regime outlawed all Marxist organizations and Frente members,
except Christian Democrats. After being mangled, labor unions and their

party sympathizers played no significant role for the remainder of the 1970s.[30]

From 1973 to 1980, the Frente Amplio was totally on the defensive. Many of its leaders, including its president, army general Líber Seregni, were arrested immediately. Thereafter the Front operated clandestinely. Members met furtively at their place of work or study. In 1977 they patched together a Coordinating Committee in exile in Madrid. That committee fomented international solidarity against the dictatorship, following orders from the Directorate of the Frente Amplio still underground in Uruguay. The FA maintained more unity than did the Chilean UP and always kept it clear that the real leadership remained within Uruguay.[31]

The most important labor party—the Communists—suffered the worst persecution, having been banished for the first time since the party's birth in 1921. After arresting its top leaders in 1973, the armed forces completed the demolition of its middle- and lower-level cadres in 1975–76. Underground, the PCU struggled to keep alive the historical memory of working-class conquests under democratic auspices. Even minor acts, such as painting city walls with slogans or distributing mimeographed leaflets, acquired mounting political significance and attracted retribution from the security forces.

Some CNT and PCU leaders went into exile in Eastern Europe. With support from comrades there, they beamed radio broadcasts back to boost the spirits of the faithful, as the Communists did in Chile and Spain. The Uruguayan Communists also forged new alliances, especially with progressive Blancos, which eventually helped weave together the Democratic Convergence.[32]

Some Colorados and numerous Blancos joined the Christian Democrats and other center-left and leftist parties in the opposition. From exile, and with assistance from the Carter administration in the United States, these politicians formed the Convergencia Democrática Uruguaya (CDU, the Uruguayan Democratic Convergence) in May 1980. The organization was led by the Blancos and included the Christian Democrats, the Socialists, the Communists, and some Colorados.

Similar to the *multipartidaria* in Argentina, the CDU represented a far broader opposition coalition than anything ever knitted together in Chile. These Uruguayan politicians built a consensus around the need to reconstruct a democratic system with unrestricted participation. Although it began as mainly an external multiparty alliance, the CDU soon developed stature within Uruguay.

Parties in Uruguay, like those in Brazil, proved more effective than those in Chile and Argentina at acquiring room for maneuver. One reason was that Uruguayan parties were less tied to labor and to programs for structural change, and therefore were more tolerable to the military. Their relative lack of radicalism or polarization by class and ideology also made it easier for the Uruguayan parties to cooperate among themselves. Because of their much greater strength in the past and their much lesser oppression by the armed forces, the longstanding multiclass parties—rather than labor or the left—proved most capable of reigniting democratic activities. The two traditional parties eventually joined forces in promoting a return to electoral democracy including the Frente.

As a result of consensus and coordination, Uruguayan opposition forces—unlike their Chilean counterparts—defeated the government's plebiscite on a new authoritarian constitution in November 1980. Winning by a 57-percent majority (as compared to the government's 43%), they opened the door to redemocratization much earlier. Despite economic growth, effusive propaganda, and restrictions on opposition campaigning, the regime failed to claim majority support.

The parties succeeded in the plebiscite because a broad antidictatorial front transcended socio-ideological cleavages and included a democratic right wing. Since the mid-level leaders of the Blancos and Colorados had not been purged, they could still call forth their clienteles. The more progressive wings of the two traditional parties led the campaign for a "no" vote, while the left had to keep its peace. Nevertheless, clandestine labor leaders connected to the leftist parties helped to galvanize opposition voters.

Gallup polls indicated that a majority of the members of all parties, especially those affiliated with the Frente, voted against the military's constitutional proposal. Just as before the coup, however, those opinion samples did not turn up any sharp social correlations with voting patterns. Surveys indicated that roughly two-thirds of both the upper and lower classes in Montevideo cast negative ballots. Subsequent internal elections within the two traditional parties in 1982 showed exceptional support for the parties' most democratic and reformist factions.[33]

Redemocratization, 1980–1985

Labor in Uruguay, as in Chile, progressed from muteness to clamor under the dictatorship and then to accommodation as democracy was reinstated. In 1983, after the Uruguayan parties engineered a process of redemocratization following the 1980 plebiscite, the labor movement began to raise its voice. The PIT-CNT was the major nonparty actor pushing for redemocratization. Without party leadership, the PIT launched the first general strike in ten years at the start of 1984. The government reacted to that protest's success by declaring the PIT illegal and by issuing new restrictions on the right to strike. The parties debated whether to support such working-class militance as the best way to bring down the tyrants.[34]

The PIT-CNT also helped to propel democratization by lending support to those fractions of the traditional parties which were most opposed to the despotic government. The labor confederation joined with those factions, with the leftist parties, and with other newly audacious social movements (mainly student organizations and human rights groups) to galvanize mass demonstrations in 1983 and 1984. They called for redress for economic grievances, for amnesty for all political prisoners, and for government negotiations with the opposition parties.

The social organizations and the political parties worked together at some times and separately at others. The opposition had to manage complex relations among intraparty factions, among parties, and among parties and social movements. Three coalitions coordinated the drive for democratization: the Intersocial Group, which brought together the social movements, chiefly labor, students, and human rights organizations; the Intersectoral Group, which linked the social movements with the political parties; and the Multiparty Group, which connected the political parties. Through the last organization, the political parties also fashioned understandings with the entrepreneurial peak organizations and between those business elites and the PIT. Social protests and multiparty solidarity soon made it clear that the vast majority of citizens wanted the armed forces to relinquish power.[35]

Then, as in the other cases discussed herein, the opposition debated whether mobilization or negotiation was the best way to end the dictatorship. Some strategists hoped that mass turbulence would accelerate and deepen democratization. Others feared that agitation would delay or even doom the restoration of civilian rule.

Some laborites argued that working-class assertiveness during the transition would assure unions a bigger role under the new democracy. Others warned that too many demands from the workers might leave labor isolated and repressed. Caution prevailed, especially as the transition approached its end. Labor leaders downplayed mobilization, trade unions bided their time, political parties took charge, and a negotiated redemocratization occurred according to the timetable acceptable to the armed forces.[36]

Those Uruguayans most opposed to confrontation preferred concertation as the path to redemocratization. They believed that understandings and compromises between proponents and opponents of the authoritarian regime, among diverse members of the opposition, and especially between capital and labor would smooth the return to democratic procedures. Even the Communists defended concertation against those leftists who charged that it was a bourgeois trap.[37]

Although much discussed, concertation never went very far in terms of concrete agreements or pacts. Nevertheless, consensus-building among political and social actors played a bigger role in the Uruguayan transition than in the rest of the Southern Cone and in Brazil. The most determined effort came in preparation for the 1984 electoral return to democracy.

Labor joined with other social movements, business groups, and political parties to forge the Concertación Nacional Programática (the National Programmatic Concert [CONAPRO]). The participants formed commissions to hammer out proposals and minimal agreements for the upcoming democratic government. Above all, these conversations served to reassure capitalists that the change in political regime would not alter the rules of the economic game. These discussions produced no firm accords but did generate some understandings between capitalists and workers, and between the leaders of business and labor and those Colorados who would soon be making government policy. One result was a meeting of the minds between Colorado politicians and Communist union leaders to assure order during the reinstallation of the democratic system. These politicians and labor leaders also concurred on the gradual recuperation of lost wages thereafter.[38]

During the transition in 1983–84, the Frente Amplio, in solidarity with the PIT-CNT, adopted a three-pronged approach: "mobilization, concertation, negotiation." It still represented several tiny parties, the largest and best-organized being the Communists. It operated as an integral member of the Multiparty Group, which influenced the military to allow the Frente to participate in the political opening. Shortly before the return of democracy, with the support of the Colorados as well as the Blancos, the Broad Front regained legality in 1984 under the banners of the Christian Democrats and the Socialists.

In the negotiations with the armed forces, the Front joined the Colorados in taking a soft-line position, while the Blancos played the hard-liners. The Frente reassured its militants that none of the movement's fundamental principles had been sacrificed in the bargaining. More than in 1971–73, however, the leftists emphasized the intrinsic virtue of formal democratic institutions.

To regain acceptance in the political arena, the FA stressed its moderation and deemphasized mass mobilization. Although on the surface the Frente appeared exactly the same as it had in 1971, it had actually become more centrist. It no longer presented any imaginable threat to democracy or capitalism, if it ever had.[39]

The restoration of democracy came in phases, as dictated by the military's "chronogram." Redemocratization resulted from a protracted series of negotiations between the armed forces and the political parties, culminating in the Naval Club Pact in 1984. The country returned to civilian rule through the presidential and congressional elections of November 1984. Centrist, moderate forces from all three main party conglomerations won those elections. A leader of the Colorados, Julio María Sanguinetti, took office as president in March 1985.

Between the 1971 elections and the 1984 elections, the Frente Amplio grew from 18 percent to 21 percent of the votes, still concentrated in Montevideo. That splendid showing, combined with the breakdown of votes among the factions of the coalition, fortified the Front's new, more pragmatic leadership and direction. It also confirmed the allocation of the electorate into definable right, center, and left camps. A tripolar array closer to the Chilean pattern replaced the old two-party lineup. When the electoral results of 1971 and 1984 are compared the general position of the FA seems to have changed little, but internally the far left declined. As in Chile, the Communist vote shriveled, from 33 percent to 28 percent of the Front's total.[40]

The journey back to democracy produced even more moderation in the leftist parties than in the unions. The balance of forces within the Frente was the opposite of that within the PIT-CNT, with the Communists dominating the latter and the non-communists the former. By the same token, the far-left current in the PIT-CNT had little resonance with the national electorate. Similarly, while declaring their devotion to democracy, the Tupamaros temporarily remained outside the Front, although they joined it before the 1989 elections. Thus the left had to reconcile its more temperate party position and its more militant labor stance, which soon became congruently moderate.[41]

In 1984 the Frente still attracted a multiclass following but relied heavily on organized labor. According to one survey, the decision to vote for the

TABLE 5.1

Percentage Distribution of Montevideo Voter Sample at Various Income Levels, by Party Preference, November 1984

Party Preference	Income Level (in pesos per month)			
	6,000 or less	6,001–12,000	12,001–20,000	20,000 or more
Colorado	36	38	18	26
Blanco	33	26	26	16
Frente Amplio	16	31	47	36
Total	85	95	91	78

SOURCES: Equipos, "Los sindicatos," *Estudios de Opinión Pública* 1:1 (May 1985), 35–39. Luis E. González, *Political Structures and Democracy in Uruguay* (Notre Dame, Ind., 1991), 121–27, 133–34. Charles G. Gillespie, "Activists and Floating Voters: The Unheeded Lessons of Uruguay's 1982 Primaries," in Paul W. Drake and Eduardo Silva, *Elections and Democratization in Latin America, 1980–85* (La Jolla, Calif., 1986), 228–41. Juan Rial, "The Uruguayan Elections of 1984: A Triumph of the Center," in ibid., 267–68.

NOTE: The totals do not add up to 100 percent because some of the interviewees responded with "other," "don't know," etc.

Front correlated more closely with youth, with higher education, and with male gender than with social class. Nor did poverty match up neatly with preferences for the FA. Among those who expressed a preference for the Colorados, the Blancos, or the Frente Amplio in polls in 1984, correlations between socioeconomic indicators and political choices were mixed (see tables 5.1 and 5.2).

Sample surveys agreed on the general interclass makeup of the parties' votes, but they disagreed on the proportions. The survey data in table 5.2 showed the Frente performing exceptionally well with skilled workers, the unemployed, and students. Another poll in 1984 also suggested that manual laborers (55%) and the unemployed (67%) identified with the Front far more than with either of the two traditional parties. However, that same poll showed strong Front support within the middle class, especially among white-collar workers and students.

Labor increasingly identified with the left in national elections. In 1985, a public opinion poll of adults in Montevideo indicated that workers not in unions had scattered their votes in 1984: 33 percent for the Frente, 30 percent for the Colorados, and 26 percent for the Blancos. However, that same poll reflected a strong connection between organized labor and the Broad Front. Those data revealed that 58 percent of organized workers had voted for the Frente in 1984, four times the percentage of trade unionists voting for the Colorados (15%) and more than twice the percentage of those voting for the Blancos (23%).

Within the adult population surveyed in Montevideo, 18 percent were organized workers: 3 percent voted Colorado, 4 percent Blanco, and 11 per-

TABLE 5.2
Percentage Distribution of Montevideo Voter Sample in Various Occupational
Categories, by Party Preference, November 1984

Party Preference	Occupational Category			
	Skilled Workers, Drivers	Laborers, Agricultural and Service Workers	Unemployed	Students
Colorado	14	37	23	26
Blanco	29	26	23	17
Frente Amplio	43	31	42	52
Total	86	94	88	95

SOURCES: Equipos, "Los sindicatos," 35–39. González, *Political Structures*, 121–27, 133–34. Gillespie, "Activists," 228–41. Rial, "Uruguayan Elections," 267–68.

NOTE: The totals do not add up to 100 percent because some of the interviewees responded with "other," "don't know," etc.

cent Frente. Since the Colorados garnered 35 percent of the total vote in Montevideo, 1 in every 12 of their votes presumably came from trade unionists, as compared with 1 in every 7 Blanco votes (27% of the total Montevideo vote), and 1 in every 3 Frente voters (33% of the total vote). The Front fared better with mainstream blue-collar workers than with laborers who were more marginal, self-employed, and/or in the informal sector.

Despite the Frente's multiclass composition, the equivalent of a labor party had begun to take shape in Uruguay. The FA dominated not only among union leaders but also among the rank and file. If workers' family members are counted among those directly influenced by the labor movement, perhaps one-half of the Frente electorate in Montevideo could be described as so influenced. Since only a minority of voting adults were organized workers, however, the Front still needed to cultivate multiclass support to achieve electoral victories. In general, Uruguayan parties were still not based on social class, but they were more class-based after the dictatorship than before, especially on the left.[42]

Although still an internally divided and fragile multiparty vehicle, the Frente had become crucial to the democratic transition. It could not only represent but also restrain disruptive social movements, especially trade unions. It could assure right-wingers that there was no leftist menace to the system. And now it could provide the Colorados or the Blancos with majorities that would enable them to pass legislation in Congress.[43]

The new Colorado government realized that one of its biggest challenges was dealing with organized labor. The administration was also aware that most of the unions were quite moderate and weak, less formidable than they had been in 1973. President Sanguinetti faced the difficult task of reactivating economic growth and improving income distribution, while honoring the towering foreign debt and restraining inflation. He maintained many elements of a neoliberal economic approach, along with gradual recuperation of employment and real wages for workers.

Although the government acted tough with unions on occasion, the economic and social situation stabilized, as did the restored democracy. Sometimes indulging in radical rhetoric, the unions complained about continuities between the new government's economic and social policies and those of the dictatorship. They mainly demanded wage increases. Although striking often under Sanguinetti, they emphasized restraint and discipline.[44]

Even when confronting the government, labor adopted a flexible, negotiable posture for several reasons: (1) workers feared that excessive agitation might bring about a return of authoritarianism; (2) economic conditions offered little room for maximal demands; (3) the Colorado government exercised no control over unions' rights to exist and strike, provided space for collective bargaining, and improved employment and real wages; and (4) the leftist parties counseled moderation. After Sanguinetti's first year, labor activism abated.[45]

By 1985, the Uruguayan labor movement's size, composition, structure, and behavior looked similar to what they had been before the coup. Unionists had recovered not only better wages but also the essence of their precoup infrastructure. Although the PIT-CNT encompassed more unions than the confederation had before the coup, PIT-CNT leaders still found it difficult to speak with one voice for their diverse membership, let alone for the working class as a whole. As in Brazil, Chile, and Argentina, the growth of the informal sector reduced the leverage of trade unions.

Unions were slightly smaller than they had been before the coup, but they still represented virtually all the important enterprises in the country, including the state. As before the coup, unions enrolled approximately 25 to 30 percent of the economically active population, although that figure declined to around 20 percent by the end of the decade. The majority of unions remained tiny, and they lacked full-time leaders, technical specialists, and centralized bureaucratic organization.[46]

In 1985, the PIT-CNT maintained essentially the same program it had prior to the coup, which was very similar to the platform of the Frente Amplio. The confederation still called for a fundamental socialistic transformation, but without the overthrow of the capitalist system. Whatever the discourse, the Communists and most union leaders favored a reformist rather than a revolutionary program and strategy.

After the transition to democracy, Uruguayan unions quickly moved away from most concertation mechanisms and understandings among labor, management, and government. As in Argentina and Brazil, corporatist economic pacts did not take hold. Instead, unions relied on traditional mechanisms, especially strikes, both specific and general. Ten general strikes rocked the country during the Sanguinetti administration. Surveys found that 63 percent of adults believed that almost all recent strikes had been justified; another 22 percent said that some had been and some had not been, while only 7 percent opined that very few or none of the strikes had been justified. When pollsters asked those same adults in Montevideo if labor conflicts affected the stability of the democratic government, 19 percent replied that they had a great effect, 33 percent said that they had some effect, and 36 percent said that they had no effect.[47]

After the military regime, as before it, no national labor code regulated unions. In 1985 the Colorado administration nullified all the union laws handed down by the dictatorship. In that same year, a public opinion survey found that only 17 percent of the adults in Montevideo thought that Congress should legislate on unions, whereas 62 percent thought that unions should manage their own affairs. Those most resistant to government regulation (82%) were interviewees aligned with the Frente Amplio.[48]

Many unions also wanted to assert their independence from political parties. As in labor movements elsewhere after redemocratization, party influence intensified. Several labor leaders bemoaned the parties' domineering, paternalistic, vertical attitude toward the unions. Still, trade unions remained far less subservient to parties in Uruguay than in Chile. According to a Communist leader of the Uruguayan port workers: "The process of unity grows out of the workers and not through political accords, as occurs for example in Chile."[49]

Although the laborers increasingly backed the same parties in national elections as in the unions, the left still had greater strength in the unions than in national elections. Most conflicts within the PIT-CNT pitted the Communists against everyone else. By 1984, persecution by the dictatorship had made the PCU less dominant in the directorship of the labor confederation. By 1985, however, the Communists once again predominated in the leadership of the national confederation, although now with more vigorous challenges.

Like the Radicals in Argentina, the Colorados hoped to "democratize"

the unions by reducing the hold of the parties already powerful in labor organizations, but those hopes came to naught. Of the two traditional parties,
only the Blancos made small inroads in the labor movement. At the PIT-
CNT congress in November 1985, an estimated 59 percent of the delegates
were Communists, representing the public sector as well as the private sector. Most blue-collar unions—for example in metallurgy, textiles, and construction—aligned with the PCU. Approximately 13 percent of the delegates sympathized with the Socialists, 11 percent with other Frente Amplio
leftists, 6 percent with the Blancos, 4 percent with the Tupamaros, and
1 percent with the Colorados, while the rest remained independent.

At that confederation meeting, the Communists won a majority of the
directors' seats. Other members of the FA captured the remainder, except
for one slot taken by a Blanco delegate. Thus, affiliates of the Front totally
controlled the PIT-CNT Secretariat, although officially and publicly none
of the confederation's leaders represented political parties.[50]

However independent, unions acted as political socialization agents for
the left and thus helped deliver votes to the Frente Amplio. A public opinion survey in 1985 found that workers who identified with "the left" were
more likely than those who identified with "the center" or "the right" to
have unions in their workplace. That same poll indicated that workers in
firms where unions existed were more prone to participate in union activities if they identified with leftist politics. Working-class respondents even
made a distinction between the Colorados and the Blancos, perhaps because the latter had become more reformist than the former in the last fifteen years and had been more hostile toward the junta. In comparison with
those workers aligned with the Colorados, twice as many Blancos, and
three times as many Frentistas, were likely to join union mobilizations.
Those laborers active in union affairs were twice as likely to sympathize
with the Blancos and three times as likely to favor the Broad Front, as compared with the Colorados. By the same token, of workers in workplaces
with unions, 45 percent of those sympathetic to the Colorados, 63 percent
of those sympathetic to the Nationals, and 79 percent of the Frentistas belonged to the union. In sum, voters for the Frente were much more likely
than voters for the Blancos or, especially, the Colorados to be connected to
and supportive of unions (see table 5.3).[51]

Despite external and internal tensions, the Frente, as a whole, cooperated with the Colorado government. Three main tendencies coexisted
within the Front, similar to the currents within the PIT-CNT. The first and
predominant position was social democratic. This category included most

TABLE 5.3
*Percentage Distribution of Sample of Montevideo Party Voters Who Exhibit
Union-Related Characteristics, 1985*

	In 1984 Voted for		
Characteristics of Respondents	Colorado	Blanco	Frente
Has a union in workplace	26	40	56[a]
Almost always participates in union activities	28	56	86[b]
Belongs to union	45	63	79[b]
Thinks Congress should enact union legislation	24	15	8[c]
Thinks almost all recent strikes are justified	45	58	86[c]
Agrees with February 1985 general strike	18	35	80[c]
Thinks labor conflicts affect the democratic government's stability			
Greatly	30	15	10[c]
Somewhat	44	35	18[c]
Not at all	17	29	65[c]

SOURCE: Equipos, "Los sindicatos," 8–24. González, *Political Structures*, 132–35.
[a]All workers.
[b]Workers with unions in their workplace.
[c]All adults.

of the Christian Democrats and Socialists, who were trying to compete with the Blancos for an eventual shot at the presidency. These groups were clearly reformist, not revolutionary, and willing to make grand sacrifices to sustain the democratic order. They were influenced by the rise of more pragmatic socialism in Western Europe, epitomized by François Mitterand in France and Felipe González in Spain.

The second posture, led by the Communists, was slightly more leftist, at least verbally. This segment put more emphasis on the demands of social groups, especially unions. Learning from the tragic experience of the Chilean Popular Unity, the Communists had no hopes of occupying the executive branch soon. For them, it seemed best to have the Frente in the opposition while they reconsolidated their own strength in the labor movement. Thus they hoped to sustain the new democracy and to use that system to press the economic demands of their members. The third sector, which was smaller, was more radical and anti-system, and included some who sympathized with the Tupamaros. This faction of the Front was shrinking among the electorate.[52]

Conclusion

Redemocratization in Uruguay represented a "restoration" more than a "renewal" for labor and the left. Although the political organizations iden-

tified with the working class had become slightly larger and more social democratic, they were essentially the same gradualist, democratic entities they
had been before the takeover by the armed forces. In many respects, the
dictatorship had been little more than a parenthesis. However, in teaching
the workers and the leftists that there was no viable alternative to subordination within a standard capitalist democracy, the military may have had a
lasting impact.[53]

SIX

Chile, 1973–1990

On the eve of the military takeovers in the Southern Cone, an assessment of the historic capacity of labor unions and their parties to turn democratic politics to the benefit of workers would have ranked the movement in Chile first, followed by that of Argentina and then that of Uruguay. Before it was destroyed, the Popular Unity (UP) government of President Salvador Allende Gossens (1970–73) provided laborers a unique opportunity for advancement. Although Chile had offered the best possible chance for working-class activism and conquests before 1973, it offered the worst thereafter.

In the months preceding the coup against Allende, it appeared that Chile's aggressive, ideological, class-conscious workers and Marxist parties were poised to confront any attempts to reverse their dramatic gains. Despite sporadic resistance by Popular Unity loyalists, however, the military quickly flattened them in September 1973. Thereafter, the dictatorship of army general Augusto Pinochet Ugarte contained them for seventeen years.

Based on the extraordinary tempo of political mobilization prior to the military takeover, expectations were high for a counteroffensive by the UP. However, between 1973 and 1982 there occurred no general strikes, no widespread civil disobedience, no significant uprisings, and no massive counterattacks by labor and the left. Of course, no trade unions or electoral parties anywhere in the world could likely have repulsed the initial blitzkrieg and the subsequent reign of terror by the armed forces. Labor's experience under Pinochet before the economic crisis of 1981–83 differed sharply from its experience thereafter, shifting from paralysis to resurgence. In the struggle to wrest the country from military rule back to democracy between

1983 and 1990, workers and their political allies reasserted themselves, but they were significantly chastened and diminished.[1]

Before the Coup

Structural Constraints on Labor

From the 1930s to the 1960s, organized labor in Chile benefited from a classic model of import-substituting industrialization. The state promoted and protected the simultaneous development of manufacturing, the working class, and trade unions in the cities. The labor parties grew as the numbers of their urban supporters and their stalwarts in the mining camps increased.

Even prior to the military takeover, however, the standard social base for blue-collar, laborite parties had stopped growing. By the 1960s, the ISI model had run out of steam. Economic growth stalled while inflation ran rampant. Since industrialization did not keep pace with the expansion of the urban workforce, the proportion of laborers in manufacturing in the economically active population stagnated, hovering around 20 percent. Workers in the manufacturing sector were surrounded by some unemployed and many underemployed compatriots, especially in the growing service sector, which accounted for about one-third of the workforce.

Institutional Constraints on Labor

By 1973, approximately one-third of Chile's economically active population belonged to unions. However, even among manufacturing workers, only 41 percent were enrolled in unions, and manufacturing workers accounted for just 32 percent of all trade union members. As in the other Southern Cone countries, those workers belonging to trade unions linked to explicitly working-class parties constituted a minority of the labor force.

Small, localized unions with scant finances and insecure leaders were the rule. For example, one survey of Chilean union presidents in the 1960s found only 10 percent who thought that unions by themselves had much impact on national issues. Those organizations divided among blue- and white-collar and urban and rural groups, as well as among competing labor parties. Most Chilean unions possessed only tenuous ties with national federations and parties. They were much less centralized and bureaucratized than their Argentine counterparts.

Through numerous federations, some two-thirds of Chile's unions promoted unity by establishing connections with the overarching Unified Workers' Central (CUT). The CUT possessed its greatest strength in manufacturing, construction, and mining. This loose amalgam of blue- and white-collar organizations had no legal standing prior to the government of Allende. Thus the CUT depended heavily on party spokespersons to exert national influence.

Party connections also benefited organized workers because the national labor code—crafted in 1924–31—left unions disadvantaged in bargaining with employers. Therefore they relied on the state to intervene on their behalf. From the 1920s to the 1940s, Chilean unions had been incorporated legally but remained autonomous politically, seeking both integration and confrontation with the prevailing order.

Traditionally, union activity in Chile aimed more at extracting benefits through the state than at seeking them directly from individual employers. Worker appeals to labor inspectors, labor courts, labor laws, and the labor ministry were used routinely to settle grievances. Collective bargaining was frequently more effective with the government than with business. That statist orientation was reinforced by extensive government intervention in the economy and by the need to cope with chronic inflation. The state regulated not only labor disputes but also wages, working hours, working conditions, job security, vacations, and profit sharing.

When regular mechanisms to resolve disputes between labor and management proved unsatisfactory, unions—with aid from their party allies—turned grievances against employers into political issues. In response, the state often pressed firms to grant union demands, thereafter compensating the companies with favors such as price or tariff hikes, especially in protected industries. This political exchange fueled inflation, which undercut worker gains and sparked new union demands in an ongoing vicious circle.[2]

Political Constraints on Labor

Historically, the leftist parties—especially the Communists (PC) and Socialists (PS)—had dominated the labor movement. Centrist parties—Radicals (PR) and then Christian Democrats (PDC)—had exerted lesser influence but had been relatively friendly toward unions when controlling the government, in contrast with rightist parties. The left, center, and right each controlled a significant share of the electorate in a democracy that endured from 1932 to 1973.

Unionists relied most heavily on parties on the national stage, often through the CUT. Laborite parties also provided leadership in the plants. Because the labor code denied union heads special security, salaries, and perquisites, party inspiration often proved necessary to convince workers to take burdensome union leadership posts.

This dependence on parties resulted in a dualistic system. Union chiefs dedicated themselves not only to the particular needs of their members at the local level but also to the political aspirations of their parties at the national level. Nevertheless, keen competition among parties for these leadership slots kept unions close to and responsive to the rank and file.[3]

In the Southern Cone, the most extensive studies of working-class political orientations were carried out in Chile. One measure, albeit imprecise, of party strength within the Chilean union movement came from the elections of directors of the CUT. In the two decades before the downfall of democracy, those returns showed persistent massive support for the Marxist parties, which usually claimed well over two-thirds or even three-fourths of the seats. However, those parties' share of the CUT directorships declined under the Allende government.

The CUT suffered tensions and conflicts—especially between leftist and centrist members—over its dual role as a mainstay of the UP administration and as a representative of concrete union concerns. In 1972–73, the Christian Democrats and maximal leftists made gains in union elections at the expense of the PS and the PC—for example, among steelworkers, copper miners, and teachers. Switching parties gave discontented workers a means to pressure a government under Socialist and Communist control. Thus the regime of Augusto Pinochet would confront a labor movement in which approximately two-thirds of the organizations were loyal to Allende's Popular Unity or kindred forces, but in which there were noteworthy fractures within union ranks.[4]

Even those laborers wedded to the Marxist parties naturally placed far more emphasis on material gains than on ideological conquests. Unions also embraced broader radical goals, but—as Socialist and Communist politicians frequently complained—these were scarcely their first priority. However, given the necessary pragmatism of most unionists anywhere in the capitalist world, what was remarkable about Chileans was not their predictable incrementalism but rather their complementary political commitment.

All polls of Chilean workers in the decade prior to the coup produced almost precisely the same results within any reasonable margin of error.

TABLE 6.1
Survey Results on Support for Marxists among Chilean Workers, 1962–1972

Year	Source	Survey Group	Percentage Supporting Marxists
1962	Landsberger	Union leaders	43
1964	Langton and Rapoport	Industrial workers	46
1968	Smith and Rodríguez	Industrial workers	41
1970	Smith and Rodríguez	Industrial workers	42
1972	Prothro and Chaparro	Lower-income persons	46

SOURCES: James W. Prothro and Patricio E. Chaparro, "Public Opinion and the Movement of Chilean Government to the Left, 1952–72," in Arturo Valenzuela and J. Samuel Valenzuela, *Chile: Politics and Society* (New Brunswick, N.J.), 67–114. Henry A. Landsberger, "The Labor Elite: Is It Revolutionary?" in Seymour M. Lipset ad Aldo Solari, *Elites in Latin America* (New York, 1967), 256–300. Brian H. Smith and José Luis Rodríguez, "Comparative Working-Class Behavior: Chile, France, and Italy," *American Behavioral Scientist* 18:1 (Sept. 1974), 59–96. Kenneth P. Langton and Ronald Rapoport, "Social Structure, Social Context, and Partisan Mobilization: Urban Workers in Chile," *Comparative Political Studies* 8:3 (Oct. 1975), 318–44.

Without going into the thorny methodological problems presented by comparing different surveys conducted using different techniques in different groups at different times, one can discern some clear patterns. Whenever a sample was taken of how many workers politically supported the Communists, the Socialists, and/or Allende, the results always fell short of a majority, and of course dwindled off dramatically among social sectors above the proletariat (see table 6.1).

Chilean survey and electoral data revealed a very persistent and enthusiastic core of working-class support for the Marxists. However, these polling results did not augur well for the creation of socialism through democratic institutions. The Marxists failed to knit together an electoral majority. They obtained 36 percent of the national votes for the presidency in 1970 and a high-water mark of 44 percent for the Congress in 1973. By comparison, some surveys in Western Europe found nearly two-thirds of the working class backing socialist (often non-Marxist) and/or communist parties.

The Allende coalition could not speak for a majority of the working class or for the working class alone. The Popular Unity had to rely on supplemental support from rural laborers, middle sectors, and regional groups. The UP was unlikely to be able to carry through its program, achieve a majority, or resist a coup without converting more workers to its camp. The only other path to a majority was through the assistance of other social and party forces, especially the Christian Democrats.[5]

Between 1937 and 1973, the PS and PC combined—without the minor parties in the UP—attracted a mean percentage of 22 percent of the national vote in the congressional elections. Their highest tallies ever came when they served jointly in coalition governments in 1941 (33%) and 1973 (35%). As the end of democracy approached in 1973, they were holding most of their solid working-class base in manufacturing, construction, and mining, while capturing some farm workers in the countryside. In addition, both parties—especially the Socialists—lured some backers among shantytown dwellers, white-collar employees, intellectuals, students, and assorted "popular" groups.[6]

Conditions on the Eve of the Coup

Prior to the Allende government, virtually all scholarly studies of organized labor in Chile portrayed a movement that was, in spite of its superficially powerful national confederation and Marxist parties, fairly weak and moderate. Between 1970 and 1973, however, the working class acquired a radical reputation that elicited brutal antilabor reactions from the armed forces, acting at the behest of the frightened upper and middle classes. How did the workers come to be viewed as such a menace, to be curbed with such draconian measures?

The main reason for the transformation of segments of the Chilean working class was that the Unidad Popular permitted and encouraged an unprecedented level of labor activism. That mobilization sometimes went farther than the government intended. Under the administrations of Eduardo Frei and Salvador Allende, in 1965–73, Chile exceeded Argentina, Uruguay, and Brazil in the increase in the percentage of workers in trade unions (a figure that rose from 23% in 1964 to 31% in 1972). During those years, it also outpaced all other Latin American countries in the number of strikes, the number of striking workers, the percentage of the economically active population taking part, and the number of working days lost to strikes.

Under Allende, working-class activism reached heights unparalleled in the history of South America. Unionization spread rapidly. The CUT became the interlocutor between the government and organized workers. Labor unions and parties had never before been so participatory in government or achieved so much through the state. The reforms that were implemented included income redistribution, and socialization of many of the means of production.[7]

By the early 1970s, the drive toward socialism, the intensity of class conflict, and the appearance of newly activated worker groups engendered some extraordinary working-class radicalism in Chile. The proletariat expressed that leftward shift through ideological and rhetorical escalation, redistributionist battles, and most importantly, property takeovers. Although the relatively pragmatic standard portrait of labor probably still was accurate for many unionists, a rising number of radical—even revolutionary—workers had emerged. Threatened more than in any of our other cases except Spain, conservatives reacted against the radical minority by punishing all labor unions and parties.[8]

During 1970–73, the presence of a vehemently prolabor government intensified politicization as well as divisions among workers. Those cleavages persisted after the coup, when they would be exploited by the military government. Although many laborers loyally heeded directives from the UP, so-called "economistic" and "radical" groups caused their government severe anxieties. The Marxist parties' traditional dual role of providing labor with clientelistic services and ideological missions proved more manageable when those parties were out of office than when they were in power.

On the one hand, Allende encountered disruptions created by economistic worker groups demanding bread-and-butter benefits. The most famous example was the striking copper miners in 1973, who received backing from the Christian Democrats. On the other hand, the UP confronted radical laborers who desired full-scale revolutionary change. That vanguard, comprising workers who were independently seizing some factories and forming "industrial cordons" spanning industrial areas, was encouraged by Socialists and others to the left of Allende.

Although radical and autonomous working-class activism was highly significant, its scale and import tended to be inflated in the months prior to the coup. Amidst rising consciousness and conflicts, the mobilization, politicization, and radicalization of the labor movement were doubtless exaggerated. These inflated estimates stemmed from alarmists on the right trying to justify military intervention, from optimists on the left claiming growing mass support for accelerated proletarian advances, from the UP warning rightists against the dangers of igniting a civil war, and from observers impressed by the creativity, spontaneity, and potential for worker liberation of these new forms of participation.

These emergent groups, however, possessed neither the numbers nor the strategy required to push through a socialist project or to block a military takeover. In Chile's political system, the left had been tolerated for decades partly because it provided an institutional outlet for worker discontent. Now, increasingly independent actions by laborers—whatever their relative strength—were what most disturbed the opposition to the UP.

The Pinochet coup took place against a working-class union and party movement that had become more aggressive and more successful at marching toward socialism than any other in all of South American history. Even in Chile, however, that movement was increasingly divided, debilitated, and defensive by the time of the coup. Labor was worn down by the economic and political errors of its government as well as the blows from its adversaries. Although a minority of Chilean workers became the only workers in the Southern Cone to resort to armed resistance to the military takeover, neither red battalions nor any Spanish-style civil war appeared. After disposing of the Allende government, the armed forces quickly stamped out isolated pockets of resistance in the factories and working-class neighborhoods.[9]

After the Coup

From the 1930s to the 1970s, Chilean development had been characterized by the growth of industry, unions, the state, the welfare system, political parties, leftist organizations and programs, and democracy. Now the armed forces reversed all those trends. Far more than in Brazil or Uruguay, the Chilean military takeover unleashed instantaneous, massive, savage repression against the labor movement.

Labor parties and unions immediately became the principal victims of the Chilean coup. The armed forces and their accomplices murdered, imprisoned, tortured, and/or exiled thousands of labor leaders, followers, and politicians. That firestorm rendered any systematic resistance by workers unthinkable; thus, their leaders and parties retreated into clandestinity or exile.

Under military rule, the labor movement experienced divergent conditions before and after the economic crash of 1981–82. Its trajectory under Pinochet went through six phases: (1) devastation and hibernation (1973–76); (2) recomposition (1976–79); (3) constrained collective bargaining (1979–81); (4) crash and withdrawal (1981–83); (5) protests (1983–86); and (6) transition back to democracy (1986–90). Through these phases, labor passed from (1) suffering near total intimidation and immobility; to (2) overcoming fear to try to work within the parameters set by the regime, and then encountering frustration; to (3) struggling to end the dictatorship as the only way to meet the needs of the workers.[10]

Structural Constraints on Labor

After the stunning coup and the subsequent nights of terror, Pinochet sent workers reeling with the most extreme free-market policies in the Southern Cone. He began the economic shock treatment in 1975. As a result, the industrial workforce became smaller, poorer, more heterogeneous, and less strategic in the economy.

To begin with, the government carried out stabilization at the expense of workers. Through tight budgetary and wage policies, Pinochet by 1978 had reduced the rate of inflation from over 600 percent to less than 40 percent and workers' real wages by approximately 30 percent. Take-home pay was determined by government readjustments rather than by collective bargaining. Real wages and salaries went from an index of 100 in 1970 to 133 in 1972 to 90 in 1980 (in manufacturing they went from 100 to 145 to 106); after falling drastically in 1974 and 1975, real wages rallied to a certain extent between 1976 and 1981 (see table 6.2).

The increasing concentration of income in the hands of the wealthiest 20 percent of the population diminished the likelihood of political alliances across class lines. At the same time, uninhibited market forces produced a salary and wage structure that was increasingly differentiated by type of work. Thus, coalitions and unity among wage earners or between the working and middle classes became ever more difficult.

The reduction of the state also undercut labor, especially the public sector unions. Between 1974 and 1978, the dictatorship terminated over 20 percent of government jobs. Along with the ending of most price controls for consumers, the elimination or privatization of many social services punished many workers, although some gained from the transfer of social security to the private sector. Between 1974 and 1982, per capita government

TABLE 6.2
Annual Growth Rate of Real Wages in Chile, 1965–1983

Year(s)	Growth Rate (%)	Year	Growth Rate (%)
1965–72	6.5	1979	8.3
1974	−19.2	1980	8.4
1975	−3.2	1981	9.0
1976	2.9	1982	0.0
1977	10.4	1983	−9.4
1978	6.4		

SOURCE: Guillermo Campero and René Cortázar, "Logics of Union Action in Chile," working paper no. 85, Kellogg Institute, Oct. 1986.

social expenditures were 20 percent lower than in 1970. Abandoned by the state, many laborers became too concerned with individual survival in the marketplace to engage in spirited collective action.

The traditional nuclei of Chilean unionism—mining, construction, and industry—waned, while nonproletarian, typically nonunionized enterprises—finance, commerce, and migratory agriculture—waxed. Those activities that were on the rise did not generate strong alternative unions to challenge the shrunken traditional core. Therefore, the classic proletariat remained the bastion of trade unionism.[11]

The number of industrial firms and their number of workers shrank in the late 1970s. Whereas in the 1960s Chilean manufacturing output rose nearly 6 percent per year, in the 1970s it declined or stagnated. Manufacturing dwindled from 25 percent of GDP in 1970 to 21 percent in 1981.

Employment in manufacturing had increased an average of 3 percent per year in the 1960s, but it decreased by the same annual rate in the 1970s. Between 1972 and 1980, the percentage of Chile's economically active population employed in industry fell from 20 percent to 16 percent, the percentage employed in mining from 3 percent to 2 percent, and the percentage employed in construction from 7 percent to 5 percent. In absolute terms, the national labor force in industry only dropped slightly, from 561,000 in 1972 to 524,000 in 1980. Despite losses, those workers retained potential for collective action because they were concentrated in the large firms that had managed to survive the "shaking out" period from 1975 to 1978.[12]

Industrial restructuring as well as deindustrialization damaged the labor movement. Those industries that survived free-market policies had to become more competitive, especially to produce for export. They usually became leaner by reducing the cost, size, and organizational capacity of the workforce—in part, by introducing new technologies. Decentralization of the economy dispersed a labor force previously more concentrated in Santiago, Valparaíso, and Concepción. Even when new industries rose to replace fallen old ones, workers had already lost job security and venerable strongholds of left-wing unionism.[13]

Chile increasingly became an economy centered on services. The agricultural workforce echoed the manufacturing workforce by shrinking from 20 percent of national employment in 1972 to 16 percent in 1980. Meanwhile, commerce jumped from 12 percent to 18 percent, and the service sector bulged from 31 percent to 35 percent. The percentage of the labor force producing goods (workers in agriculture, mining, manufacturing, and construction) fell from 50 percent in 1972 to 39 percent in 1980, while the share producing services (workers in services, commerce, transportation, and communication) rose from 50 percent to 61 percent.[14]

By promoting, liberalizing, and diversifying foreign trade, Pinochet slashed the leverage of workers producing for domestic consumption and of workers in the copper mines. The government removed most tariffs and subsidies for industries, resulting in deindustrialization. Total imports and nontraditional exports approximately tripled in value between 1970 and 1978. Even though the value of copper production also rose throughout the 1970s, the reduction of copper's share of exports diminished the bargaining power of the miners; copper's percentage of the value of all Chilean exports fell from 76 percent in 1970 and 1974 to 46 percent in 1980 and 43 percent in 1987. Employment in the copper industry dropped from 32,800 in 1974 to 24,886 in 1986. Nevertheless, copper miners retained more national strategic and symbolic power than did other workers.[15]

Unemployment joined repression as one of workers' greatest fears, paralyzing union activities. The scaling down of the state and of the economic sectors most conducive to job creation—particularly manufacturing and construction—boosted unemployment and underemployment. Total national unemployment exploded from 91,000 in 1972 to 418,000 in 1980; the total rate of unemployment rocketed from 3 percent in 1972 to 16 percent in 1980 (12% nominal plus 4% in the government's make-work program).[16]

By the start of the 1980s, Pinochet's structural changes had reversed the historic assumption underlying any socialist project. Leaders of the PS and PC could no longer assume that capitalist growth would produce an ever-larger, more homogeneous, more powerful working class. Consequently, some former UP supporters speculated that their movement's resurrection would have to rely less on the classic proletariat and more on popular elements among the service-sector workers, the self-employed, the unemployed, and the white-collar employees.[17]

From the depression of 1982 until the return of democracy in 1990, many economic conditions continued to disfavor Chilean laborers and their political leverage, even though some major improvements occurred after recovery began in 1985. When Pinochet's open, vulnerable economy reeled from the blast from the international recession, the downward spiral became worse than during the Great Depression of 1929–32. In 1982, economic output shrank by at least 14 percent, and real unemployment reached a third of the workforce. Between 1979 and 1983, employment in manufacturing fell by 30 percent.

The crash of 1981–82 rendered futile even the limited collective bargaining and striking that had emerged under the new labor code during 1979–81. Consequently, Chilean workers turned to political protest. Their anger rose as the government reacted to the crisis by reducing workers' incomes to encourage exports and discourage imports. Between 1982 and 1986, real average wages fell by 13 percent and the minimum wage by 35 percent. Between 1986 and 1988 average wages recovered to their 1980 level but still remained below their 1970 level.

The official unemployment rate—which did not include those in the government's make-work programs—went from 5 percent in 1973 to 12 percent in 1980 to 20 percent in 1982 to 11 percent in 1988. The employment situation was particularly grim in manufacturing and construction. The collapse of some industries and the need for others to become more internationally competitive through mechanization slashed job opportunities.

Unionization was also undercut in the 1980s by the multiplication of varieties of precarious employment: subcontracting, temporary work, seasonal work, piecework at home, and the like. Chilean workers engaged in these survival strategies as the economy tried to become more competitive by making the workforce cheaper and more flexible. In the mid-1980s, more and more laborers ended up in the informal sector, which came to account for over one-third of the workforce, normally beyond the reach of unions. In a 1986 poll, 48 percent of workers said that their family's economic situation had worsened in the last three years; that survey also found that 42 percent of respondents ranked unemployment as the top national problem.[18]

To recover from the depression and to pay the astronomical foreign debt, the government clung to the neoliberal model but adjusted it pragmatically. Those modifications resuscitated some of the traditional bailiwicks of the labor movement. During recovery, employment improved dramatically but wages improved only slightly. The regime emphasized exports, especially fruits and copper, increasing the latter's strategic importance. Industrial exports also grew, as did industry in general, partly because the foreign exchange squeeze made it attractive to promote domestic production in preference to imports. That same constriction, however, limited industrial growth by making it difficult to acquire imported ingredients.

Industry's share of Chile's total GDP (around 20% by 1986) and of national employment (around 15% by 1986) recovered, though it remained far below the levels of the 1960s. Between 1970 and 1991, manufacturing's share of GDP fell from 25 percent to 21 percent. In the late 1980s, imports and investments from abroad began to rebound. As military rule came to an end in a context of prosperity, labor remained structurally debilitated, although not as emaciated as it had been at the beginning of the decade.[19]

After stressing reforms in the national economic and political systems during the crisis of 1982–85, labor emphasized instrumental demands during the recovery and growth of 1986–90 — as it had during 1976–81. As the authoritarian regime played its last cards, unionists tried to combine emphases on the needs of the nation and on their own needs. They hoped that the impending civilian government would implement economic plans more favorable to the working class.[20]

Institutional Constraints on Labor

The military regime deprived unions of any effective role so that workers would subsist at the mercy of the marketplace. By nullifying national leaders and organizations, the government tried to molecularize the working class. The intention was that the labor movement would at most survive on the shop floor.

Without completely banishing unions, the regime tried to eliminate their organization above the enterprise level, their capacity to act on behalf of their members, and their political participation. To begin with, the military executed, exiled, detained, or otherwise removed or intimidated numerous unionists sympathetic to the UP. Raids on their factories and communities terrorized workers.

At the same time, the junta's initial decrees outlawed national federations and the CUT, denied all unions and their leaders most associational or bargaining rights, and forbade any collective or political activities. The armed forces seized the assets of several labor organizations linked with the Marxists. Pinochet allowed meetings only with police approval. Although most unions suffered, white-collar and Christian Democrat organizations received more lenient treatment than did UP affiliates.[21]

Pinochet tried to create a new, non-Marxian generation of labor leaders by banning most UP sympathizers from office. Those loyalties proved so deeply ingrained, however, that, beneath the surface, many trade unionists remained aligned with the left. Between 1973 and 1979, the Ministry of Labor and the military governors of provinces filled vacant posts in union organizations. Shortly after the coup, the junta, having abolished union elections, simply ordered many former Popular Unity leaders replaced by the oldest union members. But those elder workers frequently turned out to have equally strong Marxist propensities, particularly in Communist unions.

Unlike party and CUT leaders, very few Popular Unity union heads fled the country immediately after the coup. Normally representing the moderate faction of the UP, those unionists tried to resume their duties quietly after the storm. In late 1974, the International Labor Organization estimated that a majority of union officials were carryovers from the Allende period.

As the junta stepped up its purge of the labor movement, some Marxists, especially Socialists, willingly ceded their posts to Christian Democrats so as to alleviate government harassment of their union. Consequently, the PDC and even more conservative unionists made substantial gains, notably as official and public leaders of the labor movement. For some unions, switching to the Christian Democrats constituted a true political conversion; for others, it represented a marriage of convenience; in either case, most unions remained hostile to the government.

Especially in its first six years, the junta tried to coax some non-Marxian unions over to its side. In 1976–77, Pinochet and his ministers met with directors of progovernment unions to promote clientelistic ties. The regime won support from a few anti-Allende, Christian Democrat, and white-collar groups, for example, organizations of truck owners, bank employees, and copper workers.

Government efforts to court unions soon encountered snags. The regime refused to give them significant rights or benefits, feared the politicization of even friendly forces, and maintained economic policies inimical to workers. The monetarist, market-oriented model adopted in 1975 made populist or corporatist appeals to labor impossible. An attempt to create a progovernment national labor confederation in 1978 floundered. The dictatorship increasingly came into conflict even with cooperative unions and drove most of them into the opposition.

As the new labor code emerged in 1978–79, the government confidently allowed some plant-level elections with only four days' notice. It barred formal candidates and workers with former political or union leadership experience. Nevertheless, the balloting in most organizations replicated unionists' pre-coup party alignments.

The Communists, Socialists, and Christian Democrats each accounted for almost one-third of the newly chosen leaders, with progovernment forces comprising the small remainder. In the first post-coup elections in unions in copper, railroads, and most other basic industries in 1980, workers rejected leaders who had been imposed by the dictatorship. Even during the best economic years for the military regime, the vast majority of trade unionists remained loyal to the opposition.

In 1978–79, the regime codified its systematic discrimination against unions in the Labor Plan. One reason was that unions, despite all the mistreatment, refused to disappear. After soaring from 361,000 in 1966 to 628,000 in 1970 and to 939,000 in 1973, total membership in legally registered unions dipped to 917,000 by 1977. The greatest shrinkage (14%) occurred among organizations of industrial workers.

Some interunion organizations also clung to a precarious existence. In 1978 the government again called for the abolition of the national labor federations in mining, metals, textiles, construction, and some farming areas. The regime expressed dismay at their persistent organizing and lobbying and their unrepentant devotion to Marxism.

A second reason for codification of the labor system was the apparent success of the free-market model and the consolidation of Pinochet's personal authority in 1977–79. The time seemed ripe for general institutionalization of the new economic and political order. Vis-à-vis labor, the regime tried to move from destruction and coercion to containment. A third factor, international pressure, especially a boycott threatened by the AFL-CIO in the United States, convinced the dictatorship to issue a legal charter for unions.[22]

The Labor Plan extended the neoliberal economic model to the social sphere. The new laws essentially abandoned most laborers to the caprice of owners. "Market unionism" hamstrung labor organizations and activities while removing the central government from disputes with management. Although the code recognized the legality of voluntary membership in unions, federations, confederations, and international organizations, it allowed significant union activity only at the plant level. Even there, the regime restricted collective bargaining, outlawed the closed shop, severely limited strikes (though it did permit them, for the first time since 1973), and prohibited all political involvement. For employers, it allowed lockouts. It also made it easy to fire workers without significant justification and with only token severance pay.

In conjunction with this hobbling legislation, the dictatorship dealt further blows to labor. Pinochet scrapped the eight-hour day, shortened holidays, encouraged the hiring of workers under twenty-one or over sixty-five years of age, reduced state social services, and eliminated labor courts. He also harassed even some conservative unions, such as that of the dockworkers, and expelled key Christian Democrat labor leaders and sympathizers.[23]

Although unions uniformly condemned the regime's legislative package, they used it to become more active. In 1979–81, taking advantage of the small space that had been opened up, they engaged in collective bargaining in their individual enterprises. They also made use of their restored right to elect their leaders, replacing many progovernment directors with opposition representatives. Under the revamped code, unionists also found new openings to issue manifestoes about the lot of workers. Although the law encouraged parallel unions and autonomy by enterprise, laborers recreated the traditional union structure: single unions organized by factory and profession, with links to national federations. They tried to resurrect unity based on class consciousness.

Only slowly did the unions begin to recover from the wreckage caused by the military takeover. After initial suicidal resistance by a minority of workers, laborers reacted to the junta's bombardment from 1973 to 1975 by lying low in order to survive. As the pogrom against Marxists became more systematic and permanent, more and more unions converted to PDC bosses. By the time the labor movement started to resurface in 1976, perhaps 80 percent of the public leadership positions had passed into the hands of Christian Democrats.

During the second half of the 1970s, labor unions reemerged from their shrunken local bases. They also reorganized into broad, albeit flimsy, federations to speak out on government policies and worker needs at the national level. Although the dictatorship refused to recognize them, it did not prevent their existence. Like the forbidden political parties, these federations struggled to establish their representativeness within the uncertainty of an authoritarian context.

The two most important alliances became the Group of Ten (born in 1976) and the National Union Coordinator (CNS; created in 1978). Partly reproducing pre-coup divisions within the labor movement, the anticommunist Ten primarily identified with conservative Christian Democrats. After originally cooperating with the junta, the Group of Ten moved into the opposition in 1976 at the same time as the rest of the Christian Democrat party was doing so. The Ten then capitalized on the legitimacy given it previously by the dictatorship to lead public criticisms of the regime. Backed by the AFL-CIO from the United States, it soon became the Democratic Union of Workers (UDT) in 1981 and then the Confederation of Democratic Workers (CDT) in 1984.

The CNS, which was larger than the Group of Ten, was also led by a Christian Democrat—Manuel Bustos, a former CUT director who had been imprisoned by the junta. Despite his party affiliation, the CNS tended to include most of the older, stronger, blue-collar unions historically wed-

TABLE 6.3
Annual Numbers of Strikes and Strikers in Chile under Pinochet, 1979–1990

Year	Legal and Illegal Strikes	Strikers	Year	Legal and Illegal Strikes	Strikers
1979	38	10,895	1985	40	4,468
1980	52	18,256	1986	39	3,816
1981	82	24,504	1987	126	34,160
1982	11	1,070	1988	113	32,568
1983	40	5,605	1989	152	293,841
1984	39	3,685	1990	228	36,148

SOURCE: J. Samuel Valenzuela and Volker Frank, "The Labor Movement and the Return to Democratic Government in Chile," *Latin American Labor News* 5 (1992), 9–11.

ded to the leftist parties, especially in industry and construction. Bringing together Marxists and more progressive Christian Democrats, the CNS and its leaders endured constant persecution by the government, which accused the confederation of being a Communist front organization. From the late 1970s onward, the CNS received increasing cooperation from the Ten and from independent unions, such as that of the copper workers. As the junta's antilabor economic, social, and political policies continued, former PDC and UP unions—although still quarreling—developed more coordinated positions and activities than did the parties themselves.[24]

The CNS, the Ten, and similar smaller federations could not command the labor movement or bargain effectively with employers or the state. They did, however, issue declarations denouncing the government's labor code, human rights violations, and economic favoritism for the well-to-do. Coming mainly from the CNS, most of these manifestoes focused on unemployment and job insecurity.

In the late 1970s, some individual unions also met quietly, presented employers with discrete demands, and provided welfare assistance to members. Brief work stoppages, slowdowns, absenteeism, and strikes occurred on rare occasions, for example at the El Teniente copper mines in 1977 and 1980. The government usually responded with repression, primarily the firing or arrest of union activists.

After strikes regained a limited legality in 1979, they initially rose in number, then dropped off as a result of the 1982–85 recession, skyrocketed following the 1988 plebiscite victory, and finally pulled back during the 1990 return to democracy (see table 6.3).

It was mainly through their own efforts that these labor organizations recaptured a voice in national affairs. They also had significant aid from international labor organizations, the Roman Catholic Church, and the forbidden parties. The AFL-CIO, the Interamerican Regional Organization of Labor, the International Confederation of Free Trade Unions, and the ILO pressured the junta to respect union rights, delivered financial and advisory assistance to Chilean labor, and squeezed concessions from the government by on-site visits. The exiled CUT, the UP parties, and the Christian Democrats helped forge these connections between external and internal unionists, far more elaborate linkages than existed before 1973. In the mid-1980s, the U.S. National Endowment for Democracy donated financial aid to union confederations, especially the CDT. Throughout the Pinochet years, assistance from overseas proved valuable to Chilean workers, but it sometimes aggravated existing factionalism because of the anti-communist motivations of many of the foreigners.[25]

The Roman Catholic Church, sometimes working in conjunction with the Christian Democrats, also helped to rally international backing for organized labor under Pinochet. It shouldered some of the functions of the proscribed parties in speaking for and protecting unions. The church provided workers with legal defense and social services, and made protests on their behalf. This church assistance bridged the longstanding political division between proclerical and anticlerical reformers, the latter historically strongest in the labor movement; it presaged the greater cooperation between Christian Democrats and Socialists in the 1980s.

By the start of the 1980s, the union movement had endured the harshest treatment it had received since the early years of the twentieth century. It was more undernourished than it had been in fifty years. Between 1973 and 1983, the percentage of the workforce in unions fell from 27 percent to 8 percent. Desyndicalization mainly resulted from the rise in unemployment, the growth of the providers of services and the correlative decline of the producers of goods, and the smashing of unions.

By undercutting the ability of the trade unions to function on their own, however, Pinochet left them looking to political parties as allies. Thus he failed to depoliticize unionists. As one labor leader in the construction industry said during the economic crisis of 1981–82: "The political parties should present themselves more. They should not do so much of their work in hiding, because our people are very politicized. Today the parties are indispensable."[26]

During the 1982 crash, the government constricted even the few rights that unions had under the Labor Plan in order to reduce the costs of labor. Unionists turned to political protests. The limited opening for economic bargaining during 1979–81 had reactivated and frustrated unions, preparing them for political mobilization in 1982–83. The unionists struggled both within and against the Labor Plan. They resumed their pre-coup dual role of defending workers' interests both at the plant level (through legal channels) and at the national level (through political action).

Labor became more active in the promotion of redemocratization in Chile than in Argentina or Uruguay. As workers switched from defense to offense, they taught their fellow citizens to overcome fear and challenge the dictatorship. Unions transcended many of their occupational and ideological divisions by uniting around the desire for an end to military rule. Virtually all agreed on their antipathy toward the authoritarian regime, the neoliberal economic model, and the individualistic Labor Plan.

Union pronouncements escalated from the incrementalist demands of the late 1970s to include more calls for massive changes in the national labor, economic, and political systems. Addressing such comprehensive issues, the Chilean labor movement recaptured its historical symbolic power to speak in general on behalf of the working class and social justice. As the president of the petroleum workers argued, "In the period of the dictatorship, the union movement assumes an eminently political role, one that goes far beyond sectoral demands to make only one fundamental demand, that is democracy."[27]

Spearheaded by the copper miners, Chilean organized labor detonated widespread social protests in 1983–86. In the throes of the snowballing demonstrations, unionists formed the National Workers' Command (CNT) in 1983. It temporarily pulled together the CNS, the UDT/CDT, and independent unions. Like the reactivation of the CUT in 1988, the forging of this confederation reflected the deepening political cooperation between Christian Democrats and Marxists, along with minor opposition parties. Nevertheless, ideological differences remained, and the CDT soon distanced itself from the CNT.

Since widespread unemployment made general or lengthy strikes unsustainable, the antigovernment demonstrations sustained themselves by spreading to the middle sectors and the shantytowns. Soon the outlawed parties seized command, and labor took a back seat. By 1986, government intransigence made it clear that social mobilization would not bring down the dictator, so the protests tapered off.[28]

During the mobilizations of the mid-1980s, it became evident that the oppression of the Pinochet years had affected workers' political roles in contradictory ways. To oversimplify, the split was reminiscent of the pre-coup division between "economistic" and "radical" workers. Most laborers, especially in the trade unions, had reacted to the defeats at the hands of the military by lowering their expectations and demands in a quest for survival and security. For others, especially among the young and unemployed in the shantytowns, deprivations had bred desperation and radicalism. The most politicized were those who had developed ties with the clandestine parties. As the transition toward democracy gathered momentum, the pro-labor parties strove to incorporate all types of workers.[29]

In addition to staging protests, some unions tried to move the country toward democracy by promoting "concertación" between capitalists and workers. These initiatives came chiefly from Christian Democrat organizations, particularly the CDT. Discussion among social actors, however, could only build consensus so far before understandings among political parties became necessary.

Although both unions and parties debated whether to choose strategies of confrontation or conciliation, the parties moved more decisively to switch to negotiations. They sought to bring about redemocratization through the regime's own institutions. As the debate focused on political institutions and the rules of the game rather than on social demands, the terrain became naturally more congenial to parties. Unions expressed reluctance to get too involved in the institutional struggle to the neglect of social issues. Neither did they want to be so strident on social questions as to upset the legal timetable for a return to civilian rule. As the 1988 plebiscite drew closer, conversations among party leaders increasingly overshadowed networking among social organizations, although the latter had laid the groundwork for the former.[30]

After shriveling during the recession of 1982, labor organizations grew during the rest of the decade. Between 1981 and 1987 the number of unions and union members rose from 3,977 and 395,951, respectively, to 5,883 and 422,302 (still less than half the pre-coup membership figures). The number of federations climbed from 62 (with 630 affiliated unions with a total of 85,727 members) to 180 (with 2,308 affiliates with a total of 221,642 members). The union movement remained strongest in mining, industry, and construction, especially in the larger enterprises.

Despite gains, at the end of the 1980s only 11 percent of the total labor force was unionized, less than half the percentage unionized in 1970. Sixty-five percent of the workers in mining, 20 percent of those in manufacturing, 10 percent in construction, 4 percent in the service sector, and 4 percent in agriculture belonged to unions. Atomization still prevailed, since the average number of members per union had dwindled from 140, in 1972; to 73, in 1981; to 71, in 1989.[31]

In a 1986 poll, the decline of labor organizations was reflected in the 18 percent of Chileans who had no opinion of unions. In spite of all their problems, unions received a "good" to "very good" rating from 57 percent of the people surveyed (only 14% labeled them "bad" to "very bad"). Of all institutions, only the Roman Catholic Church, student federations, and small business ranked higher in public esteem, while big business, banks, and the armed forces trailed behind, with the government finishing in last place.[32]

By the end of the 1980s, three trends dominated labor in Chile. One segment remained unionized, linked to national federations and confederations, highly politicized, and concentrated in the shrunken traditional preserves of the union movement. These workers bargained at the national level, mixing concrete demands with ideological appeals. A second group belonged to nonpolitical unions and exhibited strength in more modern, technical enterprises. Downplaying national issues, they bargained at the plant level, emphasizing higher wages in preference to lower unemployment. A third faction stayed outside unions and relied on individual bargaining in the marketplace. They had imbibed the regime's propaganda against collective action and political parties.

Although in better shape at the end of the 1980s than in the darkest days of the 1970s, unions remained frail, weakly attached to their own followers, and poorly connected to sectoral and national organizations. The Pinochet years left unions more independent from federations and confederations as well as from political parties. Surveys of union presidents and members in the second half of the 1980s showed an overwhelming focus on local and bread-and-butter concerns, not on national or political issues. In the run-up to the 1988 plebiscite, the labor movement, without abandoning its commitment to mobilization on behalf of democratization, concentrated on rebuilding its own organizations.[33]

Political Constraints on Labor

Under military rule, four political tendencies developed in the Chilean labor movement. First, many unions remained loyal to the Marxist parties and struggled to recreate the old labor movement. Second, more trade unions than before aligned with the Christian Democrats, who were divided between forming their own separate camp or cooperating with the

Marxists. Third, a small and shrinking number of unionists—including, in the first couple of years of the dictatorship, some of the more anti-communist Christian Democrats—sided with the government. Fourth, some laborers and their organizations cherished their independence from partisan politics.[34]

Enforced demobilization led to the "Argentinization" of the Chilean labor movement. Whereas before the coup unions in Chile had worked through political parties, during the first decade of military rule the parties worked through the unions. Since parties could not "make politics" through the state, they turned to society. As in the rest of the Southern Cone under military rule, unions appeared increasingly economistic and independent from party control, but they were also playing politics for and with their parties in new ways.

In the second half of the 1970s, organized laborers had to develop more autonomous skills because the military had so thoroughly dismembered their political allies. While the previous powerful electoral and parliamentary strengths of the UP parties proved useless against the tyrant, those parties' prior weaknesses—especially disunity—dragged them down. Their feuding also exacerbated divisions within union ranks. By closing down the opposition parties' electoral and congressional arenas, the government did not eliminate those parties. It did, however, reinforce their factionalism and polarization, freeze their leadership and ideas, and keep them on the defensive for a decade.

Even though severely restricted, labor parties retained significance for workers. Those organizations still provided identities, networks, allies, international connections, and support services. Until the economic crash in 1981–82, however, Chilean labor parties and unions experienced less progress toward a democratic opening than did their counterparts in the other Southern Cone nations. Far more than in the other cases, they were still viewed by the regime and its capitalist supporters as a formidable foe to be kept down.[35]

Because the regime did not adopt corporatist, populist, or state party instruments to take over the groups and functions previously monopolized by the political parties, it left those areas open to them—albeit subterraneanly until the early 1980s. That the parties lost some—but by no means all—of their influence in the 1970s was revealed through union activities and the 1980 plebiscite. Although unions operated much more autonomously after the coup, they still heeded party cues. For example, copper unions linked to the Christian Democrats did not mobilize against Pinochet's policies until the PDC itself moved solidly into opposition by 1976. And in union elections, the opposition prevailed with increasing frequency.

Although the government rigged the 1980 plebiscite on a new constitution against any valid showing by its adversaries, it apparently had majority support. At the same time, it conceded that one-third of the voters responded negatively to the constitution that allowed Pinochet to stay in office for up to seventeen more years. Both the Marxists and the Christian Democrats, as well as the CNS and the Group of Ten, had called for a negative vote. Those "no" votes mainly came from the time-honored strongholds of labor and the left, such as the far north and south, the mining zones, and the working-class districts of Santiago. This limited evidence suggests that the Marxist parties, with their long history of a social base sharply defined by class and ideology, were preserving much of their hard core.[36]

The plight of Chilean labor parties after the coup reflected not only the government's repression but also their own longstanding characteristics. Both before and after the end of democracy, the Socialists failed to discipline their ideologically and socially diverse ranks. As some of its key upper- and middle-level leaders fled or died, the Socialist Party lost contact with many of its nuclei. By the late 1970s, the PS had shattered into at least six subparties. It divided into ideological camps, personalistic factions, older and younger militants, intellectuals and workers, and exiled and domestic components. When this mitosis reached its peak in 1979, the PS and the UP essentially dissolved.

At the start of the 1980s, the splintering of the Socialists rendered them ineffectual and useless as allies. Gradually, however, this fragmentation began yielding some positive results. The dissolution of the old PS and UP opened the way to a renovation of the Socialist Party and its coalitions. By the early 1980s, some leaders began trying to construct new thinking within the PS, new unity among its factions, and new alliances between it and other progressive movements. Despite the damage the Socialists had suffered during the 1970s, the party faithful still hoped that the enduring popularity of many of their past programs, symbols, and leaders, their martyrdom since 1973, and their very factionalism, diversity, and elasticity might allow the PS to adapt and rebound in a future democratic opening. Like their Spanish counterparts, the Chilean Socialists almost disappeared during the dictatorship but then sprang back to life, transformed, during redemocratization.[37]

Although enduring even more atrocities and persecution than the Socialists, the Communists remained intact to a greater degree under Pinochet. Their durability stemmed from their disciplined organization, deep roots in the labor movement, prior underground experience (most recently 1948–58), and international backing. From 1973 to 1980, the PC, more than the PS, reportedly retained many of its labor militants—for example in mining, textiles, and construction. It also increasingly branched out from unionists to the informal sector and shantytown dwellers, especially the young and unemployed. Until the end of the 1970s, the PC emphasized maintaining the Unidad Popular and reaching an accord against the dictatorship with the Christian Democrats, but those efforts to forge an "antifascist front" failed.

After the 1980 plebiscite undergirded Pinochet's continuation, the historically gradualist PC endorsed armed struggle as one approach to toppling the tyrant. Although the party did not instigate working-class uprisings, it did spawn a small guerrilla group, the Manuel Rodríguez Patriotic Front (FPMR). It also developed closer relations with the insurrectionary Movement of the Revolutionary Left (MIR), which it had previously scolded as adventurist.

Apparently, the PC's endorsement of "popular rebellion" appealed more strongly to youth and to shantytown inhabitants than to its traditional working-class core. Despite their revolutionary posture, the Communists in the early 1980s—like the Socialists—mainly counted upon international pressures, economic grievances, labor demands, multiparty coalitions, and the regime's own contradictions and mistakes to bring down Pinochet. During the second half of the decade the party became schizophrenic, trying to juggle both its radical line and its reintegration into normal party politics.

Historically, both Marxist parties had displayed a talent for surviving intimidation and fragmentation. While competing and cooperating, they had retained their individual resonance within the working class. Indeed, continuity had been one of the most striking features of Chilean party politics since the early 1930s. Throughout half a century, the PC stubbornly maintained its working-class foundation, even while outlawed during 1948–58. Meanwhile, the PS inflated rapidly (1932–41), deflated as dramatically (1942–53), and reflated thereafter (1957–73).

The durability of the Marxist parties could not be explained merely by their usefulness to organized labor, which was drastically attenuated and even reversed by Pinochet. Their persistence also stemmed from their lengthy and profound ideological and social penetration of a working-class subculture that inculcated these party loyalties through socialization in the family, the neighborhood, the workplace, and the union hall. Although the leftist parties had never faced such duress as they encountered under Pinochet, the historical odds were against Pinochet's attempt to obliterate their influence.[38]

Meanwhile the Christian Democrats, suffering less persecution from the government, came to represent more laborers. The PDC publicly defended the rights of workers. Cooperation between its unionists and those loyal to the Marxists opened up the possibility of new understandings between the centrist and leftist party opponents of Pinochet. Like the ex-UP parties, the PDC underwent agonizing self-reappraisal about its social base, immobility, and future agenda after the 1980 plebiscite. It became increasingly willing to align with the left so long as the Communists were excluded, a position many Socialists came to accept.[39]

Redemocratization

After the social protests petered out in 1986, the opposition regrouped to defeat Pinochet through the most venerated vehicles for mass participation in Chile: unions, parties, and elections. As the parties took command, they set their sights on the 1988 plebiscite mandated in the Constitution of 1980. For the plebiscite, the unions helped to mobilize the "no" vote against Pinochet's continuation, but they left most of that campaign to the political parties. As in the final phases of peaceful transitions to democracy in most other nations, labor went from aggression to restraint during 1986–90.[40]

Despite the length of Chile's authoritarian experience, its politicians managed to reproduce much of the traditional political culture of the working class. As the parties positioned themselves for the 1988 plebiscite on Pinochet's claim to eight more years in office, they exhibited significant continuities with as well as changes from the 1970s.[41]

The Socialists were divided between two main camps, one more "social democratic" and aligned with the Christian Democrats, the other more "Marxist-Leninist" and linked to the Communists. As the 1988 showdown approached, however, the various factions grew closer together in favor of the "no" vote. The non-Leninist position came to prevail. As in Spain, that takeover by the moderate, "renovated" elements was supported by European social democrats and socialists, along with the Socialist International.[42]

Whereas the Chilean Socialists had been more leftist than the Communists under Allende, they reversed their positions under Pinochet. Because of their endorsement of violence as one way to bring down the dictator, the Communists became increasingly isolated, especially after the failed attempt on his life in 1986. In Chile as in Portugal, Spain, and Greece, the dictatorship's denunciation of the PC as its principal enemy exaggerated the party's importance. And the Chilean Communists, like their Spanish counterparts, emphasized mass mobilization as the best way to topple the regime. Although trying to reassert its old authority over unions, the PC lost significant strength among organized laborers. Even where the Communists retained strength, it was more diluted by other political groups, especially the Christian Democrats.[43]

The PDC became increasingly willing to collaborate with "renovated" Socialists in the labor movement, the plebiscite, and the upcoming civilian government. The PDC's expansion among unionists was assisted by the growth of the service sector and white-collar unions. In May 1988, a poll of workers in Santiago found the most respected labor leader to be the Christian Democrat Manuel Bustos (selected by 35%), followed by "don't know" (25%), and "none" (24%), with Socialists and Communists not even registering above 1 percent.[44]

That same poll showed 63 percent of the laborers in favor of a new CUT, 95 percent planning to register for the plebiscite, and 52 percent intending to vote "no" (compared to 11% "yes," and 32% not saying). Although mainly for the opposition, workers were not demanding an immediate rupture with the authoritarian regime, as the Communists had proposed. When asked what they would like to have happen in the event of a victory for the "noes," 33 percent of those polled responded that Pinochet should leave office immediately, while 43 percent said that the changeover should wait a year as required by the constitution.

One month before the plebiscite, the unions finally recreated a single national confederation, the CUT (Unitary Workers' Central). Its formation was orchestrated by the political parties, which increasingly reasserted their domination over trade unions, though without as much discipline and control as they had exerted sixteen years before. The CUT played little role in the plebiscite, partly because Pinochet kept its president, Bustos, in internal exile.

Politicization reminiscent of pre-coup days permeated the first election for the CUT executive board. The political coloration of the resulting lineup of directors was very similar to that prevailing before Pinochet: 64 percent were for the parties formerly identified with the UP and kindred

TABLE 6.4
*Percentage Distribution of Elected CUT Executives,
by Party Affiliation, 1953–1991*

	Party Affiliation	
	Unidad Popular and Other Leftist Parties	Christian Democrats
1953	61	6
1957	79	15
1959	80	15
1962	68	18
1965	81	12
1968	80	10
1972	71	26
1988	64	36
1991	54	45

SOURCES: Alan Angell, *Politics and the Labour Movement in Chile* (London, 1972), 84–85, 216–19; idem, "Unions and Workers in the 1980s," in Paul W. Drake and Iván Jaksic, *The Struggle for Democracy in Chile, 1982–90* (Lincoln, Neb., 1991), 198–200. Francisco Zapata S., "The Chilean Labor Movement under Salvador Allende, 1970–1973," *Latin American Perspectives* 3:1 (winter 1976), 85–97. Patricio Frías, *El movimiento sindical chileno en la lucha por la democracia, 1973–1988* (Santiago, 1989).

NOTE: The CUT leaders not included in these percentages were normally Radicals or independents.

leftists, and 36 percent were for the PDC. Although elections were not conducted exactly the same way over the years, a comparison of pre-coup and post-coup, old and new CUT elections showed both continuing strength for the Marxists and big gains for the Christian Democrats (see table 6.4).[45]

Despite those political continuities, the new CUT emitted much more moderate declarations than had its predecessor in the 1960s and 1970s. It eschewed any calls for class struggle against capitalism. Instead, the CUT program emphasized liberal democracy, human rights, and specific union demands such as reform of the labor code. It also expressed a desire for greater autonomy from political parties, but they had clearly reasserted their influence over the labor movement.[46]

The yes-or-no referendum on Pinochet finally produced unity among opposition parties. For labor groups, the most significant innovation was the alliance of the Christian Democrats and the more moderate Socialists in the "Command for the No," which also included fifteen micro-parties. While the Command represented many unionists, so did the Broad Party of the Socialist Left (PAIS), dominated by the more militant Socialists, the Communists, and the MIR. Although separate, both coalitions campaigned successfully against Pinochet in the plebiscite (October 5, 1988) and for a Christian Democrat, Patricio Aylwin, in the subsequent democratic elections (December 14, 1989). In both contests, they won with 55 percent of the votes.[47]

The presidential and congressional elections of 1989 revealed some profound changes from 1973: a stronger right, an enduring center, and a weaker left. The decline of the labor movement was reflected in the diminution of the leftist parties in the 1989 elections. In the lower house of deputies, the right captured 40 percent of the seats, the Christian Democrats 33 percent, and the left roughly 22 percent. That tally for the leftists fell far below their 44 percent in 1973 but actually approximated their historical average. Although several Socialists won election as deputies and senators, not one Communist succeeded. Voters tended to reject extremes on both the left and the right.

Thereafter, the center-left party panorama solidified. The Christian Democrats remained the largest single party in Chile, and they won the first two postauthoritarian presidential elections in league with the Socialists. The Socialists reunited in the PS while many of their colleagues joined the new Party for Democracy (PPD), a more social democratic electoral vehicle also headed by the Socialists.

Meanwhile, the Communists floundered. In Chile as in Spain, their belief that the dictatorship might be ended by rupture rather than reform proved incorrect. In similar fashion, their role as the most militant opposition against the dictatorship did not translate into a powerful position in the new democracy.

In contrast with the transitions from military rule in Spain, Brazil, and the other Southern Cone countries, Chile's first civilian government included parties with strong labor backing. Thus it represented aspirations not only for political democracy but also for social reform. However, the victorious parties warned the workers to lower their expectations so as not to upset political or macroeconomic stability.[48]

As democracy returned to Chile, the labor movement faced the dilemma of trying to recover rights and benefits for its members while restraining their demands. Although workers knew that they had paid for recovery from the 1981–83 recession with low wages, they were willing to be patient so as not to endanger noninflationary economic growth. In the 1988–90 transition to democracy, trade unionists wanted political rights, a higher standard of living, and a more favorable labor code for future organization and bargaining. Their main economic demand was for stable jobs at decent wages. Without proposing an alternative economic model, they called for greater state action, especially to meet the basic needs of the poorest segment of the population.

The ruling coalition—now known as the Concertation for Democracy—vowed to try to meet those demands. Like Sanguinetti in Uruguay, Aylwin (1990–94) presided over economic growth and gradual recuperation of income for the needy, without abandoning the dictatorship's neoliberal formula. The government raised wages and social spending. It also reduced unemployment and the number of indigents.

In contrast with the other cases discussed in this book, labor benefited more in Chile because redemocratization took place during prosperity and because its political allies held office. The CUT reached agreements with business and government on consensual economic policies, mainly support for private property, market-oriented growth, and modest wage increases. Since labor would likely have encountered similar economic conditions in any case, concertation really had little effect on the standard of living of workers, as we have seen in our other cases. The government felt a greater necessity to placate capitalists than to accommodate laborers.

The new administration improved the lot of the working class, but it changed little of the labor legislation. It moved cautiously because the right blocked reforms in the Senate. At the same time, the Concertation accepted the neoliberal concept of labor-market flexibility as essential to economic growth. Aylwin maintained the principle that workers and managers should solve most of their differences one-on-one, with the state playing a secondary role.

The government did make it slightly harder to lay off workers; it raised severance pay and discouraged lockouts. However, laborers remained easy to fire and easy to defeat at the bargaining table. The disappointed unions called for greater protection against layoffs and for increased government participation in labor-management negotiations.[49]

Since the Concertation embraced both neoliberalism and labor, its competitors had nowhere to go. As in most of our other cases, the center-left triumphed, while the right and the Communists slumped in the doldrums. The adoption of neoliberalism by the leading labor parties in Chile, as in Spain and Argentina, inhibited political alternatives from trade unions, the far left, and the right. By the same token, governments that included labor parties proved unusually successful at sustaining neoliberal programs. Because they were less likely to incur labor's wrath, they could provide control over inflation in exchange for wage restraint, and they could credibly offer workers economic growth and some participation in its benefits.[50]

The Chilean labor movement, though returned to life, seemed destined to play a smaller, more muted role in the 1990s than it had done before the advent of capitalist authoritarianism. Although not adhering to an economistic North American model, unions seemed less politically combative than in earlier populist or socialist periods. They moved closer to a European social-democratic style of cooperation with the state to balance democracy, growth, and welfare. The authoritarian experience had not depoliticized labor, but it had changed labor politics.

The number of unions and union members in Chile continued to grow, as they had ever since recovery from the 1982–83 depression. Between 1990 and 1993, union affiliations increased 40 percent. Unionization rose from 9 percent in 1983 to 13 percent in 1990 and then to 16 percent of the economically active population by 1993, about half the pre-coup density.[51]

Especially after Aylwin's first year, laborers struck, but not inordinately or disruptively. Although collective bargaining and strikes multiplied following Pinochet's departure, labor agitation under the restored democracy was probably less intense in Chile than in any of our other cases. The unions held back because they were weak, their parties were in power, and the economy was in good shape. Following two decades of trauma, workers were willing to sacrifice in order to avoid any return to the instability under Allende or the repression under Pinochet.[52]

Labor retained great respect. A 1991 poll on how well leading political institutions had behaved during the first year of the democratic government found 60 percent of the respondents rating unions favorably. That level of approbation was well behind that of those groups with the most prestige (bishops with 76%, and deputies and senators with 74%) but well ahead of those at the bottom (military personnel with 40% and judges with 37%). As they had for several years, respondents listed unemployment as the most important national problem.[53]

Despite greater autonomy, labor remained heavily reliant on political parties. The Concertation, especially the Christian Democrats and Socialists, dominated trade unions. At the CUT Congress in 1991, the elections to the National Executive Committee delivered 45 percent of the votes to the Christian Democrats and 34 percent to the Socialists, as well as 20 percent to the Communists.[54]

Although the Communists lost ground among unionists, they retained more of a following among the trade unions than in the national electorate. The dejected and divided PC opposed the government. It criticized Aylwin for insufficient action on human rights abuses, military independence, and social inequalities. The party was torn between those who wanted to follow the Socialists' transformation into social democrats, and those who denounced the Socialists for abandoning Marxism and revolution.[55]

With its centrist approach to democratization, economic growth, and social justice, the government retained majority support. The 1992 municipal elections delivered 54 percent to the multiparty Concertation, including 29 percent to the Christian Democrats and 18 percent to the Socialists (the PS and the PPD, although not all of the PPD voters were necessarily Socialists). The Communists and some other, tiny leftist groups netted 7 percent.

With the backing of Christian Democrats, Socialists, other minor parties, and organized labor, the renamed Coalition of Parties for Democracy won the presidency again in 1993 with an even higher proportion of the vote: 58 percent. The victor was Eduardo Frei, a Christian Democrat and son of the former president. In the contest for the Chamber of Deputies, the Coalition took 55 percent of the votes and 58 percent of the seats. The Christian Democrats captured 27 percent of the votes and 31 percent of the seats; the PS and the PPD, combined, received 24 percent and 25 percent; and the Communists, 5 percent and 0 percent.

While the two parties led by the Socialists steadily increased, the Christian Democrats and Communists leveled off, and the right sank, somewhat as occurred during the postauthoritarian situation in Spain. If all the 1993 deputy votes for the PS and the PPD could be considered "socialist" in some sense, the descendants of Allende were doing better than ever and improving their position within the ruling alliance. With minor nuances and modest gains, the 1993 elections duplicated the 1988 and 1989 watershed results for the democratic forces. If the 1993 congressional votes were reconfigured to more or less match the pre-coup tripolar party alignment and nomenclature, it looked as though little had changed since 1970; each of the three poles was supported by about a third of the electorate: 37 percent for the right, 27 percent for the Christian Democrats, and 31 percent for the Socialists and Communists. Although their ideas and leaders had changed, the parties had retained most of their electoral shares despite the execrations from Pinochet.[56]

Conclusion

Under the Chilean dictatorship, most unionists apparently had decided that authoritarianism rather than capitalism was the principal enemy. During redemocratization, workers in general sought conciliation, participation, and compensation, instead of class conflict, revolution, and revenge. When the civilian government took office in 1990, laborers wanted to integrate into the national system, not to overthrow it.

Before 1973, the labor movement in Chile had tried to reconcile the quest for worker demands and for socialism. After years of repression, it sought to balance the struggle for worker needs and for democracy. Whether labor's new social and political agendas were mainly compatible or conflictual remained to be seen. But that dilemma, after all, afflicted all capitalist democracies. What was more significant was that Chilean workers and their fellow citizens had recaptured their democratic heritage.[57]

SEVEN

Argentina, 1976–1983

After Juan Perón established his labor movement in the 1940s, Argentine politics split between Peronists and anti-Peronists. Following the banishment of Perón and his party by the armed forces in 1955, his unions kept the movement alive, despite repression. For two decades, neither labor nor capital could impose its political will for long. Each side vetoed the other in a "reciprocal blockade."[1]

With Perón in exile, weak political parties and governments co-existed with powerful functional organizations, chiefly trade unions and the military. The most important political bargaining and brawling took place outside the formal arena of parties and elections. All efforts to crucify, co-opt, or incorporate the Peronists failed to produce political and economic stability. Between 1955 and 1973, attempts at effective government were made by the armed forces and the centrist Radical Party, but the unionists continued to resist and disrupt. During 1973–76, the last-ditch effort to allow the Peronists themselves to restore political order and economic growth ended in catastrophe.

The 1976 coup d'état ushered in the maximal attempt by the armed forces and the economic elites to break the impasse by deactivating and recasting organized labor. Although modifying the behavior of trade unions, the right-wing groups once again failed to transform the fundamental battle lines in Argentine politics. The workers' movement, also unable to prevail, nonetheless survived—bent, but not broken. When democracy returned in 1983, the stalemate continued, albeit with labor steadily losing ground.[2]

Before the Coup

Structural Constraints on Labor

Prior to the coup, organized workers in Argentina had more leverage than those in the rest of South America. They operated in a tighter labor market in a more industrialized economy, in which unemployment was not a significant factor. Nevertheless, organized labor began losing power before the exhaustion of democracy in 1976.

In that year, the military takeover would accelerate structural changes that were already under way by the 1960s. The import-substituting-industrialization coalition forged between laborers and manufacturers in the late 1940s by Perón became increasingly untenable in a stalled economy. From 1954 to 1974, industry's share of the nation's economically active population stagnated at slightly over one-third. Manufacturing lost its dynamic ability to provide employment. Industrial laborers in Buenos Aires found their strength diluted by growing numbers in the middle class and the service sector, and among the self-employed. The working class also became less highly concentrated in Buenos Aires, as other industrial centers, notably Córdoba and its metallurgical factories, gained in size and importance.[3]

Institutional Constraints on Labor

From the 1950s to the 1970s, Argentine labor also had advantages over its counterparts in the Southern Cone because of its sturdy union organizations and bureaucracy. Approximately 34 percent of Argentina's economically active population belonged to trade unions. More than 60 percent of all industrial laborers were union members, and industrial workers comprised 34 percent of all union members. Legal unions possessed a monopoly on representation in their industry and supplied social services to their members.

Their situation epitomized a type of political unionism in which the union and the party fused. Argentine labor's cohesion derived not from any radical ideology but from unity behind a single political banner—albeit one tattered by internal squabbling. From 1955 to 1973, Peronist unions took the place of their outlawed party as the mobilizing agent for the working class on political as well as job issues. Those trade unions represented labor demands, expressed class conflict, and provided political socialization.

Argentine unions' greater size and discipline—by comparison with their

Uruguayan and Chilean counterparts—meant that they could also more effectively bargain directly with employers. Labor usually conducted collective bargaining by sector, rather than by individual shops and factories. Except for the advocacy of Peronism, their demands remained overwhelmingly incremental and defensive. They eschewed loftier ideological goals, unlike their Marxian counterparts in Chile.

Although Argentine unions flexed their own muscle vis-à-vis capitalists, they also relied heavily on pressuring the government to gain their objectives. Public policies—for example, decisions on exchange rates—were crucial to workers in an economy shaped by massive state intervention. Moreover, opposition governments frequently suspended collective bargaining rights, reminding workers how important the state was to their legal, political, and economic achievements.

After years of interdiction of their Peronist party, Argentine unions had developed much more autonomous power than had unions in Uruguay or Chile. They boasted unparalleled pre-coup experience at cooperating, negotiating, or—more commonly—clashing with dictatorships. Often regardless of party proclamations, individual unions adopted different positions toward hostile governments for their own pragmatic purposes. Some even reached accommodations with dictators, notably during the military regime in 1966–73.

Repeated persecution also drove most union leaders and union members close together. Union officials wielded great authority. From the 1950s to the 1970s, unions' governing bodies usually perpetuated themselves through controlled elections with only one list of candidates. Although the bosses brooked little dissent from the rank and file, more and more workers complained about unrepresentative, corrupt, and conservative union and party leaders.

In Argentina as in Chile and Brazil, unions possessed representational monopolies. The Argentines outshone their counterparts in Chile, Brazil, and Uruguay with their inordinate prowess at the national level of the federation and confederation. Argentine workers profited from organizational solidarity within the overarching General Confederation of Labor (CGT), which took pride in being the "backbone" of Peronism. The CGT maintained firmer lines of authority and greater capacity to mobilize a wide spectrum of labor than did any other national confederation in South America.

Beneath superficial solidarity, festering divisions existed between sectors of labor, between national and local organizations, and between some leaders and members. As industry became more decentralized in the 1960s, so did unions. Regional branches proliferated, balking at control from Buenos Aires. Many cleavages among unions reflected disputes over how to relate to the Peronist party and to governments. Those disagreements erupted into open conflicts after the return of Perón in 1973 proved disappointing.

Because of its ambivalence, labor legislation from the first two Peronist administrations (1946–55) provided a double-edged sword. The labor code endured because it attracted both prolabor and antilabor groups. After non-Peronist governments discarded the laws' original corporatist orientation, the state played a circumscribed role. That evolution distinguished the Argentine situation from the full-blown corporatist model in Brazil, wherein juridical rights carried with them government control over unions. Argentina's system of labor-industrial relations also differed from the liberal model in the United States, wherein state legitimation played no part. Argentina, like Chile, was an intermediate case on a scale ranging from state domination to unfettered autonomy.

A built-in tension existed between the unions and the government with regard to the implementation of the legal system. By imposing a single union organization for each economic sector, the code encouraged union unity, toughness, and independence. Labor welcomed laws through which the state recognized the legal standing of centralized, national, industry-wide unions. That legislation also provided safeguards against dismissals of union leaders.

Although workers faced a less confining labor code in Argentina than in Brazil or Chile, Argentine laws gave administrations great potential control over union elections, finances, and activities. The Ministry of Labor had the authority to certify, cancel, or modify the rights of unions to represent their sectors. Prior to 1976, however, governments usually experienced little success at exercising those controls.

In spite of the state's potential for supervision, unions repeatedly displayed their autonomous capabilities to deflect or disrupt government initiatives. They pressured presidents—partly through friendly politicians—to exercise generosity in interpreting labor legislation. The importance of how the executive branch applied the laws was demonstrated when the third Peronist administration tipped the legislation in favor of the unions during 1973–76. Thereafter, the military dictatorship would tilt the balance decisively against organized labor.[4]

Political Constraints on Labor

By comparison with their Chilean counterparts, Argentine social actors were not well incorporated into political parties. The Radical Party (PR), rooted in the middle class, was poorly organized and unable to win a majority after the arrival of Perón. The Peronist party (known officially as the Justicialist Party [PJ]), exerted little power in comparison with its charismatic leaders or its trade unions.

Scholars carried out few attitudinal or ecological studies of political alignments in Argentina. Nevertheless, some slender evidence suggested that workers there identified with and voted for Peronists even more solidly than workers in Chile supported the Socialists and Communists. Apparently, great continuity prevailed in the electoral base of Peronism from 1946 to 1973. A clear majority of urban laborers cast ballots for the party in elections in both of those years. But almost half the Peronist votes in 1973 came from groups outside the working class, mainly in the poorer provinces. In contrast with Chile's Popular Unity, the Peronist movement attracted a much larger following and relied much more on other social strata, especially white-collar employees. Both a laborite and a multiclass party, the Peronists could neither command the entire union movement nor speak solely for workers.[5]

For workers, their unions and politicians had always been more important than any party. The PJ primarily played an intermittent role as an electoral vehicle. Dominated from the top down by Perón, it developed very little life and very few leaders of its own. Like the labor movement, the party was run by numerous clientelistic bosses, some of whom were also union officials.

The populist, nationalist, redistributive program of Peronism kept workers within the capitalist system and also made them players to be reckoned with. By supporting tandem state action on behalf of industrialization and social welfare, Peronism enlisted laborers in the cause of reform, not revolution. It overshadowed appeals from the left, whether the older Communists and Socialists or newer insurgents. In Argentina more than in any other country in South America, one party clearly spoke for the working class and cornered an electoral plurality.[6]

Also, as elsewhere in the Southern Cone in the 1960s and 1970s, insurrectionary leftist groups—both inside and outside Peronism—appeared more powerful than they actually were. They owed their cachet to the

Cuban Revolution. Argentina's would-be revolutionaries were more appealing to young people than to organized laborers.

Many of these leftists saw the traditional union bureaucracy as an impediment to their pulling Peronism and the proletariat in a socialist direction. That conflict was epitomized when, on the eve of Perón's return to the presidency, a guerrilla group known as the Montoneros assassinated the secretary general of the CGT. Despite these hostilities between the left and labor, many conservatives feared that these Castroites and the workers chafing at their established leadership comprised a dangerously inflammable mixture.[7]

Conditions on the Eve of the Coup

The armed forces finally allowed the Peronists to return to power in 1973, after enough military leaders had become convinced that the party and its union adherents were, at most, reformist. Just prior to Perón's return, those unions were divided because some had cooperated with the outgoing military government (1966–73), which others had opposed. Whatever tactics they adopted, most Argentine unionists did not seem terribly threatening to the established order. Instead, they appeared to some elites as an antidote to the eruption of small leftist groups among students and workers. Bringing the Peronists back into legal, electoral politics had the potential to create a vigorous, legitimate reform government and thus isolate the more insurrectionary elements on the fringe of Peronism. Despite their anti-communist credentials, however, the Peronist labor leaders had by 1976 come to be seen as a target for harsh repression.[8]

On the eve of the 1973 election, polls found 80 percent of Peronist voters identifying their party as the true representative of the working class. Of all Peronist voters surveyed, 41 percent were themselves blue-collar workers. With his wife Isabel (María Estela Martínez de Perón) as vice president, Juan Perón returned to the presidency with 62 percent of the ballots, very close to the 64 percent he had received in 1951. According to one poll, 84 percent of the working class voted for Perón in 1973. The Peronists also scored very well with the lower middle class.[9]

At the beginning of his return to power in 1973, Perón recreated a classic populist alliance of industrialists and workers in support of his statist, nationalist economic program. However, his "Social Pact" between entrepreneurs and unionists, instituted to control prices and wages, quickly unraveled. Real wages (expressed in terms of an index that equalled 100 in 1970) rose from 96 in 1972 to 136 in 1974, while unemployment fell from 7 percent to 3 percent. As in Chile and Uruguay, unbridled inflation fueled class conflict. Many property owners became convinced that labor's excesses had to be curbed. After Juan Perón's death and the ascension of his wife in 1974, economic policy swerved to the right. Isabel Perón favored capitalists, lowered wages, and combated inflation. Production and employment fell during 1975–76.

The government of Juan and Isabel Perón did not recast the basic labor legislation, but it did revise that fundamental law to fortify union capacities. It especially enhanced the power of the CGT and the national federations vis-à-vis the state and vis-à-vis local unions. The reforms hardened the monopolies of labor organizations over their economic sectors.

The Peronist government also strengthened the autonomy of unions with regard to the Ministry of Labor, permitted them to participate in political campaigns, improved their fund-raising abilities, and allowed union bosses to hold their offices longer and protected them against firings. Furthermore, it sweetened worker benefits, such as vacations and health care. Union membership rose dramatically, as Peronist domination reached a historic high.[10]

A large majority of trade unions remained leashed to mainstream Peronism. For the most part, that movement pursued short-term material goals for the workers and downplayed any vision of social upheaval. As in Spain, Brazil, and Chile, however, the presence of the prolabor government inspired a wave of worker unrest. The post-1955 tradition of Argentine unions acting outside normal party and government channels vexed the Peronist administration.

In Argentina as in Chile and Brazil, a dilemma arose between the unions' need to seek concrete benefits for their members and the labor party's need to mollify broader constituencies and to manage macroeconomic variables. That problem was especially acute in Argentina because Perón tried more than Salvador Allende did to satisfy numerous nonlabor interests. He especially courted industrialists and segments of the middle class. By the same token, Perón did not go nearly as far as Allende did in carrying out radical redistributions to the working class.

As in Chile under Allende, official labor leaders participated in the Peronist administration and supported government policies. Therefore, workers who opposed those policies also denounced those leaders. Such discontent provided fertile ground for a few leftist laborites, both inside and outside Peronism. Their inroads were not enough to challenge the hard-core Peronists but were sufficient to stoke right-wing paranoia.

After the death of Juan Perón in July 1974 and the elevation to the presidency of his wife, conflicts between the mainline unions and the government escalated. Isabel Perón had dissipated most labor backing by the end of her administration. Her increasingly conservative policies trapped Peronist labor leaders in an irreconcilable position between their government and their followers.

In pronouncements, demonstrations, and bursts of strikes in 1975–76, Peronist workers demanded wage hikes and greater participation in policy making. This conflict created the impression among anti-Peronists that the government was too weak and the unions too strong. As in Chile and Brazil, adversaries charged that a prolabor government had unleashed extreme worker expectations and agitation. Some of this strife resembled the clashes of the Allende government with "economistic" and "radical" laborers.

Responding to labor's challenge, the Peronist administration underwent a volte-face against its core supporters. The government adopted antilabor economic and political policies on a piecemeal basis before the military took over completely. Repression of the more leftist, defiant unions began before the coup. In Argentina as in Uruguay, the civilian rulers gave the armed forces increasing latitude to fight against the guerrillas and other dissidents.

As in Chile, labor's struggle against its enemies in the higher social strata coincided with an internecine fight for control of the worker movement. From the beginning of his return, Perón clashed with the Peronist unions. He did not want them exercising either domination over his multiclass political movement or autonomy from his political direction. After spending years surviving with their legendary leader at a comfortable distance, the unionists bristled at his interference. After his death, a battle for control of the CGT raged among mainline Peronists. This scuffle grew out of an older fight over the degree of authority to be exercised by the central union bureaucracy over federations, locals, and members.

Throughout the three-year Peronist administration, moderate union leaders jousted not only with the Peróns and each other but also with radical younger workers. Those newcomers rebelled against the party and union bureaucracy. They demanded more dramatic sociopolitical changes, sometimes in concert with leftists inside and outside Peronism. The elites feared that such workers might burst out of the bounds imposed by the established unions and their deals with governments. The CGT secured government help in purging many of the upstarts on the grounds of their being pro-communist.

By the time of the coup, the labor movement faced two bleak alternatives: either the conservative government of Perón's spouse or the conservative government of the armed forces. Having already given up on Isabel Perón, the unions greeted the predictable military takeover with passivity. The armed forces easily cowed unionists demoralized by their most recent governing experience, divided internally, and losing ground on wages. The ostensibly awesome labor movement looked dejected, disoriented, and disgraced. Like many other populist movements in Latin America, it had functioned much more effectively in the opposition than in the government.[11]

After the Coup

In 1976, the Argentine military launched the "Process of National Reconstruction," under the leadership of army general Jorge Rafael Videla. To a lesser extent than in Uruguay, the armed forces had already defeated many of the guerrillas before the coup, but it took three more years to eliminate them completely. More important for national politics, the campaign to stamp them out brought in its wake another purpose: the shredding of the labor movement.

Now Argentine labor endured the worst persecution in its history. The military engaged in the most brutal and vast repression during the "Dirty War" from 1976 to 1979. According to human rights organizations, between one-third and one-half of the thousands who disappeared were workers and union members. After the most barbaric phase, the regime used more selective violence and placed more emphasis on trying to restructure the union movement.

The military most frequently assaulted unionists who were on the left, or those with the greatest capacity to interfere with market-driven economics. The armed forces feared that leftists at the base of the unions might link up with the guerrillas, so deaths and disappearances occurred more at that level than among the top leadership. At the same time, the military imprisoned the majority of mainstream Peronist labor leaders. The victims of these arrests or kidnappings most often came from the more powerful unions in the industrial and state sectors. Extermination at the base and incarceration at the peak resulted in the obliteration of leftists and the silencing of Peronists.[12]

Structural Constraints on Labor

Like its counterparts in the Southern Cone, the Argentine junta committed itself to both the national security doctrine and market-oriented economics. By applying the national security doctrine against the labor movement, it removed that obstacle to the economic program. In the view of the armed forces, many laborers were linked—or at least vulnerable—to subversives and wedded to state activism, both of which the military opposed in the name of order and growth.

Jorge Videla's economic policies had six main, interconnected objectives: (1) to brake inflation; (2) to reduce the income and the bargaining strength of the working class; (3) to shrink the role of the state as an instrument for populist movements; (4) to undercut protected industrialists who relied on expansion of the internal market and who forged alliances with organized labor; (5) to stimulate capital accumulation, the financial sector, and production for export; and (6) to open the economy to foreign traders and investors.[13]

The dictatorship's anti-inflation campaign did not become as extreme or as successful as its counterpart in Chile. When Videla took office, he designated the curtailment of inflation as his highest economic priority. Arrogating to itself the power to set wages, the junta pursued stabilization by compressing the pay of workers, whittling down the public sector, ending price controls, and devaluing the currency. In addition, the government and many industries hiked working hours to raise efficiency and productivity.

The annual growth in consumer prices dropped from 335 percent in 1975 and 348 percent in 1976 to 170 percent in 1978, 140 percent in 1979, and 88 percent in 1980, thereafter rebounding to 131 percent in 1981. After rising from a base index of 100 in 1970 to 105 in 1975, real wages had plunged to 63 by 1978. Real wages in industry fell from 116 in 1975 to 74 in 1976 and 67 in 1981. The participation of wage earners in the gross domestic product dropped from 48 percent in 1975 to 29 percent in 1980. After peaking at 49 percent under the second Perón government in 1950–55, wages and salaries as a percentage of national income declined until 1974–75, when they reached a second high point of 47 percent under the third Perón government; then they dived to 36 percent under Videla in 1976–80.

As in Uruguay, the main economic policy that harmed labor in Argentina was the lowering of real wages. By reducing the income of workers and expanding wage differentials, government policies decreased the unions' power and unity. In the face of persistent inflation, unionist protests over the declining value of take-home pay continued at the plant level and in conversations between the government and the more cooperative unions.[14]

And as in Chile, deindustrialization eroded the foundation of the labor movement. The Argentine government not only reduced the size and protection of industry but also tried to make it more efficient and competitive. During 1975–80, industrial output fell by 3 percent, and industrial employment by 26 percent. Industry's share of GDP dropped from a peak of 38 percent in 1974 to 34 percent in 1980, and to 25 percent in 1984. While overall employment stayed high under the military, industrial employment decreased, as more and more workers became self-employed. Between 1974 and 1980, industry's share of the economically active population fell from 37 percent to 30 percent, while the service sector grew from 27 percent to 28 percent. The percentage of the economically active urban population that was self-employed rose from 21 percent in 1976 to 22 percent in 1979, and to 24 percent in 1981.

Although the relative growth of the service sector reduced the leverage of industrial workers, it did not slash the size of the union movement dramatically. Trade unions absorbed numerous employees outside of manufacturing. Thus, organized labor became less representative of blue-collar sectors and more representative of white-collar sectors. Between 1965 and 1985, the industrial sector's share of total union members dropped from 38 percent to 31 percent, while the service sector's share rose from 28 percent to 31 percent.

The government's preference for free trade also undermined manufacturing firms and workers. As in Chile and, to a lesser extent, Uruguay, the dictatorship in Argentina pared down protective barriers against externally manufactured goods. Thus Videla forced domestic industrialists to meet foreign competition by lowering their prices and wages. At the same time, trade promotion and currency devaluation transferred income from urban workers to agricultural exporters.

Adaptations by industrialists further damaged the traditional labor movement. When industries tried to become more competitive and adopted more modern technology, they employed fewer workers. They also increased salary and skill differentials among those who remained, thus undermining labor unity. Workers also became more heterogeneous as the use of piecework by contract and of work at home expanded. While the industrial sector trimmed its sails, manufacturing enterprises became smaller and more dispersed geographically, reducing the concentration of the proletariat. The government favored that dispersion to fragment the working class and to energize the poorer provinces.

Unlike Pinochet, Videla only wanted to discipline industry and its workers, not to decimate them. Some regime leaders still hoped to lure labor away from Peronism and the left through state paternalism. The dictatorship wanted to avoid creating massive unemployment that might radicalize the workers. By 1978, the Argentine government had backed away from an all-out crusade against inflation which was eliminating jobs. The total national unemployment rate hovered around 3 to 4 percent during the dictatorship. Indeed, by 1979 high employment combined with economic growth and reduced salaries to ignite a growing number of strikes, in a scenario similar to the Brazilian one.[15]

Much more than in Chile, industrialists in Argentina prodded the government to reverse or tone down its free-market approach. They were not willing to be sacrificed in order to cripple the working class. Argentine manufacturers were larger and more powerful than their Chilean counterparts, who had been weakened by expropriations under Allende. Chilean industrialists, although discontented with some neoliberal policies, remained far more fearful of the workers and their Marxist parties. Consequently, they were less willing and able to restrain antilabor programs under the dictatorship. Before the coups, populist alliances across class lines had been abandoned far more decisively in Chile than in Argentina.

In Argentina, unlike Chile and Uruguay, neoliberal economics did not generate enough growth to satisfy producers. Entrepreneurs criticized the government's anti-inflation campaign for driving many of them out of business. They also complained that wages had fallen so far that consumption and sales had plummeted. By the turn of the decade, the military regime had gradually shelved its program for stabilizing prices and opening the economy to international market forces.

Argentina was buffeted by a recession that began in 1980, accelerated in 1981, and continued through the return to democracy. Between 1980 and 1982, its GDP contracted by 11 percent. In 1981–82, regardless of the government's desires, unemployment approximately doubled, although it still did not exceed 6 percent. By 1982 the industrial workforce was about one-third smaller than it had been in 1975. The informal sector ballooned, as labor became more segmented and individualized. Inflation mounted, soaring over 400 percent by 1983.[16]

All along, most union leaders denounced the neoliberal program as "economic terrorism." In 1980–81, they tried to reconstruct an alliance with industrialists against free-market policies. As soon as the Falklands/ Malvinas war ended in 1982, laborers spearheaded strikes and street demonstrations demanding simultaneous economic recovery and redemocratization. However, the economic disaster bequeathed by the military and compounded by the staggering foreign debt left little room for redress of labor's grievances.[17]

Institutional Constraints on Labor

As under previous dictatorships in Argentina, the junta's policy toward organized labor vacillated between atomization and, to a lesser extent, cooptation. These two approaches posed an inescapable dilemma. On the one hand, the military wanted to disarticulate and disaggregate the union movement. But an extremely scattered labor sector would be hard to discipline from the top down. Moreover, constant repression would be costly.

On the other hand, if the armed forces tried to encapsulate labor the way it was, it would be too powerful an entity. The despots could not figure out how to conjure up weakened but still effective union leaders who could both obey the junta and represent the workers. Following the initial state of siege and reign of terror, the dictatorship tried both confrontation-atomization and cooperation-cooptation with little success.[18]

After enjoying a zenith of mobilization and power from 1973 to 1976, the Argentine labor movement sank to its lowest point in decades between 1976 and 1982. The unions mounted no resistance to the March 1976 coup. The call for a general strike on the day of Isabel Perón's overthrow had no impact. During the initial four years of the dictatorship, workers became almost totally impotent. Unions suffered not only from demobilization and factionalism but also from a crisis of leadership.

The military set out to eliminate the national power of the union movement by dismantling the CGT, and to stamp out radicalized local groups by intervening in targeted factories. Videla aimed to deactivate labor from above and below. The junta divided the union leadership and isolated it from its social base, while imposing a climate of fear on all workers. The armed forces took advantage of the weaknesses of a labor movement that already exhibited fissures among its leaders, and between its leaders and the rank and file.

Like Pinochet, Videla first unleashed naked coercion, including incarceration, kidnapping, torture, and assassination. The military justified this onslaught on the grounds that they were eradicating "corruption" and "subversion" among unionists. As part of the general assault, the armed forces attacked labor at all three levels: confederation, federation, and local. They primarily wanted to erase the ability of the trade union movement to exert national influence through a centralized command structure, so they outlawed the CGT and jailed its leaders.

At the same time, the army occupied most major union offices, and the junta announced that union meetings or elections could be held only with military authorization. The state took social welfare programs away from the unions and seized control of union funds. Numerous interventions, arrests, and disappearances took place not only among militant Peronists in the confederation and federations but also at the plant level. Factory owners and the armed forces worked in tandem to eliminate troublemakers, especially leftists.[19]

Like its counterparts in the Southern Cone and Brazil, the Argentine military hoped to change the leadership and political orientation of the labor movement. In one of its first acts, the dictatorship suspended several existing union affiliations and called for the affected workers to declare anew their union ties. The next day, 95 percent of those workers confirmed their previous affiliations.

Unhappy with the outcomes of union elections, the Argentine junta simply froze most existing union leadership arrangements or took them over. Those officials who kept their posts found it hard to pose as legitimate, either as agents for the workers or as intermediaries for the regime. To avoid reprisals against their leaders, unions sometimes rotated their representatives, so that a different delegate attended every meeting with the factory owner.

The armed forces intervened in unions representing 75 percent of the labor movement, often replacing elected directors with military commanders. They removed those who had been the most prominent leaders under the Perón-Perón government, the heads of the most powerful unions, and the hard-line Peronist bosses. Some of these leaders languished in prison for several years, but others regained their freedom after brief sentences.

As a result of military interference, the big unions became weak and factionalized with regard to the issue of leadership. Without democratic participation and validation from the rank and file, it was impossible to tell who truly spoke for the working class. Disputes raged among displaced leaders, new claimants who sought to take their place, and local bosses asserting autonomy.

Although the numbers of detained leaders were not vast, the removal of those individuals intimidated other union chieftains or gave competitors an opportunity to replace those hauled away. The opportunists included leaders of locals and of smaller unions, which were normally less militant groups. Some old and new federation union officials cooperated with the military interveners and served as interlocutors between government representatives and the workers. They found it difficult, however, to function both as handmaidens of the regime and as spokespersons of the working class.

The interventions divided union officials into two groups: confrontationists and cooperators. The leaders of unions in which there had been no intervention at least had the legitimacy of having been elected in the past, although their authority waned when no new elections were held for several years. Moderate, fearful of military intervention, and often conciliatory with the dictatorship, these leaders headed the first unions that were able to speak out even mildly against the government's policies.[20]

The dictatorship practiced some restraint because a few of its leaders desired to restructure an exhausted labor movement under state paternalism. They planned to take charge once the leftists and more intransigent Peronists had been expelled or subdued. The armed forces hoped to place equivalents of the Brazilian "pelegos" at the head of the union structures. They wanted to convert the hierarchical labor movement into a mechanism for control rather than representation.

The junta faced the quandary that its own repression had left it with few valid intermediaries between itself and the working class. Therefore some leaders of the military and the capitalists preferred to normalize union structures as soon as possible after the purge. They wanted to reestablish legitimate officials who could impose discipline on the workers. The junta wavered because it wanted to "democratize" the unions internally to loosen the grip of Peronism, but that would have allowed expressions of discontent from the rank and file. The dictatorship sought to exert control over the membership through a more compliant centralized bureaucracy, but that would mean restoring some leaders it had ousted as corrupt.

Although very ineffectual, the union leadership provided one of the only voices critical of the armed forces. The union officers responded to the dictatorship by trying to salvage themselves, their organizational structure, their unity, and their function as a communicator with the state. They primarily played a reactive role, responding to state initiatives such as invitations to discussion, announcements of economic measures, or decrees of new labor legislation.

In Argentina more than in any of the other countries discussed here, unions maintained an important dialogue with the government and the armed forces throughout the dictatorship. This interaction reflected the original alliance between the military and the unions under Perón in the late 1940s. Ever since Perón's fall in 1955, some trade union leaders and even a few military officers had been trying to recreate the coalition between the unions, the armed forces, and the state.

The dialogue under Videla also grew out of the conflicts, conspiracies, confrontations, and compromises between soldiers and workers during the period 1955–76. For two decades, the labor movement's reaction to hostile governments had divided it between "participationists" and "combatives." In 1976, some leaders of the CGT and the armed forces shared a desire to expunge the more leftist unionists who had arisen in the 1960s and 1970s. After the first six months of virtually total retreat, a few unions reached an accommodation with the military government.

Union responses to the dictatorship were basically divided between negotiation and confrontation, although with many blurred lines. Cooperation and conflict characterized two different approaches to the junta more than two different groups, since particular unions changed their approach from time to time. Those favoring collaboration were led initially by the twenty-one key nonintervened unions. This schism split the CGT, which, despite legal prohibition, continued to speak for many workers.

Argentine labor leaders realized that they did not have the power to win a clash with the armed forces by themselves. Therefore most unionists pressed their demands within the boundaries of behavior tolerable to the military, while seeking political and social allies to stretch those limits. Their strategy was, of necessity, moderate and gradualist. They also behaved pragmatically because they had no alternative ideological project tied to a political party with a vision of transformation.[21]

Through the manipulation of repression and dialogue, the Argentine armed forces had more success at dividing the labor movement than did their counterparts in Uruguay and Chile. In 1976–77, several unions that had not been subject to intervention met with Videla, exchanged ideas with the ministers of labor and the economy, and tried to cooperate with the government. When the dictatorship refused to heed their demands, some unionists tried pleading their case with individual commanders of the air force and the navy, with equally unsatisfactory results.

Even cooperative unionists experienced frustration because their list of basic grievances was so long. They had to urge the government to (1) reveal the whereabouts of disappeared union bosses; (2) release imprisoned labor leaders; (3) honor unions' legal rights, especially for collective bargaining and striking; (4) permit union elections; (5) terminate government intervention in numerous unions; (6) allow national confederations; (7) restore control of their social welfare programs to the unions; (8) return unions' offices and assets; (9) modify the conservative economic policy; (10) protect national industries; (11) assure stable employment; and (12) improve wages and salaries.

All Argentine unionists, whether mainly conciliatory or combative, were eager to reestablish labor unity. Since Peronism permeated so much of the working class, it proved hard for the junta to keep labor divided permanently into progovernment and antigovernment camps. Even most moderate or conservative Peronists were reluctant to abandon that political umbrella to endorse the regime's antilabor economic and social policies.

The junta's efforts to co-opt segments of labor did not succeed for long. By 1978, cooperative union leaders were cautioning the government that they could not be compliant much longer. They warned that the poor wage situation and other mistreatment of labor made them look like traitors to the workers, and they feared that they were in danger of being replaced by less patient leaders. As time went on, more and more unions adopted a confrontationist posture, as also occurred in the rest of the Southern Cone.[22]

In 1977–78, the unionists divided into two grand coalitions, mixed groups with ill-defined and shifting positions. Unions were torn between the two confederations, and many held membership in both associations. Both collectivities contained unions from diverse previous factions of Peronism, both sought dialogue with the regime, and both criticized the government's economic policies, especially on wages. The only relatively clear distinction between the two organizations was a struggle for turf among union leaders and a debate over hard-line or soft-line tactics toward the dictatorship. The government tolerated these loose confederations because it sought collaborationist unions, or at least moderate labor spokespersons.

The heterogeneous Commission of Twenty-five primarily represented the old CGT and hard-line Peronists. It criticized the government stridently, calling for a freely elected replacement. The Twenty-five also maintained stronger ties with international labor organizations. Its rival, the National Commission of Workers (CNT), was an amalgam of seventy-one unions and took a more flexible stance toward the government. It claimed to be less politicized and purely professional.

Repeated attempts to unify the two organizations in 1978 and 1979 achieved only partial success. In November 1980, the Commission of

Twenty-five partially reconstructed the CGT, mainly representing dyed-in-the-wool Peronist unions. Its rebirth marked the rising willingness of unionists to challenge the regime's existence. Several more moderate unions, particularly those descended from the CNT, temporarily stayed out of the CGT. In 1981 they formed a more conciliatory alternative confederation, the Intersectoral.[23]

Neither confederation displayed much effectiveness. The CGT called for general strikes in 1979 and 1981, but turnout was sparse. The government responded with repeated arrests of CGT leaders. The unionists closer to the CNT and then the Intersectoral hoped for a social pact among unions, entrepreneurs, and government authorities, similar to the arrangement forged during Perón's return in 1973. However, in 1981 conversations among the union soft-liners, the capitalists in the Industrial Union, and the Ministry of Labor foundered on the intransigence of the industrialists. Thereafter the moderate unionists backed away from compromises and aligned more closely with the militants in the CGT.[24]

Before the Argentine military rewrote the labor laws in 1979 (the same year the labor code was revised in Chile), unions suffered from a loss of their previous legal rights. Given government and employer hostility as well as union devastation, it became almost impossible to exercise such previously won prerogatives as the right to decent working conditions, fair procedures for determining salaries and promotions, negotiated work quotas and rhythms, reasonable working hours, breaks and vacations, and so forth. In one of its first acts, the junta suspended the most significant trade-union legal rights, especially those governing collective bargaining and strikes. It also prohibited all political activities by unions. In short, the dictatorship left the workers at the mercy of owners.

Since it was hard to sustain unrelenting repression, and since strikes and protests proliferated, the regime recast labor legislation in 1979. The partially new labor code was an attempt to dilute the hegemony of monolithic Peronist unions, curb their bargaining power, and roll back their benefits. For example, it prohibited the closed shop, long terms and job security for union officials, political affiliations on the part of unions, and numerous state and employer welfare provisions, especially union control over social service programs.

The code encouraged unions that were organized by enterprise in preference to those organized by federated sector or confederation. It allowed plant unions and professional federations but not the CGT, and it enhanced the power of the Ministry of Labor over unions. Although designed for at-

TABLE 7.1
Annual Number of Strikes in Argentina, 1973–1980

Year	No. of Strikes	Year	No. of Strikes
1973	214	1977	100
1974	330	1978	40
1975	300	1979	188
1976	154	1980	261

SOURCE: Edward C. Epstein, "Labor Populism and Hegemonic Crisis in Argentina," in
Edward C. Epstein, *Labor Autonomy and the State in Latin America* (Boston, 1989), 26–27.

omization, this legislation did not go as far toward individualization and
emasculation as did the Chilean plan. The government claimed that these
regulations would democratize and professionalize the unions, while the
trade unions denounced them as an assault on their rights and liberties.

In Argentina as in Chile, the revamped labor code simultaneously gave
unions a new opening for their operations and motivated them to mobilize
to overturn that legislation. Some individual unions started adjusting to the
new laws and working within them. The major result of the legislation,
however, was to produce greater labor activism and unity against the
government. It also inspired labor to collaborate more closely with opposition political parties in order to align them against the code as well as the
regime.

In protest against the new laws and against declining real wages, strike
activity escalated in 1979 (see table 7.1). Many unions refused to obey the
code, which proved very difficult to implement. Both the Peronist and Radical parties castigated this "punitive" legislation, as did international labor
organizations. Along with the International Confederation of Free Trade
Unions and the Interamerican Regional Organization of Labor, the International Labor Organization criticized the laws and pointed out conflicts
between them and previous international agreements on union rights
signed by Argentina. With so much resistance, the code did not fulfill the
regime's hopes of spawning a new labor system and a new group of labor
leaders.[25]

Throughout the dictatorship, Argentine unions lacked strong international or church support, especially by comparison with Chilean unions.
The CGT was traditionally introspective and suspicious of foreign connections, given its nationalism and its antipathy toward both the United States
and the Soviet Union. Nevertheless, the authoritarian experience brought
the trade unions closer to international entities and to the Roman Catholic
Church.

From 1976 on, the labor movement turned to international linkages as a means of survival—for example, using foreign forums to denounce the dictatorship. Involvement in international labor organizations also provided training for new union leaders during the enforced inactivity under the authoritarian regime. Fortunately for the CGT, it had just joined the social-democratic ICFTU in 1975. As a result, Argentine unions received some solidarity from abroad under the dictatorship and became more cosmopolitan after the return to democracy. Whereas prior to the 1970s the unions had been isolated, a poll of union leaders in 1984 found that 74 percent of them had participated in international labor congresses abroad and 52 percent of them belonged to unions affiliated with external organizations.

Much more than its Chilean counterpart, the Argentine government tried to maintain cordial relations with the ILO and the ICFTU. The dictatorship's need to send authentic but subservient union leaders to the annual meetings of the International Labor Organization provided occasions for discussions—even negotiations—between the unionists and the regime, and for jockeying for place among unionists. Argentina persuaded the ILO that it was moving toward normalization of labor relations, and thus it did not end up on the "blacklist" of countries violating union rights until late 1981.

The government capitalized on nationalism to convince many unions not to attack it too severely either at home or abroad. The unions did not want to appear "anti-Argentine"—or worse, "communist" or "terrorist." However, complaints from unions, although cautious, elicited denunciations of the government from the ILO, which provoked some liberalization toward moderate trade unions in 1980. Unionists also complained about their detained and "disappeared" associates to the Commission of Human Rights of the Organization of American States.

Interventions by international labor representatives helped the unions. In 1977 the AFL-CIO dispatched to Argentina officials who protested to Videla about the disappearance of labor leaders. These officials' visits with union chiefs from the Commission of Twenty-five, which spoke for the majority of the unions affiliated with the CGT and was usually ignored by the government, helped legitimize the Twenty-five.

Delegations from the ICFTU and its Latin American branch, the ORIT, also bestowed recognition on the Twenty-five and expressed concern about detentions and disappearances to the minister of labor and to President Videla. In addition, the World Confederation of Labor (CMT, a Social Christian organization) sent delegations and decried violations of human rights. Its interventions were facilitated by the growing role of the Roman Catholic Church as a spokesperson for persecuted unionists.[26]

Relations between labor and the Roman Catholic Church had not been close in the years leading up to the military takeover. After the coup, most church officials maintained a prudent neutrality toward the dictatorship and the unions. The unionists appealed to the church, to its social justice encyclicals, and to the pope for support. The CGT boasted of "Christian" inspiration, and Peronism claimed to embody "the Social Doctrine of the Church." In response, the workers received some succor from progressive segments of the local church hierarchy.

Although most of the clergy remained conservative, the church pronounced in favor of trade union freedom at the end of the 1970s. It convinced Videla to release some detained union leaders on the grounds that Argentine unionists were anti-communist. In 1980, some church leaders decried disappearances, mistreatment of unions, low wages, and the social costs of the economic program. These criticisms were also voiced by human rights organizations.[27]

Although aided by international entities, the labor movement for the most part survived on its own. The government failed to destroy or completely declaw the unions because of their stout bureaucratic structures, their resilience from previous experiences with military regimes, and their immunity against the use of anti-communism as a rationale for wide-scale atrocities against workers. In contrast with their counterparts in Chile and Uruguay, unionists in Argentina participated not only in more dialogue with the government but also in more strikes against firms. This schizophrenic behavior sometimes reflected a division between conformist union bureaucrats and the contentious rank and file.

Given the suppression of federations as well as confederations, local unionists had little alternative but to act on their own. Even without much assistance from the CGT or the PJ, Peronist workers continued to build upon their heritage of combat to launch strikes and protests from the factory floor. In Argentina as in Chile, unions displayed more resistance capabilities than did their dispirited party allies during the more repressive days of the dictatorship, before redemocratization began to unfold.

In addition to striking, some unionists fought back with work slowdowns and stoppages, absenteeism, sabotage, public demonstrations, and even a few plant occupations. Most of this defiance, however, was localized at the workplace and lacked national organization or repercussions. As the regime and its economic program lost momentum, general strikes occurred

during 1979, 1981, and—most effectively—1982, when workers staged the
first major street demonstration under military rule.

In a few factories, union affairs proceeded normally under the dictatorship. In other firms, unions continued partial operation, although often un-
recognized by management. In still other plants, the destruction and reconstruction of unions occurred repeatedly. And in numerous businesses,
the authorities totally liquidated regular union activities. Nevertheless, so-
called inorganic ("wildcat") strikes still erupted.

Under the junta, conflicts without official union participation may have
comprised the majority of labor-industrial disturbances. Some of these actions were spontaneous or were hatched by new labor leaders arising under
the dictatorship. Others were orchestrated covertly by seasoned Peronist or
leftist bosses. The government expressed exasperation at being confronted
with strikes that had no visible leaders.

During most of the Argentine dictatorship, the unions emphasized concrete objectives, not political goals that directly challenged the regime. As
in the rest of the Southern Cone, labor's behavior became increasingly defensive. Workers stressed job security and retention of previous "historic
conquests." As the labor movement resurfaced in 1979–82, it mainly demanded higher wages, expanded employment, restoration of legal rights,
and protection for national industries.

The decline in pay spurred the vast majority of labor-management disputes under Videla. One study of 287 industrial conflicts during 1977–80
found that 200 concerned wages. Whereas centralized union federations
had previously struggled for equitable remuneration, now decentralized
unions extracted highly differentiated pay scales.[28]

In Argentina, as in Chile and Uruguay, the labor movement really began
to remobilize in the wake of the new legal code and, above all, the 1980–81
economic crisis. Strikes and street demonstrations by organized labor gathered momentum from 1979 to 1982. These activities wove new bonds between many union leaders and the alienated rank and file.

By 1982, the CGT and other worker organizations increasingly emphasized redemocratization as a fundamental demand. Working-class protests,
although milder than those in Chile, undermined the free-market program,
upset the order imposed by the armed forces, exacerbated divisions within
the regime, resonated with discontented industrialists, and aroused broader
civilian demands for democracy. Labor demonstrations reached a crescendo
on the eve of the 1982 Malvinas War.

During the skirmish with Great Britain, the Peronist trade unions and party backed the government for reasons of patriotism. Both the CGT and the Intersectoral hailed Argentina's invasion of the Falkland Islands with manifestoes and rallies. They stressed, however, that their demands for social justice and democracy would remain the same once the international conflict had ended.[29]

Following humiliation by England's armed forces, the dictatorship imploded. Government controls over union and party activities evaporated quickly. Ignoring the constricting labor regulations, union leaders swiftly reconstructed their organizations and launched protests. And the junta, restoring some of the old labor legislation, annulled the law prohibiting strikes. In 1982–83, general strikes became increasingly effective.

However, union pressures on the dictatorship were not necessarily more significant than those coming from other organizations, such as human rights groups and political parties. Given its suffering, its traditions, and its strategic importance, the labor movement actually seemed fairly restrained in 1982–83. Many union leaders still maneuvered gingerly for good relations with the military, for victory in the upcoming national elections, and for an eminent role under the new regime thereafter. Some unionists tried to cut a deal with the armed forces to allow the Peronists to return to power and to protect the military from retribution.

When redemocratization took hold in 1982–83, labor remained split between negotiators and belligerents, but both groups campaigned for the electoral triumph of the Justicialist Party. The PJ embraced both worker factions but primarily supported the more pugnacious CGT. As the authoritarian regime fell, the Peronist unions wary of concertation or cooperation with the military came to prevail.

While the armed forces were preparing to return to the barracks, they allowed the normalization of most unions. The military's attempt to foster a new set of union leaders had failed. Most of the same bosses who had held office in 1976 retook command of their organizations in 1983. Two weeks before the 1983 presidential and congressional elections, the major unions forged a reunited CGT, similar to the reconstruction of the CUT in Chile. It brought together moderates and militants. They hoped that their combined action could assure more economic benefits for workers and an electoral victory for Peronism. Just as the rift between unions had reflected a conflict within the PJ, so unification of the unions coincided with the Peronists pulling together to try to reclaim the presidency.[30]

Political Constraints on Labor

Upon taking power in 1976, the armed forces destroyed or neutralized most leftists outside as well as inside Peronism. The military hunted down Marxist groups and the Peronist left but allowed the regular Peronist, Radical, Christian Democrat, Socialist, and even Communist parties to maintain most of their leaders and structures so long as they suspended their activities. The Communists were so docile that they declared support for Videla on the grounds that he was not as bad as the more "fascist" groups in the armed forces or as Pinochet in Chile. Neither the Peronists nor other political parties played any significant role against the dictatorship during its first five years.

Under the authoritarian regime, most laborers clung loyally to Peronism as well as to past union officials. Although other parties—Communists, Socialists, and Radicals—claimed adherents within the labor movement, they remained minuscule compared to the Peronists. When the dictatorship arrived, the Justicialist Party was a hollow shell, dominated by Isabel Perón and by the unionists. The core of the PJ remained a loose conglomeration of labor leaders and provincial bosses.

Now that Juan Perón had passed away and his widow had lost credibility, no magnetic personality could unify or galvanize the workers, let alone hold aloft the hope of a successful political alternative. The leadership and activities of the Justicialist Party were moribund under the junta. Many of the party's mid-level and local leaders, especially those connected to the unions or the left, suffered persecution, imprisonment, exile, and even execution.

Although largely ineffectual, the Peronists continued to speak for workers, both to the government and to other opposition parties, with much greater freedom than did the labor parties in Chile or Uruguay. Led by the Peronists and Radicals, the opposition formed a broad democratic coalition, the "Multipartidaria," in 1981. Both soft-line and hard-line unionists threw their support to the multiparty alliance.[31]

Between 1980 and 1982 the political parties, especially the Peronists and Radicals, became more important in the drive to unseat the government. They increasingly supported the demands for change from the more militant unions. Parties and unions cooperated, but Argentine parties did not command unions to the extent that Chilean parties historically did. In Argentina, the parties followed the initiatives of social organizations and then began to assert party primacy for electoral battles. In 1981–82, this political reawakening coincided with liberalization by the dictatorship, which expanded its openness to dialogue.

Despite their enmity toward the government, the Peronists supported the military in the Malvinas on the grounds of nationalism and anti-imperialism. So did the Montoneros, the Communists, and the Multipartidaria. Once the debacle on the islands had shamed the armed forces, most observers assumed that the other major power in Argentine politics—the labor-based Peronists—would recapture the presidency.[32]

Redemocratization

From the end of the 1982 war until the 1983 elections, the parties, unions, and other opposition groups pressed for full democratization. They convoked massive street demonstrations and general strikes, the largest since 1976. Individual unions and the rank and file protested more loudly than did the often-softspoken CGT. Many middle-class organizations of professionals and white-collar employees seemed more fervent than industrial workers in their demands that authoritarianism be done away with.

Although adamant on labor questions, most trade unions did not play a prominent part in campaigns on the issue of human rights. Instead, many unionists appeared more interested in reaching minimal understandings with the armed forces to assure an orderly election and transfer of power, presumably to the Peronists. As in the other countries discussed above, labor exercised restraint as the tyrannical regime stepped aside.

Within Peronism, the labor organizations had survived with greater vitality than the party machinery. Always weaker than the unions, the PJ had withered during the authoritarian regime, and leftist groups that had arisen within Justicialism in the early 1970s had vanished by the early 1980s. The old union chiefs who had reigned during 1973–76 dominated party decision making during redemocratization. To their surprise, the unionists soon discovered that much of their Peronist constituency, as well as a majority of the electorate at large, wanted a political movement that was younger, more pluralistic, more open, and more democratic.[33]

The centrist Radical Party's presidential candidate, Raúl Alfonsín, blamed both the Peronists and the armed forces for the curse of authoritarianism. He denounced Peronist union chieftains for concocting a secret "military-union pact" with segments of the army. He charged that the military, as it eased out of office, was restoring old Peronist leaders to control over labor in exchange for promises that there be no prosecutions for

TABLE 7.2
Percentage Distribution of Presidential Votes by Sample of Argentine Male Workers in Córdoba and Tucmán, 1973 and 1983

	Córdoba		Tucumán	
	1973	1983	1973	1983
Peronist	41	31	66	45
Radical	22	51	9	45
Total	63	82	75	90

SOURCE: Jorge Raúl Jorrat, "Las elecciones de 1983: ¿'Desviación' o 'realineamiento'?" *Desarrollo Económico* 26:101 (Apr.–June 1986), 89–119.

NOTE: The totals are less than 100 percent because votes for "other" are not shown.

human rights violations. Although the PJ denied it, this accusation pulled together in the public mind the widespread disgust with the recent dictatorship, with the previous Perón-Perón government, and with all the clashes and conspiracies between soldiers and unionists during the last four decades. That image, along with the bankruptcy of the Peronist program, helped Alfonsín sweep into the presidency.[34]

In October 1983, the Peronists lost the presidency—and numerous working-class votes—to the resurgent Radical Party in a vote of 40 percent to 52 percent. For the first time since 1946, many working-class districts cast a majority or large plurality of their ballots for a Radical instead of a Peronist. Nevertheless, polls and ecological studies showed that the sociological character of the Peronist electorate had changed little from 1973. The urban lower classes remained the hub of the movement, along with mixed groups in the interior provinces.

Probably a majority of Argentine laborers still supported Peronism, and certainly a majority of the Peronist votes came from workers. However, that working-class support had clearly become more conditional. Having dominated the Justicialist electoral effort and having tried to deliver the usual proletarian votes, the orthodox Peronist unions took much of the blame for the defeat.

Survey results revealed a decrease in worker support for the Peronists between 1973 and 1983, as well as a continuing reliance of the PJ on working-class voters. The distribution of votes from different social sectors can be seen in the polling data in tables 7.2, 7.3, and 7.4. Polls on other attitudes found that most workers in general, and Peronist voters in particular, were moderate ideologically, self-defined as "centrist," committed to democracy, antagonistic to communism, and only slightly more dedicated to egalitarian measures than was the population as a whole.

TABLE 7.3
Percentage Distribution of Sample of Presidential Vote, by Party, in Argentine Urban Centers, 1983

	Unskilled Workers	Skilled Workers	All Voters
Peronist	69	45	40
Radical	27	47	52
Total	96	92	92

SOURCE: Edgardo Raúl Catterberg, *Los Argentinos frente a la política* (Buenos Aires, 1989), 108.
NOTE: The totals are less than 100 percent because votes for "other" are not shown.

TABLE 7.4
Percentage Distribution of Sample of Party Votes in Argentina, by Social Class of Voter, 1983

	Upper and Upper-Middle Class	Middle Class	Lower Class	Total
Peronist	7.5	28.6	63.9	100
Radical	8.8	53.4	37.8	100

SOURCE: Edgardo Raúl Catterberg, "Las elecciones del 30 de octubre de 1983: El surgimiento de una nueva convergencia electoral," *Desarrollo Económico* 25:98 (July–Sept. 1985), 259–67.

In Argentina as in the other countries discussed here, laborers exhibited enduring but weaker ties to their old political parties after the end of authoritarianism. Communists and Socialists urged voter support for the Peronist presidential candidate, to little avail. As in Chile, the PC failed to elect a single congressional deputy. The Argentine left was now more moderate and even punier than before the coup.

In the 1983 elections for congressional deputies, the Radicals claimed 48 percent and the Peronists 39 percent. In large part, the Radical Party won because it embodied democracy, antimilitarism, and a repudiation of the past. On all these points, the stance of the Peronist party and union leaders was ambiguous. The Peronists lost because of the erosion of the proletariat and the labor movement, their party's previous association with failure and authoritarianism, their divisions, their lack of vision, and the absence of a leader with the stature of Perón. In subsequent elections in 1985 and 1987, however, both skilled and unskilled workers returned to the Peronist fold in large numbers.[35]

As democracy returned, Argentine labor leaders faced a novel situation. For the first time since 1946, they confronted a non-Peronist government that they considered legitimate and that they could challenge only within the accepted rules of the game. They had to become a loyal opposition.

There was no Juan Perón to rally the unionists, no military dictatorship to repress them. They neither held power in the state nor suffered oppression from the state. Now they had to learn to function effectively in a democracy, with no coherent political protagonist or nemesis. In Argentina as elsewhere in the Southern Cone, union leaders placed greater emphasis than before the coup on the importance of democracy as a national political system and as a mode of operation within the labor movement.[36]

Union membership had shrunk by approximately 1 million since 1976. Although reliable data were unavailable, one plausible estimate showed the labor movement declining from approximately 5 million members in 1976 to roughly 3.5–4.0 million in 1983. A sample of union affiliates revealed that industrial union membership fell by 23 percent between 1973 and 1985, while unions in the service sector grew by 17 percent, for a net decline of approximately 5 percent.

By the mid-1980s, the unions still enrolled approximately 48 percent to 56 percent of all Argentine wage earners. That was the highest level in Latin America, and far higher than levels in the United States or much of Europe. By 1984, 67 percent of all wage earners in the Argentine industrial sector belonged to unions. Of all Argentine union members, 31 percent came from manufacturing, 31 percent from services, 15 percent from commerce, and the rest from diverse occupations. According to another form of calculation for 1984, 4 percent of unions came from the primary sector, 34 percent from the secondary, and 62 percent from the tertiary. The types of unions, and the distribution of unions among these types, were much as they had been prior to 1976.[37]

Although the unions had lost some credibility, they retained broad public support, as also seen in other countries emerging from authoritarian persecution of labor. An opinion poll in 1984 found that 81 percent of the Argentine public viewed unions positively. At the same time, only 30 percent saw union leaders in a favorable light. A survey of workers in 1985–86 found that 82 percent gave positive ratings to foreign companies and 62 percent to labor unions but that reactions to Argentine business, large landowners, and the military were unfavorable (positive ratings were given by 38%, 32%, and 22%, respectively).[38]

A survey of Argentine laborers in 1985–86 found overwhelming support for a democratic type of government and much weaker support for populist, socialist, military, or conservative governments (68% versus 17%, 5%, 3%, and 0%, respectively). They expressed the strongest party preferences for the Peronists (45%) and the Radicals (37%). The workers included in the sample reported their plurality support for the Peronists (67%) in the 1973 presidential election, for the Radicals (56%) in the 1983 presidential race, and for the Peronists (50%) in the 1985 congressional contest.

The interviewees indicated very little affinity for leftist movements. When asked if communism offered any solutions for Argentina, 78 percent said no, 9 percent yes. Eighty-nine percent criticized the guerrillas. When queried about the military's crusade against subversion under Videla, 38 percent of the workers opposed it, while 52 percent voiced support. Despite this positive response, they exhibited generally negative attitudes toward the armed forces and their reign, with 60 percent condemning the 1976–83 government. Placing themselves on an ideological spectrum, 3 percent of the workers interviewed chose the left, 8 percent the center-left, 42 percent the center, 12 percent the center-right, and 17 percent the right, while 19 percent elected "other" or "don't know."[39]

In union balloting in 1984–85, the Peronists maintained their domination, albeit with greater pluralism than in the past. Within the union movement, debates became freer and contests more competitive, although most of the contestation took place among different branches of Peronism. In 1984–85, the Peronists won 90 percent of the union elections.

In Argentina as in the rest of the Southern Cone, the dictatorship had very little success in changing the basic political identifications of organized labor. Peronists still controlled around three-fourths of the unions, as well as the executive committee and secretary generalship of the CGT. A smattering of Radicals and Socialists performed slightly better than they had prior to the junta, but candidates farther to the left fared poorly. A poll of union general secretaries and adjunct secretaries in 1985 found that 75 percent were Peronists, 4 percent Radicals, 4 percent Socialists, 9 percent independents, and 9 percent unidentified.[40]

As also occurred in Uruguay, Chile, and Brazil after the return of democracy, some unions demanded greater independence from confederations, from parties, and from the state. Non-Peronist and provincial unionists asserted their autonomy most strongly. Thus the Argentine labor movement became slightly more decentralized than it had been in 1976.[41]

Under President Alfonsín, attempts to forge a concertation on macroeconomic guidelines among government, business, and labor bore little fruit. Persistent economic problems deterred unionists from accepting government proposals for extended compromises with capitalists. As in Brazil and Uruguay, hammering out such a consensus was difficult because labor unions and parties were not part of the government.[42]

Argentine labor leaders succeeded at channeling worker grievances within the system, but they failed at changing the economic model or significantly boosting paychecks. After a brief recovery in 1983–84, real wages and levels of employment fell under Alfonsín, as they had under the dictatorship. Stagflation took hold, as the government lurched from one unsuccessful economic program to another, swerving between hyperinflation and stabilization.

Labor in Argentina, as elsewhere in the Southern Cone and in Brazil, succumbed to international pressures for austerity and debt payments. In vain, the CGT kept advocating an anachronistic Peronist program in favor of populism, nationalism, and the welfare state. As a result of working-class disappointment, unions struck frequently. Thirteen general strikes perturbed the Alfonsín period, but never approached the abyss of destabilization.[43]

As in Chile, labor gave high priority to reinstatement of its previous legal rights. Showing that it was still more vigorous than some critics supposed, the CGT convinced Congress to reject Alfonsín's proposal to democratize unions internally and thus diminish Peronist hegemony. However, the new government—like its counterparts in Brazil and Chile—did not move quickly to undo all the military's labor laws. Reforms for unions took a back seat to consolidation of a fragile democracy in an economy wracked by recession, inflation, and debt. The government returned the CGT's assets and funds for social services, but it only restored full labor rights bit by bit. For example, it did not reestablish uninhibited collective bargaining until 1988.[44]

Under the new democracy, the CGT was handicapped by the structural changes wrought by the dictatorship, by the poor performance of the economy, by the continuation of many of the institutional hobbles installed by the military, by the absence of a dynamic national leader of Peronism, by its obsolete populist program, and by the confusion of the Justicialist Party after its first loss in an honest competitive election. Tension continued between the CGT and the PJ as to who really controlled Peronism. The union confederation initially held the upper hand, as it had most of the time since 1955, while the divided party sorted out its new identity and mission.[45]

Like other labor parties after authoritarianism, the Peronists underwent a process of profound self-examination and redefinition. Within the PJ, mainline "verticalists," or "orthodox," who had dominated under the Perón-Perón government, struggled against "antiverticalists," or "renovators," who had spearheaded protests against the dictatorship. In most cases, the antiverticalists were less wedded to the CGT, more dedicated to participation from the rank and file, and more committed to democratic procedures within unions and in national politics.

Not unlike the Socialists in Chile and Spain, renovated Peronists captured control of their party and advocated a social democratic program. They exhibited more willingness to compromise with the Radicals to stabilize the new regime. They believed that their party had to grow stronger than ever before, now that all political competition would take place within a legitimate democratic order. At the same time, they realized that the Peronist unions could not win public elections, govern, or attract as diverse a constituency as could the Peronist party.[46]

Peronism had always defined itself more as a movement than as a party, with the unions as its spine. The unionists tried to continue that role under Alfonsín, but they learned that an effective labor party was indispensable in a durable democratic system. In a classic dilemma for labor parties, the trade unionists wanted to build the party up without surrendering their autonomous clout; they wanted to endow it with independent muscle without losing their domination; and they wanted it to encompass sectors beyond unions without diluting its dedication to organized labor. Relying on the party and on charismatic leaders offered labor important political opportunities. But it also presented the risk that the politicians could subordinate the unions and their demands.[47]

In 1989, the Peronists recaptured the presidency under Carlos Saúl Menem. Between 1983 and 1989 the Peronists increased their share of the vote from 40 percent to 47 percent, while the Radicals stumbled from 52 percent to 33 percent, mainly because of the economic chaos fueled by astronomical inflation. Labor celebrated its victory and awaited promised wage hikes.

But, like Felipe González in Spain, Menem turned the tables. He did so mainly because the economic situation—particularly hyperinflation, stagnation, and the foreign debt—gave him little choice. After preaching populism on the hustings, Menem pushed through neoliberal reforms in office. He completely reversed the historic mission of Peronism. Unions were torn over their party's switch to reducing the state, privatizing public companies, liberalizing trade, promoting free enterprise, courting foreign capital, and advocating growth more than redistribution.

Menem had one of the greatest successes with that market-oriented program that any democratic president in Latin America achieved. He could constrain many of the unionists while he stole the right's thunder. Restrict-

ing the right to strike and other legal prerogatives, he also divided and
weakened the CGT. Whereas labor had united against similar policies carried out by inimical governments in the past, now it lost its direction under
a Peronist administration, as it had done earlier under Isabel Perón. As in
most of the other countries we have studied, organized labor ended up disoriented and bereft in the face of the neoliberal juggernaut, especially when
those policies were embraced by its own political paladins.[48]

Conclusion

How had the dictatorship changed the Argentine labor movement? The
industrial working class had shrunk, while the self-employed had increased
in number and the service sector had grown. Workers were poorer, and
unions were weaker. Trade unions had become more independent, participatory, and pluralistic. Within the CGT, smaller organizations, which had
been less oppressed by the military, now played a bigger role alongside the
traditional Goliaths. Some new leaders who had emerged under the dictatorship now functioned alongside the old guard. As in Chile, the labor
movement had developed stronger international ties.

The dictatorship had failed to eliminate Peronism. But oppression and
changing times had turned the Peronists and the proletariat into more
moderate forces that no longer jeopardized the institutional, social, or economic status quo. Like most of society, the labor movement now placed a
higher value on formal democracy. Diverse political currents became more
cooperative with each other. Consensus proved easier to achieve because
the military had eliminated left-wing contenders. Also, as democratization
underwent consolidation, working-class groups had no plausible alternative to the neoliberal model.

Alongside changes, many of the traditions of the labor movement persisted. Despite their diminution in numbers and leverage, it was still the industrial workers who had spearheaded strikes and demonstrations against
the capitalists and against the military regime. Thus they had soon attracted
other social sectors to the cause of democratization. Unionists had divided
over tactics under the dictatorship, but they had remained united in their
class cohesion. In the main, they clung to the CGT and to Peronism. Once
again, their tenacious movement, however battered, had survived.[49]

EIGHT

Labor Movements after Capitalist Authoritarianism

This concluding chapter draws out some generalizations about the roles of labor movements during and immediately after redemocratization. It places this study within the context of the vast comparative literature on authoritarianism, regime transitions, and democratization. It concentrates on three key questions. Since there were universal fears that organized workers, once unchained, would upset the transition to or the consolidation of the new democracy, why did these workers prove to be a stabilizing force in every country? Following the restoration of democracy, why did the working class receive so few of the reforms it expected? And what were the main strengths and weaknesses of the labor unions and their political parties in the aftermath of capitalist authoritarianism?[1]

In every case studied in this book, redemocratization began with liberalization, however tepid. The authoritarian regime tried to loosen its grip just enough to broaden its base and to divide the opposition between soft-liners and hard-liners. Instead of shoring up the autocracy, those small openings heartened and energized its adversaries. Working-class organizations usually took the initiative in the early stages. Then the dictatorship's opponents pressured it to stretch those meager openings and to move on to full democratization.

During redemocratization, the labor movement faced three main dilemmas, all closely related. The first problem was representation. Could labor leaders reestablish and reassert their claim to speak for their followers? Should those leaders represent older labor traditions or newer labor realities? Should they champion only organized workers or a broader social spectrum? And should they emphasize representation or regulation of the working class?

The second dilemma faced by the labor movement was mobilization. In the cause of democratization, unions debated whether to stress activism or quiescence, social mobilization or social control, and confrontation or concertation. Should they expect mass demonstrations (as the Communists initially predicted) or peaceful negotiations (as most Communists eventually preferred) to bring down the autocratic regime? In most cases, democratization eventually came about through reform, not rupture. In order to keep the return to civilian rule on track and their interests on board, labor leaders had to calculate how to time charges and retreats, how to navigate between mobilization and concertation.

The third dilemma was demands. The laborites agonized over whether to emphasize socioeconomic demands or democratic consolidation, redistribution or macroeconomic stability, and short-term or long-term goals.[2]

During the journey back to democracy, unions renegotiated their relationships with workers, each other, the nonunionized poor, employers, parties, and the state. Resistance to the dictatorship helped generate unity among very diverse unions, and among disparate social and political actors. Trade unions retained some symbolic power to speak for the broader working class. As democratization drew nigh, unionists ceded leadership of the opposition to the political parties. Most laborers subordinated their class interests to the broader campaign to do away with authoritarian rule. As the dictatorship neared its end, unions usually changed their stance from vociferous to demure.

As soon as the seemingly entrenched and impregnable dictatorship began to fade away, large segments of its institutions, authority, and followers disappeared with surprising celerity. When the authoritarian curtain lifted, parties proliferated, claiming to represent constituents although their support had not been tested. Politicians tried to rise to the top with personalism. Great confusion spread about loyalties and programs.

Very quickly, however, the more venerable parties reasserted themselves, and the electoral menu filled out. In most cases, the right wing of the spectrum was weaker than expected, the center stronger. In all of the countries under discussion except for Greece and Brazil, there were noteworthy continuities between the postauthoritarian party system and the pre-coup system, especially among leftists and laborites. However, those familiar names and positions masked important changes in leadership, ideas, and behavior. Most significant was the moderation of many leftists and their new endorsement of centrist policies. Those transformations helped make the restoration of electoral democracy both procedurally successful and substantively limited.

Restraint by Labor Unions and Labor Parties

In spite of or because of widespread fears and warnings from politicians and intellectuals, the labor movement did not knock democratization off course anywhere. Furthermore, after the reestablishment of democracy, nowhere did workers desert the new political system or provoke the authoritarians into a reversal. Laborers did not behave seismically even when many of their basic socioeconomic goals were not met. In light of its severe losses under the military-based government, labor's sophisticated willingness to recapture lost ground gradually was remarkable. It constituted one of the most significant factors in bringing about durable redemocratization.

Rather than damaging democratization, laborers made major contributions to reinventing and stabilizing that political order, partly through concertation. After the installation of democracy, worries about labor's role overestimated the disruptive impact of normal union activities. And those concerns underestimated the resilience of democratic systems, even when newly born.

In large part, the labor movement did not upset democratization because of its legacies from the authoritarian experience: (1) its fear of a recurrence; (2) the economic constraints on its leverage; (3) the weakness of its institutions; (4) the moderation of its beliefs, programs, and comportment; and (5) its heightened appreciation for classic liberal democracy. When that political system returned, working-class groups were still inhibited by shell shocks from the dictatorship. They were held back by the structural, institutional, and political constraints that had hampered previous reform efforts and that had been intensified by the despots.

One intimidating legacy from the dictatorships was fear. The traumas and nightmares experienced under authoritarianism caused labor unions and friendly parties to exert restraint during the first elections and early phase of the resuscitated democracies. After suffering more than most groups from despotism, workers knew that they were particularly vulnerable to renewed repression.

A second reason that laborers did not capsize democratization was the debilitating economic legacy from the dictatorship. The continuation and even intensification of antilabor macroeconomic policies after democratization kept the working class on the defensive. Many unions complained about the perpetuation of market-oriented programs under civilian rule, but they did not try to overturn the system. Labor leaders had no clear alternative development strategy, especially because of the discrediting of populism and socialism. In some cases, worker activism also lagged because of unpropitious economic circumstances, chiefly recession and unemployment.

Under neoliberalism, workers' leverage with the state was less than it had been and meant less than it had meant previously because the government played a smaller role in determining their lot. Therefore, in some countries, laborers accepted a new "implicit social contract." They supported or tolerated the capitalist system in return for some benefits from growth, stability, and participation in even a shrunken welfare state. In the years following authoritarianism, these accommodations in parts of Southern Europe and the Southern Cone meant that the dictatorship's goal of eviscerating organized labor and obliterating any alternative to market-driven capitalism was at least partially realized.[3]

A third carryover from authoritarianism was labor's institutional weakness. In the Southern Cone, workers realized that their organizations were smaller and poorer than before the coup and therefore less likely to extract major concessions all at once. Even the breakdown of the harshest antilabor regimes did not generate massive and radicalized labor mobilization. Extreme repression had left the atomized unions in particularly fearful and frail condition, as seen in the contrast between working-class tranquility in Chile and working-class volubility in Brazil. Unionists had made gains under corporatism in Brazil and Southern Europe, in contrast with the Southern Cone dictatorial experience, but they were still not formidable bargainers. At the same time, labor's weaknesses in the cases under discussion reflected the general decline of unions in the West from the recession of the 1970s through the neoliberal restructuring of the 1980s and 1990s.

In the Cono Sur and in Spain, authoritarianism had made the labor movement much more moderate. Although the rhetoric of some union bosses—more in the confederations and federations than in local organizations—was still radical, it belied their prudent behavior. Most of them muted or discarded previous calls for class struggle against capitalism. Instead, they advocated liberal democracy, human rights, and specific reforms for their organizations, such as changes in labor legislation. This moderation was crucial to the installation and consolidation of constrained democracies acceptable to the economic and military elites.

Throughout most of Latin America, almost regardless of regime type, unions in the 1980s became more independent of the state, their own federations and confederations, and political parties. They were more committed to collective bargaining with employers, and more interested in negotiating with the government than clashing with it. Increasingly, they mainly concentrated on local, economistic job issues.

At the same time, most labor parties reinforced the working-class propensity toward moderation because they had also been tempered by the dictatorship. Socialists and Communists became more conservative, and the latter melted with the thawing of the Cold War. Whereas prolabor parties became less aggressive in the Southern Cone and Spain, some became more assertive in Portugal, Greece, and Brazil. In all of our cases—except briefly in the Portuguese "revolution"—apprehension that outbidding wars among unshackled laborite parties would generate extraordinary conflict and radicalism turned out to be unfounded. *Restraint* and *reconciliation* became the bywords for most politicians. Those terms primarily meant that unions and their party allies—especially in the Southern Cone and Iberia—had to jettison the maximal, ideological beliefs and goals that had dominated their movements prior to the coups.[4]

Workers also held themselves in check because, after years of mistreatment, they saw electoral democracy as a higher priority. For unions, the lifting of oppression alone was a tremendous achievement. They viewed civilian rule as an enormous collective good obtained through strenuous collective struggle. Laborers were willing to postpone some of their own agenda in order to solidify the new democracy. For the long run, they believed that democracy was the best way to obtain their lost rights, benefits, and wages.

The possibility that union combativeness might upset economic and political stability was countered by the positive contributions that labor's conduct made to democratization. Rather than an impediment to reinstatement of democracy, the labor movement was one of the mainstays. When plotting their actions, workers strove for a delicate balance and for appropriate timing.

When the dictatorship displayed its first signs of weakness, working-class mobilization propelled democratization by challenging the regime and inspiring other opposition groups to come forth. Labor demands pushed the political opening beyond a pact between soft-liners in the government and in the opposition intended to implant a restricted democracy. Insistence from below helped guarantee that workers, their unions, their parties, and their issues would be included in the new political system.

During the transition, labor throttled down to reassure its enemies who feared social upheaval. At the same time, it kept up enough pressure to impel liberalization on toward full-fledged democratization. Although not halting all activities, laborers stopped short of inciting a backlash.

For workers, speaking softly during the exit of the armed forces helped facilitate democratization when it was most in danger of being halted. The unionists pulled their punches because they would be able to reassert themselves with less risk after the military had returned to the barracks. Following an elaborate extrication by the authoritarians, it would have taken a very high threshold of disorder to bring the soldiers back to center stage, and labor had no intention of supplying such turbulence. Through their steadfast support for the new democracy and their vow to defend that political system, laborers also served as a deterrent to would-be coup makers.

As civilian rule was restored, carefully modulated labor activism revived the political participation of workers, who resumed their normal role in democratic give-and-take. Since that activism took place through legal union and party channels, it reconnected laborers with their leaders and fortified democratic institutions. Containing working-class militance within legitimate, orderly conduits obviated elite fears of social upheaval. Thus to an extent, unions benefited capitalists and the government by organizing the workers and making sure that inevitable conflicts were conducted within acceptable boundaries. Thereafter, so long as labor politics stayed within standard limits, it became an accepted, routine feature of democratic life.[5]

By the same token, most capitalists tolerated the return of democratic trade union activity because they had come to realize that (1) labor activism did not necessarily indicate radicalism; (2) most union demands were economic rather than political; (3) unionists could be less disruptive if standard organizational rights were granted; and (4) agreements (on wages, working conditions, flexibility, technology, productivity, etc.) reached with free and representative unions were more likely to hold up. Many entrepreneurs also converted to democratization because it not only defused social conflicts but also facilitated integration with the world's leading economies.

Large, dense, unified, centralized labor organizations controlled by moderate political parties appeared most capable of assuring order during democratization. However, such organizations were difficult to achieve in most of the countries discussed herein. Those prime conditions proved unnecessary because workers almost everywhere were determined to facilitate the transition back to democracy. In the cases of Portugal, Spain, Brazil, Greece, Uruguay, and Chile, unions exercised caution to secure stable democratization even though they were quite decentralized and pluralistic.

Many unions initially counted on concertation and pacts to give them a voice in the new democracy. By reining in worker demands and actions so as to cooperate with democratization, Southern European and South American trade unions created situations modeled after the neocorporatist deals cut in Western Europe among labor, industry, and the state. In the countries under discussion, the most explicit pacts and legal measures enabling the state to ensure a class compromise and labor's rights were in the formerly corporatist cases of Portugal, Spain, and Greece.

In South America, similar postauthoritarian tripartite consensual arrangements among workers, capitalists, and governments were more effective in Uruguay and Chile than in Brazil or Argentina. Having outlasted the dictatorship, Uruguay's traditional pluralistic, gradualist labor unions, political system, and welfare state made the achievement of concertation and democratic stability relatively easy. In the immediate aftermath of authoritarianism in South America, only Chile came close to a European social-democratic model in which a government including labor parties assured working-class peace. In Brazil and Argentina, the need to safeguard incomes and jobs in a context of high inflation threw labor on the defensive.

In most of the countries I have discussed, labor often withdrew from concertation proceedings because it was asked to pay too high a price in the short term for uncertain benefits in the long term. In many cases, consensual policy making and pacts proved short-lived, as workers realized that they were the primary actors being restrained and making sacrifices. Consequently they began downplaying accords with management and government and started emphasizing traditional bargaining tactics.[6]

Worries that labor tantrums would shatter the new democracies exaggerated the tremors set off by normal, controlled union activities. When shorn of any fundamental class-based or ideological challenge to the prevailing order, reasonable demand-making by trade unions was tolerable to most elites, even when a prolabor party held office. The workers made sure that their initiatives could not be misconstrued as any radical threat to the new order.

As labor union and party leaders pointed out, prudence was important, but restrained activism did not cross the threshold beyond which it would have provoked a coup. After having experienced the deprivations of authoritarianism, unionists backed away from the traditional political bargaining technique of engaging in brinkmanship in order to wring concessions from the government by jeopardizing its hold on power. Since that gamble was too dangerous, they emphasized economistic bargaining.

The new democracies were actually so resilient that in many cases labor was quite confrontational without evoking repression. Shortly after the return of civilian rule, significant strikes and demands erupted. General strikes convulsed Brazil, Uruguay, and Argentina, where the labor parties did not form part of the government as they did in Chile.

Before and after the grimmest years of military rule, Brazil, Uruguay, Chile, and Argentina exhibited some of the most intense strike activity in Latin America. That renewed turmoil sprang mainly from base-level demands that wage scales lost under the dictatorships be recuperated. Heightened strike activity reflected not only pent-up economic grievances but also the new freedom for unions to compete with each other.[7]

The final reason that unionists did not dynamite democratization was that the transitions from authoritarian rule were neither so fragile as they appeared at the time nor so easily rolled back. In fact, most democracies—even new ones—are usually quite hardy. Among the sturdy Latin American and Southern European democratic systems that had looked frail at birth were those that held power in Uruguay (in 1903–73), Chile (in 1891–1925 and 1932–73), Colombia (in 1910–48 and 1958–95), Costa Rica (in 1948–95), Brazil (in 1945–64), Venezuela (in 1958–95), the Dominican Republic (in 1965–95), Portugal (in 1974–95), Greece (in 1974–95), Spain (in 1975–95), and Ecuador (in 1979–95).

Understandable concerns about the brittleness of the restored democracies were perhaps due to extrapolation from the highly unusual Argentine case. Argentina's history of violent alternations between populists and praetorians in the context of a tight labor market and an extraordinarily interventionist military was not typical. Even there, redemocratization in the 1980s came off without a hitch. And predictions in the mid-1990s about the continuation of democratic regimes in the Southern Cone and Southern Europe looked fairly safe for the foreseeable future.[8]

Reforms for Labor Unions and Labor Parties

With their restraint, unionists had more success at facilitating democratization than at pursuing fundamental reforms. None of the unbound labor movements obtained big changes in the balance of power or the socioeconomic order, except briefly during the Portuguese revolution. In most countries, the working class failed to transform basic macroeconomic policies. The new governments hoped that marginal gains for workers would be sufficient by contrast with the hideous conditions under the dictatorship.

TABLE 8.1
Human Rights Accountings by New Democracies

Countries	Level of Atrocities	Strength of Democracy	Government Actions
Portugal, Spain, Brazil	Low	Low	None
Uruguay	Low	High	Minor
Greece	Low	High	Major
Chile	High	Low	Minor
Argentina	High	High	Major

Another reason that labor realized only minor benefits was the new regime's attempt to placate the right, the greatest threat to redemocratization.

None of the labor unions or parties obtained satisfactory retribution for the military's violations of their human rights. Nor did the other victims. Under civilian rule, retrospective human rights policies were mainly determined by the prior level of atrocities and the initial balance of power between the new democracy and the armed forces. In relative terms, the lower the level of human rights violations under the military and the lower the level of leverage of the new democracy with the military, the lower the level of likely government action on the issue. By contrast, the higher the levels of human rights violations under the military and of subsequent democratic powers, the higher the probability of government action (see table 8.1).

In Portugal, Spain, and Brazil, democratic officials did virtually nothing to respond to the call from labor leaders, leftists, human rights activists, and others for truth and justice for the victims of the armed forces. Almost the only consolation to the victims was that private citizens published shocking accounts of torture and other heinous crimes. Even though abuses in Spain were spectacular, that country's level of atrocities is rated as low because the worst outrages occurred a long time ago and were committed by both sides in a civil war.

In Uruguay and Chile, the central government did little except to allow some trials to proceed through the courts. However, President Patricio Aylwin did issue an official study of deaths and disappearances. Since the military retained extraordinary powers after the renewal of democracy in Chile, that country exhibited the widest gap between the high level of "war crimes" before the transition and the minor governmental response thereafter.

Only Greece and Argentina carried through with significant punishment for the perpetrators. However, in Argentina the labor movement did not march in the forefront of the human rights struggle, and the sentences for the culpable officers did not last long. Greece does not really fit the scheme shown in table 8.1: even though grisly barbarities and murders under the dictatorship were comparatively few, the colonels were tried and convicted.[9]

The resurrected democracies also did little to comply with the unions' biggest institutional demand: wholesale revision of the authoritarian labor code. Along with better wages, the unionists ranked changes in the labor-industrial relations system as their highest priority. Although the former proved slightly easier to obtain than the latter, both demands encountered firm resistance from a business class that had grown stronger under the dictatorship. Typically, the new democracies granted minor concessions to labor but delayed designing a new legal code.

In most cases, the restored democracy or the unions themselves found some features of the authoritarian labor legislation worth preserving. The governments usually wanted to keep some of the free-market provisions, whereas both the government and the unions opted to retain some of the corporatist aspects. In some corporatist cases, those features included state recognition of unions, broad national collective agreements, compulsory dues, and social insurance.

Revival of Labor Unions and Labor Parties

In most of the countries we have examined, the restored party alignment echoed many features of the pre-coup setup. The most common changes from one democracy to the next were the disorganization and declining fortunes on the right, the strengthening and domination of centrist parties, the survival and restraint of populist parties, the slight shrinkage of the left, the moderation and growth of the Socialists, and the fading of the Communists. Without a violent social eruption overthrowing the dictatorship, the labor parties that had been the principal enemies of the regime were unlikely to succeed it immediately. Instead, moderate centrists or conservatives intermediate between the diametrically opposed camps were likely to preside over democratization. This pattern was seen in Spain, Greece, Brazil, Argentina, Uruguay, and Chile, the latter a mixed case with the Socialists joining the Christian Democrats in the successor government.

Soon after playing a subdued role in the first flush of democratic restoration, labor and its party allies began to revive. Following a period of reorientation and reorganization, unions experienced increases in their membership, status, and leverage. However, that resurgence was nowhere near as pronounced as they had been hoping for, and it was sometimes short-lived. Unions remained more independent from parties than they had been in the days before the coup.[10]

Nevertheless, party influence increased dramatically between the transition from authoritarianism and the stabilization of the new democracies. The labor parties had to reassert their claim to represent the working class and once again make that claim a reality. They also had to reach out to new coalitions with nonunionized groups and with centrist parties. Moderation was reinforced by the growing influence among laborers of catch-all parties, such as the Blancos in Uruguay, the Christian Democrats in Chile, and the Radicals in Argentina.

Unionists welcomed the return of their party partners, but they complained about the extent of the takeover of labor by parties, especially in Chile and Argentina. After the reinstatement of democracy, most unions gravitated back to their pre-coup political affiliations. Government attempts in Uruguay and Argentina to "democratize" unions, by loosening the grip of the parties that had dominated them traditionally, bore little fruit. In Greece and Brazil, where strong labor parties had been absent prior to the coups, new parties made inroads with the working class.

During democratization, the traditional leftist parties performed a delicate tightrope act—holding on to some continuities with their ideological past while edging toward a more moderate future. They placed a higher value on liberal democracy and archived their antipathy toward liberal capitalism. Almost everyone discarded any hint of a resort to armed struggle, or else they were rapidly marginalized. Even far leftist groups—such as the Tupamaros in Uruguay and the Montoneros in Argentina—toned down their rhetoric and, even more so, their behavior.

In most of the cases I have discussed, the main labor unions and parties adopted a "social democratic" posture. The Socialists in Portugal, Spain, Greece, and Chile evolved into pragmatic parties with eclectic programs and constituencies. Although the Socialist organizations increasingly became catch-all parties, they remained attached to the working class, which provided the largest percentage of their votes.[11]

Among labor parties, Marxist organizations—especially Communists and groups farther left—withered away around the globe in the 1980s. They were destroyed by anti-communism, U.S. animosity, shrinkage of the classic proletariat, ideological rigidity, outdated programs, competition from social democrats, and the collapse of the Soviet Union and its satellites. For the Communists, it proved very difficult to make the transition from underground resistance to electoral combat. In every country we have studied, the PC waned in national elections, but it retained a hard core of supporters, particularly in the union halls.

The more Socialists and other labor parties evolved in a social-democratic direction, the more hostile became their relationship with the Communists, even though the latter also softened their positions as democratization unfolded. Coalitions between Communists and other prolabor parties (particularly Socialists) had been possible—albeit difficult—before the dictatorships, especially in Spain and Chile. But such alliances became impossible after redemocratization, notably in Portugal, Spain, Greece, and Chile.

Laborites captured the executive branch surprisingly rapidly, or at least made giant strides toward doing so. After the mainstream labor parties revamped their programs, leaders, machinery, and images, they were more likely to win the presidency. Rejuvenation came quickly, with the takeover of the Socialists in Portugal, Spain, and Greece, their participation in the governing coalition in Chile, the return to power of the Peronists in Argentina, and the rise in leftist votes in Uruguay and Brazil. During the evolution of the postauthoritarian electorate, some of the biggest winners were some of the main groups loathed by the armed forces.[12]

Conclusion

In most instances, structural variables outweighed institutional or political factors in determining the lot of labor. In structural terms, the dictatorships succeeded in preserving capitalism and erasing any hint of its replacement by socialism. Even without their brutality, however, revolution had never been in the cards in most cases. The extent of their responsibility for the economic paths taken was also cast in doubt because the market-oriented approaches favored by the tyrants engulfed the globe regardless of regime type. Institutionally, they weakened trade unions, but that too was a worldwide trend. Nevertheless, all these tendencies were certainly intensified and hastened by the actions of the autocrats.

Although the extent of the dictatorships' success in instituting socioeconomic transformations can be called into question, there is little doubt about their ability to withstand most attacks from below. Overwhelmingly, repression worked, whether engineered by corporatists or by atomizers. The labor unions and parties were much more successful at outlasting these regimes than at battling them.

It is not surprising that the workers manifested little capacity to destabilize or dethrone these right-wing governments. Opposition unity was crucial but very difficult to achieve because of ideological and strategic divisions, especially with the Communists. Armed struggle proved in vain everywhere. Although nonviolent opposition was also thwarted in many ways, it was more successful at pressing the despots to depart according to their own timetable or even sooner.[13]

Changes in the external environment or within the reactionary coalition were normally required to drive the regime out, although those changes frequently responded to pressures from the dictator's antagonists. Disunity within the authoritarian camp proved very helpful to redemocratization. Once democracy was restored, the main contours of the political landscape often looked so familiar that some of the autocratic regimes appeared—at least superficially—to have been a parenthesis. Although the authoritarians took credit for the increasing moderation of the labor unions and parties, that, too, was a global phenomenon that might have occurred eventually without the tyrants' staggering violations of human rights.

Perhaps the most enduring legacy from the dictators was the national memory of the enormous direct and collateral damage they had caused. With that nightmare in mind, workers and many other citizens were determined that despotism would "never again" ("nunca más," as it was expressed in the Southern Cone) return to power. The reinstated democracies did little to punish the dictators for their past abuses, but they did try to protect civil liberties for subsequent generations. They sought to safeguard the years ahead by making sure that capitalist authoritarianism would not reappear.

Although these military-based governments bequeathed a debilitating situation to their nemeses, the labor unions and parties refused to disappear. Moreover, those worker organizations often took power fairly quickly after the dictators withdrew. The new civilian governments carried out few of the reforms desired by workers, but they did give labor greater freedom. Under the adverse conditions created by capitalist authoritarianism, the survival and revival of these laborite groups were more remarkable than their deterioration. In all cases, the opponents of dictatorship—especially labor unions and parties—encountered many more defeats than victories. Nevertheless, they eventually regained a democracy, with all its opportunities and constraints, promises and perils.

Notes

ONE : Proletarians and Praetorians

1. In this book I will examine authoritarian, not totalitarian, regimes. To refer to the dictatorships studied here, terms such as *despotism, autocracy,* and *tyranny* will be alternated to diversify the vocabulary. These regimes will be distinguished from the more democratic ones that came before and after, even though those democracies were sometimes flawed and limited. In this context, the term *democracy* simply refers to the standard Western system of elected, representative, civilian government. No judgment about the solidity, depth, or quality of those democracies is implied, and no reference to economic or social equality is intended. Juan J. Linz, "Opposition to and under an Authoritarian Regime," in Robert A. Dahl, *Regimes and Oppositions* (New Haven, Conn., 1973), 171–260. Robert A. Dahl, *Polyarchy: Participation and Opposition* (New Haven, Conn., 1971). Samuel P. Huntington, *Political Order in Changing Societies* (New Haven, Conn., 1968); idem, *The Third Wave: Democratization in the Late Twentieth Century* (Norman, Okla., 1991).

2. Paul W. Drake, "Urban Labour Movements under Authoritarian Regimes in the Southern Cone and Brazil, 1964–83," in Josef Gugler, *The Urbanization of the Third World* (New York, 1988), 367–98. Manuel Barrera, "Introducción," in Manuel Barrera and Gonzalo Falabella, *Sindicatos bajo regímenes militares: Argentina, Brasil, Chile* (Santiago, 1990), 1–20. Adam Przeworski, *Democracy and the Market: Political and Economic Reforms in Eastern Europe and Latin America* (Cambridge, 1991), 181–82.

3. Thomas E. Skidmore, "Workers and Soldiers: Urban Labor Movements and Elite Responses in Twentieth-Century Latin America," in Virginia Bernhard, *Elites, Masses, and Modernization in Latin America, 1850–1930* (Austin, Tex., 1979), 79–126.

4. Conceivably, other cases, such as those of Italy, Germany, the Philippines, or South Korea, might be included in the comparison. However, they would require an enormous historical stretch beyond the already risky coverage of seven countries attempted here. Moreover, other contenders lack some of the more comparable features of our seven cases and introduce highly distorting variables, such as World

War II and totalitarianism in Fascist Italy and Nazi Germany. Nicos Poulantzas, *Fascism and Dictatorship: The Third International and the Problem of Fascism* (London, 1974). J. Samuel Valenzuela, "Labor Movements in Transitions to Democracy: A Framework for Analysis," *Comparative Politics* 21:4 (July 1989), 445–72. J. Samuel Valenzuela and Jeffrey Goodwin, "Labor Movements under Authoritarian Regimes," *Monographs on Europe* 5 (1983), 1–50.

5. The authoritarian regimes discussed here bear many traits in common with the species dissected by Guillermo O'Donnell, *Modernization and Bureaucratic Authoritarianism: Studies in South American Politics* (Berkeley, 1973). Philippe C. Schmitter, "The 'Régime d'Exception' That Became the Rule: Forty-Eight Years of Authoritarian Domination in Portugal," in Lawrence S. Graham and Harry M. Makler, *Contemporary Portugal: The Revolution and Its Antecedents* (Austin, Tex., 1979), 3–46. Immanuel Wallerstein, *The Modern World System* (New York, 1974); idem, *The Capitalist World Economy* (Cambridge, 1979). Salvador Giner and Eduardo Sevilla Guzmán, "From Despotism to Parliamentarism: Class Domination and Political Order in the Spanish State," *Iberian Studies* 8:2 (autumn 1979), 69–83. José María Maravall, *Dictatorship and Political Dissent: Workers and Students in Franco's Spain* (London, 1978), 3–5. Linz, "Opposition."

6. Robert Pinkney, *Right-Wing Military Government* (Boston, 1990), 1–15. D. L. Raby, *Fascism and Resistance in Portugal: Communists, Liberals, and Military Dissidents in the Opposition to Salazar, 1941–1974* (Manchester, 1988), 266–67. A. E. Fernández Jilberto, *Dictadura militar y oposición política en Chile, 1973–1981* (Amsterdam, 1985), 436–38.

7. Two of the most influential overviews of Latin American labor history, which tried to analyze the Latin American working class in its own special terms as a product of the region's dependent position in the world economy, are the following: Hobart Spalding Jr., *Organized Labor in Latin America* (New York, 1977). Charles Bergquist, *Labor in Latin America: Comparative Essays on Chile, Argentina, Venezuela, and Colombia* (Stanford, Calif., 1986). Other standard general accounts of organized labor in Latin America include the following publications, listed chronologically: Moisés Poblete Troncoso and Ben G. Burnett, *The Rise of the Latin American Labor Movement* (New York, 1960). Robert J. Alexander, *Labor Relations in Argentina, Brazil, and Chile* (New York, 1962); idem, *Organized Labor in Latin America* (New York, 1965). Frank Bonilla, "The Urban Worker," in John J. Johnson, *Continuity and Change in Latin America* (Stanford, Calif., 1964), 186–205. William H. Form and Albert A. Blum, *Industrial Relations and Social Change in Latin America* (Gainesville, 1965). Henry A. Landsberger, "The Labor Elite: Is It Revolutionary?" in Seymour Martin Lipset and Aldo Solari, *Elites in Latin America* (New York, 1967), 256–300. Victor Alba, *Politics and the Labor Movement in Latin America* (Stanford, Calif., 1968). Irving Louis Horowitz, *Masses in Latin America* (New York, 1970). Joseph Ramos, *Labor and Development in Latin America* (New York, 1970). Raquel Meléndez and Nestor Monteagudo, *Historia del movimiento obrero* (Buenos Aires, 1971). Jorge Giusti, "Participación y organización de los sectores populares en América Latina: Los casos de Chile y Perú," *Revista Mexicana de Sociología* 34:1 (Jan.–Mar. 1972), 39–64. Stanley M. Davis and Louis Wolf Goodman, *Workers and Managers in Latin America* (Lexington, Ky., 1972). Kenneth Paul Erickson, Patrick

V. Peppe, and Hobart Spalding Jr., "Research on the Urban Working Class and Organized Labor in Argentina, Brazil, and Chile: What Is Left to Be Done?" *Latin American Research Review* 9:2 (1974), 115–42. Carlos Rama, *Historia del movimiento obrero y social latinoamericano contemporáneo* (Barcelona, 1976). Rubén Katzman and José Luis Reyna, *Fuerza de trabajo y movimientos laborales en América Latina* (Mexico, 1979). Judith Evans, "Results and Prospects: Some Observations on Latin American Labor Studies," *International Labor and Working Class History* 16 (fall 1979), 29–39. Eugene F. Sofer, "Recent Trends in Latin American Labor Historiography," *Latin American Research Review* 15:1 (1980), 167–76. Julio Godio, *Historia del movimiento obrero latinoamericano* (Mexico, 1980); idem, *Sindicalismo y política en América Latina* (Caracas, 1983). Charles Bergquist, "What Is Being Done? Some Recent Studies on the Urban Working Class and Organized Labor in Latin America," *Latin American Research Review* 16:2 (1981), 203–23. Ian Roxborough, "The Analysis of Labour Movements in Latin America: Typologies and Theories," *Bulletin of Latin American Research* 1:1 (Oct. 1981), 81–96; idem, "Issues in Labor Historiography," *Latin American Research Review* 21:2 (1986), 178–88. Alejandro Portes and John Walton, *Labor, Class, and the International System* (New York, 1981). Michael L. Conniff, *Latin American Populism in Comparative Perspective* (Albuquerque, 1982). J. Samuel Valenzuela, "Movimientos obreros y sistemas políticos: Un análisis conceptual y tipológico," *Desarrollo Económico* 23:91 (Oct.–Dec. 1983), 339–68. Pablo González Casanova, *Historia del movimiento obrero en América Latina,* 4 vols. (Mexico, 1985). Gerald Greenfield and Sheldon Maram, *Latin American Labor Organizations* (Westport, Conn., 1985). Francisco Zapata, "Hacia una sociología del trabajo latinoamericano," in Comisión de Movimientos Laborales de Consejo Latinoamericano de Ciencias Sociales (hereafter, CLACSO), *El sindicalismo latinoamericano en los ochenta* (Santiago, 1986), 17–30. Ronaldo Munck, "Labor Studies Renewal," *Latin American Perspectives* 13:2 (spring 1986), 108–14. Alain Touraine, *Actores sociales y sistemas políticos en América Latina* (Santiago, 1987). Carlos Zubillaga, *Trabajadores y sindicatos en América Latina: Reflexiones sobre su historia* (Montevideo, 1989). Edward C. Epstein, *Labor Autonomy and the State in Latin America* (Boston, 1989). Francisco Zapata, "Towards a Latin American Sociology of Labour," *Journal of Latin American Studies* 22:2 (May 1990), 375–402. Ruth Berins Collier and David Collier, *Shaping the Political Arena: Critical Junctures, the Labor Movement, and Regime Dynamics in Latin America* (Princeton, 1991). Hobart A. Spalding, "New Directions and Themes in Latin American Labor and Working-Class History," *Latin American Research Review* 28:1 (1993), 202–14.

8. In addition to the country literature cited later, two examples were: Irving Louis Horowitz, *Revolution in Brazil* (New York, 1964). Richard E. Feinberg, *The Triumph of Allende* (New York, 1972).

9. Valenzuela, "Labor Movements." Valenzuela and Goodwin, "Labor Movements." O'Donnell, *Modernization.* David Collier, *The New Authoritarianism in Latin America* (Princeton, 1979). Karen L. Remmer, *Military Rule in Latin America* (Boston, 1989), 113. Alejandro Portes and A. Douglas Kincaid, "The Crisis of Authoritarianism: State and Civil Society in Argentina, Chile, and Uruguay," *Research in Political Sociology* 1 (1985), 49–78. Alfred Stepan, "State Power and the Strength of Civil Society in the Southern Cone of Latin America," in Peter Evans, Dietrich

Rueschemeyer, and Theda Skocpol, *Bringing the State Back In* (Cambridge, 1985), 317–46. Laurence Whitehead, "Whatever Became of the 'Southern Cone Model'?" Occasional Papers Series, no. 5, Institute of Latin American Studies, La Trobe University, Aug. 1982, 1–17. Hector E. Schamis, "Reconceptualizing Latin American Authoritarianism in the 1970s: From Bureaucratic-Authoritarianism to Neoconservatism," *Comparative Politics* 23:1 (Oct. 1990), 201–20. Samuel A. Morley, *Labor Markets and Inequitable Growth: The Case of Authoritarian Capitalism in Brazil* (Cambridge, 1982), 3–16.

10. For stylistic variety, nouns such as *labor, laborers, working class, workers,* and *proletariat* will be used almost interchangeably to refer to the labor movement outlined above, even though I realize that those terms convey somewhat different meanings. The text will indicate when those words are being used to denote something other than or more than organized urban workers.

11. Torcuato Di Tella, *Latin American Politics: A Theoretical Approach* (Austin, 1990), 102–16; idem, "Parties of the People in Latin America," working paper no. 108, Latin American Program, Wilson Center, 1982; idem, "Populism and Reform in Latin America," in Claudio Veliz, *Obstacles to Change in Latin America* (New York, 1965), 47–74.

TWO : Labor Movements before Capitalist Authoritarianism

1. If numerical weights were assigned to the descriptions in the table, setting Low = 1, Medium = 2, and High = 3, simple addition would rank the four South American cases in the order expected: Argentina, 27; Chile, 22; Uruguay, 18; and Brazil, 11. However, this quantification should not be taken too seriously, since the data are soft and the factors have not been weighted or prioritized. Moreover, the table leaves out intangibles such as historical struggles and ideological commitments. Where available, country data are provided and cited in the respective chapters. Robert R. Kaufman, "Corporatism, Clientelism, and Partisan Conflict: A Study of Seven Latin American Countries," in James M. Malloy, *Authoritarianism and Corporatism in Latin America* (Pittsburgh, 1977), 109–48. David R. Cameron, "Social Democracy, Corporatism, Labour Quiescence, and the Representation of Economic Interest in Advanced Capitalist Society," in John H. Goldthorpe, *Order and Conflict in Contemporary Capitalism* (Oxford, 1984), 143–78. Gosta Esping-Andersen and Walter Korpi, "Social Policy as Class Politics in Post-War Capitalism: Scandinavia, Austria, and Germany," in ibid., 179–85. Mancur Olson Jr., *The Logic of Collective Action* (Cambridge, 1965).

2. Subbiah Kannappan, *Employment Problems and the Urban Labor Market in Developing Countries* (Ann Arbor, Mich., 1983), 168–75. Bruce E. Kaufman, *How Labor Markets Work* (Lexington, Ky., 1988), 164–65. Jorge Salazar-Carrillo, *The Structure of Wages in Latin American Manufacturing Industries* (Miami, 1982). J. Figueiredo et al., *Empleo y salarios en América Latina* (Petrópolis, Brazil, 1985).

3. Ruth Berins Collier and David Collier, *Shaping the Political Arena: Critical Junctures, the Labor Movement, and Regime Dynamics in Latin America* (Princeton, 1991). Edward C. Epstein, "Austerity and Trade Unions in Latin America," in William L. Canak, *Lost Promises: Debt, Austerity, and Development in Latin America*

(Boulder, Colo., 1989), 169–89. George R. Neumann, "Cyclical Strike Activity and Mature Collective Bargaining: Evidence from Canadian Data: 1960–1976," in Jean-Jacques Rosa, *The Economics of Trade Unions: New Directions* (Higham, Mass., 1984), 43–56. John Burton, "The Economic Analysis of the Trade Union as a Political Institution," in ibid., 123–54. Jean-Jacques Rosa, "Toward a Theory of the Union Firm," in ibid., 157–86. Peter B. Doeringer, "Unions: Economic Performance and Labor Market Structure," in ibid., 315–38.

4. J. Samuel Valenzuela, "Labor Movements in Transitions to Democracy: A Framework for Analysis," *Comparative Politics* 21:4 (July 1989), 445–72. J. Samuel Valenzuela and Jeffrey Goodwin, "Labor Movements under Authoritarian Regimes," *Monographs on Europe* 5 (1983), 1–50. Bjorn Feuer, "Mining Unionism, Political Democracy, and Revealed Preferences—The Quid Pro Quo of Labour Relations in Bolivia, Chile, and Peru, 1950–80," *Economic and Industrial Democracy* 12:1 (Feb. 1991), 97–118.

5. The sources used for this book sometimes disagree on certain economic data—for example, on the precise sectoral distribution of the workforce or the number of union members. However, that is not a crippling problem for the broad generalizations in this study so long as all indicators are moving in the same direction at more or less the same pace and magnitude. Joseph Ramos, *Neoconservative Economics in the Southern Cone of Latin America, 1973–1983* (Baltimore, 1986), 1, 46–47. Paul W. Drake, "Requiem for Populism?" in Michael Conniff, *Latin American Populism in Comparative Perspective* (Albuquerque, 1982), 217–45.

6. Richard V. Miller, "The Relevance of Surplus Labour Theory to the Urban Labour Markets of Latin America," *International Institute for Labour Studies Bulletin* 8 (1971), 220–45. Alfredo Errandonea and Daniel Costabile, *Sindicato y sociedad en el Uruguay* (Montevideo, 1969), 94–99, 170–71. Figueiredo, *Empleo y salarios*.

7. Everett M. Kassalow, "Introduction," in Everett M. Kassalow and Ukandi G. Damachi, *The Role of Trade Unions in Developing Societies* (Geneva, 1978), 5–14. J. Douglas Muir and John L. Brown, "The Changing Role of Government in Collective Bargaining," in ibid., 123–40. Walter Galenson, *Labor in Developing Countries* (Berkeley, 1962). Gary Marks, *Unions in Politics: Britain, Germany, and the United States in the Nineteenth and Early Twentieth Centuries* (Princeton, 1989). Michael Poole, *Theories of Trade Unionism: A Sociology of Industrial Relations* (London, 1981). Adam Przeworski and Michael Wallerstein, "The Structure of Class Conflict in Democratic Capitalist Societies," *American Political Science Review* 76 (1982), 215–38. Michael Wallerstein, "The Micro-Foundations of Solidarity: Protectionist Policies, Welfare Policies and Union Centralization" (Los Angeles, Apr. 1986), 1–49.

8. Errandonea and Costabile, *Sindicato y sociedad*.

9. Gonzalo Falabella, "Epílogo," in Manuel Barrera and Gonzalo Falabella, *Sindicatos bajo regímenes militares: Argentina, Brasil, Chile* (Santiago, 1990), 283–318. Efrén Córdova, "The Latin American Picture," in Efrén Córdova, *Industrial Relations in Latin America* (New York, 1984), 3–26. Geraldo von Potobsky, "Trade Unions," in ibid., 27–52. Arturo S. Bronstein and Efrén Córdova, "Collective Bargaining," in ibid., 87–108. Howard J. Wiarda, *The Transition to Democracy in Spain and Portugal* (Washington, D.C., 1989), 270–71.

10. Ruth Berins Collier and David Collier, "Inducements versus Constraints:

Disaggregating 'Corporatism,' " *American Political Science Review* 73:4 (Dec. 1979), 967–86. Collier and Collier, *Shaping the Political Arena*. Laís Abramo, "Democracia, negociación, integración," *Sindicalismo y Democracia* 4 (Nov. 1991), 2–3.

11. James Payne, *Labor and Politics in Peru* (New Haven, Conn., 1965). For a similar analysis of the Argentine "rules of the game," see Guillermo O'Donnell, *Modernization and Bureaucratic Authoritarianism: Studies in South American Politics* (Berkeley, 1973).

12. Adam Przeworski and John Sprague, *Paper Stones: A History of Electoral Socialism* (Chicago, 1986). J. Samuel Valenzuela, "Movimientos obreros y sistemas políticos: Un análisis conceptual y tipológico," *Desarrollo Económico* 23:91 (Oct.–Dec. 1983), 339–68.

13. Julio Godio, *Sindicalismo y política en América Latina* (Caracas, 1983), 5–6, 199. Torcuato Di Tella, *Latin American Politics: A Theoretical Approach* (Austin, 1990), 102–16; idem, "Parties of the People in Latin America," working paper no. 108, Latin American Program, Wilson Center, 1982. Kaufman, "Corporatism."

14. On elite misperceptions of the revolutionary potential of the labor movement in earlier years, see Carlos Waisman, *Reversal of Development in Argentina: Postwar Counterrevolutionary Policies and Their Structural Consequences* (Princeton, 1987). On the apocalyptic and polarizing discourse in Chile under Allende, see Patricio Dooner, *Periodismo y política: La prensa de derecha y izquierda, 1970–1973* (Santiago, 1989).

15. Thomas C. Wright, *Latin America in the Era of the Cuban Revolution* (New York, 1991).

16. Rudiger Dornbusch and Sebastian Edwards, *The Macroeconomics of Populism in Latin America* (Chicago, 1991).

17. These governing experiences in these countries contrasted with many recent European cases. In some more developed Western societies, the taking of power by laborite parties has produced pacts to stabilize union activity, wages, prices, and macroeconomic policies. Scholars sometimes refer to these class compromises as neocorporatism. The difference between South America and Western Europe was partly due to lower levels of economic abundance and growth and partly due to less dense and centralized union organizations. Goldthorpe, *Order and Conflict*. Przeworski and Wallerstein, "Structure of Class Conflict." Valenzuela, "Movimientos." Ricardo Sidicaro, "Elementos para un análisis sociológico de las relaciones entre regímenes autoritarios y clase obrera en Argentina y Chile," in Bernardo Gallitelli and Andrés Thompson, *Sindicalismo y regímenes militares en Argentina y Chile* (Amsterdam, 1982), 37–60. Juan J. Linz and Alfred Stepan, *The Breakdown of Democratic Regimes,* 4 vols. (Baltimore, 1978). Youssef Cohen, *Radicals, Reformers, and Reactionaries: The Prisoner's Dilemma and the Collapse of Democracy in Latin America* (Chicago, 1994).

THREE : Labor Movements under Capitalist Authoritarianism

1. Although the estimates given here may be somewhat off the mark (for example, perhaps overstating the number of exiles in Uruguay and the number of assassinations in Chile), the exact body count will never be known. Regardless of impre-

cision, these figures accurately reflect the relative magnitude of the "war crimes" in the four countries. Peter John King, "Comparative Analysis of Human Rights Violations under Military Rule in Argentina, Brazil, Chile, and Uruguay," in James Wilkie and Enrique Ochoa, *Statistical Abstract of Latin America* 27 (1989), 1043–65.

2. Genaro Arriagada, "Ideology and Politics in the South American Military (Argentina, Brazil, Chile, and Uruguay)," working paper no. 55, Latin American Program, Wilson Center, 1979. Brian Loveman and Thomas M. Davies Jr., *The Politics of Antipolitics: The Military in Latin America*, 2d ed. (Lincoln, Neb., 1989). Alain Rouquié, *The Military and the State in Latin America* (Berkeley, 1987). Abraham F. Lowenthal and J. Samuel Fitch, *Armies and Politics in Latin America* (New York, 1986). José María Maravall, *Dictatorship and Political Dissent: Workers and Students in Franco's Spain* (London, 1978), 40–41. Gonzalo Falabella, "Epílogo," in Manuel Barrera and Gonzalo Falabella, *Sindicatos bajo regímenes militares: Argentina, Brazil, Chile* (Santiago, 1990), 283–318. Karen L. Remmer, "Political Demobilization in Chile, 1973–1978," *Comparative Politics* 12:3 (Apr. 1980), 277–82.

3. On authoritarianism from the 1960s to the 1980s, see the following: Guillermo O'Donnell, *Modernization and Bureaucratic Authoritarianism: Studies in South American Politics* (Berkeley, 1973); idem, "Reflections on the Patterns of Change in the Bureaucratic-Authoritarian State," *Latin American Research Review* 13:1 (1978), 3–38. Guillermo O'Donnell, Philippe C. Schmitter, and Laurence Whitehead, *Transitions from Authoritarian Rule*, 4 vols. (Baltimore, 1984). James M. Malloy, *Authoritarianism and Corporatism in Latin America* (Pittsburgh, 1977). David Collier, *The New Authoritarianism in Latin America* (Princeton, 1979). Karen L. Remmer, *Military Rule in Latin America* (Boston, 1989). Fredrick B. Pike and Thomas Stritch, *The New Corporatism: Social-Political Structures in the Iberian World* (Notre Dame, Ind., 1974). Howard Handelman and Thomas G. Sanders, *Military Government and the Movement toward Democracy in South America* (Bloomington, Ind., 1981). César N. Caviedes, *The Southern Cone: Realities of the Authoritarian State* (Totowa, N.J., 1984). Francisco Rojas Aravena, *Autoritarismo y alternativas populares en América Latina* (San José, Costa Rica, 1982). Alfred Stepan, *The State and Society: Peru in Comparative Perspective* (Princeton, 1978); idem, *Authoritarian Brazil* (New Haven, Conn., 1973). Richard Sholk, "Comparative Aspects of the Transition from Authoritarian Rule," working paper no. 114, Latin American Program, Wilson Center, 1982. Manuel Antonio Garretón, "Proyecto, trayectoria y fracaso de los regímenes militares del Cono Sur: Un balance," *Alternativas* 2 (Jan.–Apr. 1984), 5–23.

4. Table 3.2 weighs rough and relative magnitudes. For example, although Uruguay underwent mild deindustrialization by comparison with Chile and Argentina, it still differed on that dimension from industrializing Portugal, Spain, Brazil, and Greece. Table 3.2 also emphasizes dominant trends in what were really mixed situations. For example, although many labor opponents of the corporatist regimes infiltrated the official unions, many others abstained, whereas the Southern Cone experienced much greater distance between the state and labor. By the same token, distinguishing between the general pattern of evolution of the labor movement in the first four corporatist cases and the pattern of evolution in the three Southern Cone atomization cases obscures some similarities and some ambivalent

cases, especially that of Spain. Nevertheless, the categories and facets highlighted in table 3.2 illuminate important comparisons among our countries. The type of coup ("containment" or "rollback") and the level of repression obviously reflected the strength of the pre-coup labor movements. "Industrialization" or "deindustrialization" were not necessarily intentional. "Unemployment" and "density" refer to the situation at the end of the dictatorship. Among institutional variables, J. Samuel Valenzuela labels the two strategies "corporatist" and "market." Although that nomenclature is satisfactory, "atomization" seems preferable for the latter approach, because it refers more explicitly to institutional design and because capitalist market conditions affected workers under both systems. J. Samuel Valenzuela, "Labor Movements in Transitions to Democracy: A Framework for Analysis," *Comparative Politics* 21:4 (July 1989), 445–72. J. Samuel Valenzuela and Jeffrey Goodwin, "Labor Movements under Authoritarian Regimes," *Monographs on Europe* 5 (1983), 1–50.

5. Alejandro Foxley, *Latin American Experiments in Neo-Conservative Economics* (Berkeley, 1983). Joseph Ramos, *Neoconservative Economics in the Southern Cone of Latin America, 1973–1983* (Baltimore, 1986). John Sheahan, "Market-Oriented Economic Policies and Political Repression in Latin America," *Economic Development and Cultural Change* 28:2 (Jan. 1980), 267–91; idem, *Patterns of Development in Latin America: Poverty, Repression, and Economic Strategy* (Princeton, 1987). Arthur J. Mann and Carlos E. Sánchez, "Labor Market Responses to Southern Cone Stabilization Policies: The Cases of Argentina, Chile, Uruguay," *Inter-American Economic Affairs* 38:4 (spring 1985), 19–40.

6. Steven E. Sanderson, *The Americas in the New International Division of Labor* (New York, 1985). William L. Canak, "Debt, Austerity, and Latin America in the New International Division of Labor," in William L. Canak, *Lost Promises: Debt, Austerity, and Development in Latin America* (Boulder, Colo., 1989), 9–30. Albert Berry, "Labor: Feeling the Pinch," *Hemisfile* 4:2 (Mar.–Apr. 1993), 4–5. Roger Southall, "Introduction," in Roger Southall, *Trade Unions and the New Industrialization of the Third World* (London, 1988), 1–34.

7. Hector E. Schamis, "Reconceptualizing Latin American Authoritarianism in the 1970s: From Bureaucratic-Authoritarianism to Neoconservatism," *Comparative Politics* 23:1 (Oct. 1990), 201–20. Foxley, *Latin American Experiments*.

8. Joan M. Nelson, *Intricate Links: Democratization and Market Reforms in Latin America and Eastern Europe* (New Brunswick, N.J., 1994).

9. Ramos, *Neoconservative Economics,* 52–53. Rosemary Thorp and Laurence Whitehead, *Inflation and Stabilization in Latin America* (New York, 1979). Edward C. Epstein, "Anti-inflation Policies in Argentina and Chile: Or Who Pays the Costs?" *Comparative Political Studies* 11:2 (July 1978), 211–30. David E. Hojman, *Chile: The Political Economy of Development and Democracy in the 1990s* (Pittsburgh, 1993).

10. J. Figueiredo et al., *Empleo y salarios en América Latina* (Petrópolis, Brazil, 1985). Subbiah Kannappan, *Employment Practices and the Urban Labor Market in Developing Countries* (Ann Arbor, Mich., 1983).

11. Osvaldo Mantero de San Vicente, "Flexibilización del trabajo," in Fernando Calero, *Nuevos retos del sindicalismo* (Caracas, 1988), 13–42. Consuelo Iranzo, "Cambio tecnológico y trabajo," in ibid., 43–96. Francisco Pucci, "¿Intermediación de in-

tereses o conflicto privado?" (Montevideo, July 1992), 1–28. Jean-Jacques Rosa, "Toward a Theory of the Union Firm," in Jean-Jacques Rosa, *The Economics of Trade Unions: New Directions* (Higham, Mass., 1984), 157–86.

12. Foxley, *Latin American Experiments,* 124.

13. Alfredo Errandonea, *Política económica y estructura ocupacional en el cono sur* (Buenos Aires, 1984). Robert R. Kaufman, "Industrial Change and Authoritarian Rule in Latin America: A Concrete Review of the Bureaucratic-Authoritarian Model," in Collier, *New Authoritarianism,* 165–254. Alan Angell, "Unions and Workers in the 1980s," in Paul W. Drake and Iván Jaksic, *The Struggle for Democracy in Chile, 1982–90* (Lincoln, Neb., 1991), 188–210.

14. Jeffry A. Frieden, *Debt, Development, and Democracy: Modern Political Economy and Latin America, 1965–1985* (Princeton, 1981). Paul Berks, "The Decline of Militant Unionism in Argentina: The Case of the Auto Workers' Union" (masters thesis, University of California, San Diego, 1993). Eva Paus, "Capital-Labor Relations and Income Distribution in Latin America in the Eighties" (Mar. 1994).

15. Ralph Hakkert and Franklin W. Goza, "The Demographic Consequences of Austerity in Latin America," in Canak, *Lost Promises,* 69–97. Also see Organización Internacional del Trabajo, Programa Regional del Empleo para América Latina y el Caribe (hereafter OIT, PREALC), *La evolución del mercado laboral entre 1980 y 1987* (Santiago, 1988). Nicos Poulantzas, *Fascism and Dictatorship: The Third International and the Problem of Fascism* (London, 1974), 191–94.

16. Ian Roxborough, "Organized Labor: A Major Victim of the Debt Crisis," in Barbara Stallings and Robert Kaufman, *Debt and Democracy in Latin America* (Boulder, Colo., 1989), 91–108. Howard Handelman and Werner Baer, *Paying the Costs of Austerity in Latin America* (Boulder, Colo., 1989). Jonathan Hartlyn and Samuel A. Morley, "Bureaucratic-Authoritarian Regimes in Comparative Perspective," in Jonathan Hartlyn and Samuel A. Morley, *Latin American Political Economy: Financial Crisis and Political Change* (Boulder, Colo., 1986), 38–53. World Bank, *Poverty in Latin America: The Impact of Depression* (Washington, D.C., 1986). Emilio Morgado Valenzuela, "Crisis económica y relaciones de trabajo," in CLACSO, *El sindicalismo latinoamericano en los ochenta* (Santiago, 1986), 59–72.

17. John Walton, "Debt, Protest, and the State in Latin America," in Susan Eckstein, *Power and Popular Protest: Latin American Social Movements* (Berkeley, 1989), 299–328.

18. Peter Winn and María Angélica Ibáñez, "Textile Entrepreneurs and Workers in Pinochet's Chile, 1973–1989," Papers on Latin America, no. 15, Institute of Latin American and Iberian Studies, Columbia University, 1990. Berks, "Decline of Militant Unionism."

19. For a discussion of the difficulties of consolidating democracy along with neoliberal reforms, see Adam Przeworski, *Democracy and the Market: Political and Economic Reforms in Eastern Europe and Latin America* (Cambridge, 1991). Also valuable is Luis Carlos Bresser Pereira, José María Maravall, and Adam Przeworski, *Economic Reforms in New Democracies: A Social-Democratic Approach* (Cambridge, 1993). Tom Gallagher and Alan M. Williams, "Introduction," in Tom Gallagher and Alan M. Williams, *Southern European Socialism: Parties, Elections, and the Challenge of Government* (Manchester, England, 1989), 1–9. Gonzalo Falabella, "Labor's Odd Man

Out," *Hemisfile* 2:2 (Mar. 1991), 1–2, 12. Ben A. Pettrazini, "The Impact of Privatization on Labor and Consumers" (La Jolla, Calif., 1993), 1–34. Domingo Hachette and Rolf Luders, *Privatization in Chile: An Economic Appraisal* (San Francisco, 1992). William Glade, *Privatization of Public Enterprises in Latin America* (La Jolla, Calif., 1991). Berry, "Labor."

20. Valenzuela, "Labor Movements," 448.

21. Ibid. Valenzuela and Goodwin, "Labor Movements," 7, 49. Ricardo Sidicaro, "Elementos para un análisis sociológico de las relaciones entre regímenes autoritarios y clase obrera en Argentina y Chile," in Bernardo Gallitelli and Andrés Thompson, *Sindicalismo y regímenes militares en Argentina y Chile* (Amsterdam, 1982), 50–52.

22. Valenzuela, "Movimientos," 361–67.

23. Emilio García Méndez, *Autoritarismo y control social: Argentina—Uruguay— Chile* (Buenos Aires, 1987).

24. Valenzuela and Goodwin, "Labor Movements," 18. Thomas Carothers, *In the Name of Democracy: U.S. Policy toward Latin America in the Reagan Years* (Berkeley, Calif., 1991). Abraham F. Lowenthal, *Exporting Democracy: The United States and Latin America* (Baltimore, 1991).

25. Paul G. Buchanan, "The Impact of U.S. Labor," in Lowenthal, *Exporting Democracy,* 296–328. Julio Godio, *Sindicalismo y política en América Latina* (Caracas, 1983), 4–6, 211–70. Latin American Bureau, *Unity Is Strength: Trade Unions in Latin America. A Case for Solidarity* (London, 1980), 49–51. Thomas C. Wright, *Latin America in the Era of the Cuban Revolution* (New York, 1991).

26. Scott Mainwaring and Alexander Wilde, *The Progressive Church in Latin America* (Notre Dame, Ind., 1989).

27. Paul W. Drake, "Urban Labour Movements under Authoritarian Capitalism in the Southern Cone and Brazil, 1964–1983," in Josef Gugler, *The Urbanization of the Third World* (New York, 1988), 367–98. Víctor Pérez Díaz, *The Return of Civil Society* (Cambridge, 1992). Joe Foweraker, *Making Democracy in Spain: Grass-Roots Struggle in the South, 1955–1975* (New York, 1989). Valenzuela, "Labor Movements," 445–50. Guillermo O'Donnell and Philippe C. Schmitter, *Transitions from Authoritarian Rule: Tentative Conclusions about Uncertain Democracies* (Baltimore, 1986), 26–27, 48–53. (Hereafter this work is cited as *Transitions: Conclusions.*) Gonzalo Falabella, "El rol de los sindicatos en la transición a la democracia en Chile" (Santiago, 1989).

28. Paul G. Buchanan, "Reconstituting the Institutional Bases of Consent: Notes on State-Labor Relations and Democratic Consolidation in the Southern Cone," working paper no. 160, Kellogg Institute, Notre Dame, May 1991, 1–43. Efrén Córdova, "Social Concertation in Latin America," *Labour and Society* 12:3 (Sept. 1987), 409–23. Poulantzas, *Fascism* 196–97.

29. Víctor Pérez Díaz, *Clase obrera, partidos, y sindicatos* (Madrid, 1979), 28–32.

30. O'Donnell and Schmitter, *Transitions: Conclusions,* 57–59. Valenzuela and Goodwin, "Labor Movements," 22–23.

31. Douglas Chalmers and Craig Robinson, "Why Power Contenders Choose Liberalization: Perspectives from South America," *International Studies Quarterly* 26:1 (Mar. 1982), 3–36. Jorge A. Tapia-Valdés, "'Nacional seguritismo' e inseguridad

laboral," in Bernardo Gallitelli and Andrés Thompson, *Sindicalismo y regímenes militares en Argentina y Chile* (Amsterdam, 1982), 61–90.

32. Arturo Valenzuela and J. Samuel Valenzuela, "Party Oppositions under the Chilean Authoritarian Regime," in J. Samuel Valenzuela and Arturo Valenzuela, *Military Rule in Chile: Dictatorship and Oppositions* (Baltimore, 1986), 184–229.

33. Alan Angell and Susan Carstairs, "The Exile Question in Chilean Politics," *Third World Quarterly* 9:1 (Jan. 1987), 148–67. José del Pozo, *Rebeldes, reformistas, y revolucionarios: Una historia oral de la izquierda chilena en la época de la Unidad Popular* (Santiago, 1992).

34. Liliana de Riz, "El fin de la sociedad populista y la estrategia de las fuerzas populares en el cono sur," *Nueva Sociedad* 47 (Apr. 1980), 72–79. Manuel Antonio Garretón, "Transformación social y refundación política en el capitalismo autoritario," in Rojas, *Autoritarismo*, 141–58. Tomás Moulian, "Dictaduras hegemonizantes y alternativas populares," in ibid., 159–80. Marcelo Cavarozzi, *Autoritarismo y democracia, 1955–1983* (Buenos Aires, 1983). Donald C. Hodges, *Argentina, 1943–1976: The National Revolution and Resistance* (Albuquerque, 1976), 140–66.

35. Valenzuela and Valenzuela, "Party Oppositions."

FOUR : Corporatist Precursors to the Southern Cone Regimes

1. Alan M. Williams, "Introduction," in Alan M. Williams, *Southern Europe Transformed: Political and Economic Change in Greece, Italy, Portugal, and Spain* (London, 1984), 1–32.

2. Nicos P. Mouzelas, *Politics in the Semi-Periphery: Early Parliamentarism and Late Industrialization in the Balkans and Latin America* (New York, 1986), xiv–xv, 170–83. Nicos Poulantzas, *The Crisis of the Dictatorships: Portugal, Greece, Spain* (London, 1976), 10–19. Philippe C. Schmitter, "An Introduction to Southern European Transitions from Authoritarian Rule: Italy, Greece, Portugal, Spain, and Turkey," in Guillermo O'Donnell, Philippe Schmitter, and Laurence Whitehead, *Transitions from Authoritarian Rule: Southern Europe* (Baltimore, 1986), 3–10; hereafter this title is cited as *Transitions: Europe*. Salvador Giner, "Political Economy, Legitimation, and the State in Southern Europe," in ibid., 11–44; idem, "Economía política y legitimación cultural en los orígines de la democracia parlamentaria: El caso de la Europa del Sur," in Julián Santamaría, *Transición a la democracia en el Sur de Europa y América Latina* (Madrid, 1987), 11–59. Ronald H. Chilcote, "The Theory and Practice of Transitions: Struggle for a New Politics in Southern Europe," in Ronald H. Chilcote et al., *Transitions from Dictatorship to Democracy: Comparative Studies of Spain, Portugal, and Greece* (New York, 1990), 189–206. Ray Hudson and Jim Lewis, "Introduction: Recent Economic, Social, and Political Changes in Southern Europe," in Ray Hudson and Jim Lewis, *Uneven Development in Southern Europe: Studies of Accumulation, Class Migration, and the State* (London, 1985), 1–53.

3. José María Maravall, "Economic Reforms in New Democracies: The Southern European Experience," Estudios / Working Papers, no. 22, Instituto Juan March, June 1991, 1–64.

4. Salvador Giner, "Political Economy, Legitimation, and the State in Southern Europe," in Hudson and Lewis, *Uneven Development*, 309–50. Tom Gallagher and

Alan M. Williams, "Introduction," in Tom Gallagher and Alan M. Williams, *Southern European Socialism: Parties, Elections, and the Challenge of Government* (Manchester, England, 1989), 1–9.

5. Pinochet was the only head of state to attend Franco's funeral. Paul W. Drake, "Chile," in Mark Falcoff and Fredrick B. Pike, *The Spanish Civil War, 1936–39: American Hemispheric Perspectives* (Lincoln, Neb., 1982), 245–90.

6. Adam Przeworski and John Sprague, *Paper Stones: A History of Electoral Socialism* (Chicago, 1986).

7. For general coverage, see Tom Gallagher, *Portugal: A Twentieth-Century Interpretation* (Manchester, England, 1983). R.A.H. Robinson, *Contemporary Portugal: A History* (London, 1979). Sarah Bradford, *Portugal* (New York, 1973). Douglas L. Wheeler, *Republican Portugal: A Political History, 1910–1926* (Madison, Wisc., 1978). Antonio H. de Oliveira Marques, "The Portuguese 1920s: A General Survey," *Iberian Studies* 2:1 (spring 1973), 32–40. Antonio de Figueiredo, *Portugal: Fifty Years of Dictatorship* (New York, 1976). Hugh Kay, *Salazar and Modern Portugal* (London, 1970). Philippe C. Schmitter, *Corporatism and Public Policy in Authoritarian Portugal* (London, 1975). Alexandre Vieira, *Para a história do sindicalismo em Portugal,* 2d ed. (Lisbon, 1974). Costa Júnior, *História breve do movimiento operário portugués* (Lisbon, 1964), 59–113.

8. Philippe C. Schmitter, "The 'Régime d'Exception' That Became the Rule: Forty-eight Years of Authoritarian Domination in Portugal," in Lawrence S. Graham and Harry M. Makler, *Contemporary Portugal: The Revolution and Its Antecedents* (Austin, Tex., 1979), 3–46. Michael Harsgor, *Portugal in Revolution* (Beverly Hills, Calif., 1976). Diamantino P. Machado, *The Structure of Portuguese Society: The Failure of Fascism* (New York, 1991).

9. D. L. Raby, *Fascism and Resistance in Portugal: Communists, Liberals, and Military Dissidents in the Opposition to Salazar, 1941–1974* (Manchester, England, 1988).

10. Howard Wiarda, *Corporatism and Development: The Portuguese Experiment* (Amherst, Mass., 1977), 237–50. Jorge Campinos, "La transición del autoritarismo a la democracia en la Europa del Sur: El ejemplo portugués," in Santamaría, *Transición a la democracia,* 151–98. Philippe C. Schmitter, "Liberation by Golpe: Retrospective Thoughts on the Demise of Authoritarian Rule in Portugal," *Armed Forces and Society* 2:1 (n.d.), 5–33. Peter Fryer and Patricia McGowan Pinheiro, *Oldest Ally: A Portrait of Salazar's Portugal* (Westport, Conn., 1961). Michael Derrick, *The Portugal of Salazar* (Freeport, 1938). John R. Logan, "Worker Mobilization and Party Politics: Revolutionary Portugal in Perspective," in Lawrence S. Graham and Douglas L. Wheeler, *In Search of Modern Portugal: The Revolution and Its Consequences* (Madison, Wisc., 1983), 135–50. Eric N. Baklanoff, *The Economic Transformation of Spain and Portugal* (New York, 1978). Ramiro da Costa, *Elementos para a história do movimento operário en Portugal, 1820–1975,* 2 vols. (Lisbon, 1979). Daniel Nataf and Elizabeth Sammis, "Classes, Hegemony, and Portuguese Democratization," in Chilcote et al., *Transitions from Dictatorship,* 73–130. Kenneth Maxwell, "The Emergence of Portuguese Democracy," in John H. Herz, *From Dictatorship to Democracy: Coping with the Legacies of Authoritarianism and Totalitarianism* (Westport, Conn., 1982), 231–50. M. Porto, "Portugal: Twenty Years of Change," in Williams, *Southern Europe Transformed,* 84–112.

11. Stanley G. Payne, "La oposición a las dictaduras en Europa Occidental: Una perspectiva comparativa," in Javier Tusell, Alicia Alted, and Abdón Mateos, *La oposición al régimen de Franco,* 2 vols. (Madrid, 1990), 1:51–64. Logan, *Worker Mobilization,* 136–48.

12. Kenneth Maxwell, "The Thorns of the Portuguese Revolution," *Foreign Affairs* 54:2 (Jan. 1976), 250–70; idem, "Regime Overthrow and the Prospects for Democratic Transition in Portugal," in O'Donnell, Schmitter, and Whitehead, *Transitions: Europe,* 109–37. Bill Lomax, "Ideology and Illusion in the Portuguese Revolution: The Role of the Left," in Graham and Wheeler, *Modern Portugal,* 105–35. Charles Downs, "Residents' Commissions and Urban Struggles in Revolutionary Portugal," in ibid., 151–80. Nancy Bermeo, "Worker Management in Industry: Reconciling Representative Government and Industrial Democracy in a Polarized Society," in ibid., 181–98. Lawrence S. Graham, *Portugal: The Decline and Collapse of an Authoritarian Order* (Beverly Hills, Calif., 1975). John L. Hammond, *Building Popular Power: Workers' and Neighborhood Movements in the Portuguese Revolution* (New York, 1988). Phil Mailer, *Portugal: The Impossible Revolution?* (London, 1977). Robert Harvey, *Portugal: Birth of a Democracy* (London, 1978). Rona Fields, *The Portuguese Revolution and the Armed Forces Movement* (New York, 1976). Howard J. Wiarda, *The Transition to Democracy in Spain and Portugal* (Washington, D.C., 1989). Lester Sobel, *The Portuguese Revolution, 1974–76* (New York, 1976). Juan Yrarrazával C., "La transición a la democracia en Portugal: ¿Experiencia para Chile?" in Francisco Orrego Vicuña, *Transición a la democracia en América Latina* (Buenos Aires, 1985), 185–206. Beate Kohler, *Political Forces in Spain, Greece, and Portugal* (London, 1982), 181–217.

13. Alex MacLeod, "The Parties and the Consolidation of Democracy in Portugal: The Emergence of a Dominant Two-Party System," in Diane Ethier, *Democratic Transition and Consolidation in Southern Europe, Latin America, and Southeast Asia* (London, 1990), 155–72. Lawrence S. Graham, "Redefining the Portuguese Transition to Democracy," in John Higley and Richard Gunther, *Elites and Democratic Consolidation in Latin America and Southern Europe* (Cambridge, 1992), 282–99. Thomas C. Bruneau and Alex MacLeod, *Politics in Contemporary Portugal: Parties and the Consolidation of Democracy* (Boulder, Colo., 1986).

14. Tom Gallagher, "The Portuguese Socialist Party: The Pitfalls of Being First," in Gallagher and Williams, *Southern European Socialism,* 12–33. Allan M. Williams, "Socialist Economic Policies: Never Off the Drawing Board?" in ibid., 188–216. John L. Hammond, "Electoral Behavior and Political Militancy," in Graham and Makler, *Contemporary Portugal,* 257–80. Kenneth Maxwell, *Portugal in the 1980s: Dilemmas of Democratic Consolidation* (New York, 1986). Walter C. Opello Jr., *Portugal's Political Development: A Comparative Approach* (Boulder, Colo., 1985).

15. On the Franco years in general, see Stanley G. Payne, *El régimen de Franco, 1936–1975* (Madrid, 1987); idem, *Franco: El perfil de la historia* (Madrid, 1993). George Hills, *Franco: The Man and His Nation* (London, 1967). Manuel Jesús González González, *La economía política del franquismo (1940–1970): Dirigismo, mercado y planificación* (Madrid, 1979). Ramón Tamames, *La República: La era de Franco* (Madrid, 1988). José Antonio Biescas and Manuel Tuñón de Lara, *España bajo la dictadura franquista, 1939–1975* (Madrid, 1980). E. Ramón Arango, *The Spanish Political System:*

Franco's Legacy (Boulder, Colo., 1978). Juan Pablo Fusi, *Franco: Autoritarismo y poder personal* (Madrid, 1985). Sheelagh M. Ellwood, *Spanish Fascism in the Franco Era* (New York, 1987). Joe Foweraker, *Making Democracy in Spain: Grass-Roots Struggle in the South, 1955–1975* (Cambridge, 1989), 171–83.

16. On labor under Franco, see Robert M. Fishman, "Working Class Organization and Political Change: The Labor Movement and the Transition to Democracy in Spain" (Ph.D. diss., Yale University, 1985); also published as *Working-Class Organization and the Return to Democracy in Spain* (Ithaca, N.Y., 1990). Benjamin Martin, *The Agony of Modernization: Labor and Industrialization in Spain* (Ithaca, N.Y., 1990). Sebastian Balfour, *Labour in Greater Barcelona since 1939* (Oxford, 1989). J. A. Sagardoy Bengoechea and David León Blanco, *El poder sindical en España* (Barcelona, 1982). Julio Setién, *El movimiento obrero y el sindicalismo de clase en España, 1939–1982* (Madrid, 1982). José Luis Guinea, *Los movimientos obreros y sindicales en España de 1833 a 1978* (Madrid, 1978). Manuel Tuñón de Lara, *El movimiento obrero en la historia de España* (Madrid, 1972). Manuel Tuñón de Lara et al., *Teoría y práctica del movimiento obrero en España, 1900–1936* (Valencia, 1977). José María Maravall, *Dictatorship and Political Dissent: Workers and Students in Franco's Spain* (London, 1978).

17. The phrase "implicit social contract" comes from Víctor Pérez Díaz, *Clase obrera, orden social y conciencia de clase* (Madrid, 1980), 84–87. Also see idem, "Economic Policies and Social Pacts in Spain during the Transition: The Two Faces of Neo-Corporatism," *European Sociological Review* 2:1 (May 1986), 1–19. Francisco López-Casero, "The Social Consequences of Economic Development in Spain since 1960," *Iberian Studies* 19: 1 and 2 (1990), 57–83. Alison Wright, *The Spanish Economy, 1959–1976* (New York, 1977).

18. Fred Witney, *Labor Policy and Practices in Spain: A Study of Employer-Employee Relations under the Franco Regime* (New York, 1965). César Tcach Abad and Carmen Reyes, *Clandestinidad y exilio: Reorganización del sindicato socialista, 1939–1953* (Madrid, 1986). Abel Paz, *CNT, 1939–1951* (Barcelona, 1982). Valentina Fernández Vargas, *La resistencia interior en la España de Franco* (Madrid, 1981), 17–22. Miguel A. Aparicio, *El sindicalismo vertical y la formación del estado franquista* (Barcelona, 1980). Charles W. Anderson, *The Political Economy of Modern Spain: Policy-Making in an Authoritarian System* (Madison, 1970), 66–73. Sima Lieberman, *Labor Movements and Labor Thought: Spain, France, Germany, and the United States* (New York, 1986), 85–91. Pedro Ibarra Guell, *El movimiento obrero en Vizcaya, 1967–1977: Ideología, organización y conflictividad* (n.p., n.d.). Llibert Ferri, Jordi Muixi, and Eduardo Sanjúan, *Las huelgas contra Franco, 1939–1956* (Barcelona, 1978). Foweraker, *Making Democracy,* 79–87. Fishman, "Working Class Organization," 63–216.

19. Jon Amsden, *Collective Bargaining and Class Conflict in Spain* (London, 1972). Joseph W. Foweraker, "The Role of Labor Organizations in the Transition to Democracy in Spain," in Robert P. Clark and Michael H. Haltzel, *Spain in the 1980s: The Democratic Transition and a New International Role* (Cambridge, 1987), 97–122.

20. Maravall, *Dictatorship,* 21–28, 30–51, 63–89.

21. Nicolás Sartorius, *El sindicalismo de nuevo tipo: Ensayos sobre comisiones obreras* (Barcelona, 1977). Simón Sandoval, *España despues de Franco: Comisiones obreras o sindicatos verticales* (Buenos Aires, 1975). Julián Ariza, *Comisiones obreras* (Barcelona, 1976); idem, *La confederación sindical de comisiones obreras* (Barcelona, 1977). Patricio

Cueto Roman, *Derecho laboral y transición democrática: El caso español y el caso chileno* (Santiago, 1990), 39–42. Eusebio Mujal-León, *Communism and Political Change in Spain* (Bloomington, Ind., 1983), 58–75. Balfour, *Labour in Barcelona,* 69–109, 159–61, 210–23. Maravall, *Dictatorship,* 30–33, 86–89. Fishman, "Working Class Organization," 168–83. Foweraker, *Making Democracy,* x–xi, 88–229; idem, "Role of Labor," 97–122.

22. Eduardo Martín and Jesús Salvador, *Las elecciones sindicales: Cuestiones prácticas de lucha sindical* (Barcelona, 1975). Fishman, "Working Class Organization," i–10, 321–32, 362–65, 421–39. Sagardoy and Blanco, *Poder sindical,* 24–43.

23. Maravall, *Dictatorship,* 36–41, 170; idem, *La política de la transición* (Madrid, 1985), 26–31, 170–72.

24. Juan J. Linz, "Opposition to and under an Authoritarian Regime: The Case of Spain," in Robert A. Dahl, *Regimes and Oppositions* (New Haven, Conn., 1973), 171–260. Fernando Jáuregui and Pedro Vega, *Crónica del antifranquismo,* 3 vols. (Barcelona, 1983). Sergio Vilar, *La oposición a la dictadura: Protagonistas de la España democrática* (Barcelona, 1976); idem, *Historia del anti-franquismo, 1939–1975* (Barcelona, 1984). Javier Tusell Gómez, *La oposición democrática al franquismo, 1939–1962* (Barcelona, 1977); idem, *La España de Franco* (Madrid, 1989). Hartmut Heine, *La oposición política al franquismo de 1939 a 1952* (Barcelona, 1983). Víctor Pérez Díaz, *The Return of Civil Society* (Cambridge, 1992). José María Maravall and Julián Santamaría, "Political Change in Spain and the Prospects for Democracy," in O'Donnell, Schmitter, and Whitehead, *Transitions: Europe,* 71–108. Carlos Huneeus, "La transición a la democracia en España: Experiencias para América Latina," in Orrego, *Transición,* 165–84. Manuel Ramírez, *Sistema de partidos en España, 1931–1990* (Madrid, 1991), 41–63. Pierre C. Malerbe, *La oposición al franquismo, 1939/1975* (Madrid, 1977). Richard Gillespie, *The Spanish Socialist Party: A History of Factionalism* (Oxford, 1989). Javier Tusell, "Los partidos políticos de oposición al franquismo: Un estado de la cuestión," in Tusell, Alted, and Mateos, *Oposición,* vol. 1, 37–47. Santiago Carrillo, *Memoria de la transición* (Barcelona, 1983), 17–35. Joan Estruch Tobella, *El PCE en la clandestinidad, 1939–1956* (Madrid, 1982). Gregorio Morán, *Miseria y grandeza del Partido Comunista de España, 1939–1985* (Barcelona, 1986). Víctor Alba, *El Partido Comunista en España* (Barcelona, 1979). Mujal-León, *Communism.*

25. Paul Preston, *The Triumph of Democracy in Spain* (London, 1986). Richard Gunther, Giacomo Sani, and Goldie Shabad, *Spain after Franco: The Making of a Competitive Party System* (Berkeley, Calif., 1988). Maravall, *La política,* 170–72; idem, "The Socialist Alternative: The Policies and Electorate of the PSOE," in Howard R. Penniman and Eusebio M. Mujal-León, *Spain at the Polls, 1977, 1979, and 1982* (Durham, N.C., 1985), 129–59. Mario Caciagli, *Elecciones y partidos en la transición española* (Madrid, 1986). David Gilmour, *The Transformation of Spain: From Franco to the Constitutional Monarchy* (London, 1985). Raymond Carr and Juan Pablo Fusi, *Spain: Dictatorship to Democracy,* 2d ed. (London, 1981). Víctor Alba, *Transition in Spain: From Franco to Democracy* (New Brunswick, N.J., 1978). José Vidal Beneyto, *Del franquismo a una democracia de clase* (Madrid, 1977). José Félix Tezanos, Ramón Contarelo, and Andrés de Blas, *La transición democrática española,* 2 vols. (Madrid, 1989). John F. Coverdale, *The Political Transformation of Spain after Franco* (New

York, 1979). Carlos Huneeus, "La transición a la democracia en España: Dimensiones de una política consociacional," in Santamaría, *Transición a la democracia,* 243–86; idem, *Unión de Centro Democrático y la transición a la democracia en España* (Madrid, 1985). Edward Malefakis, "Spain and Its Francoist Heritage," in Herz, *From Dictatorship to Democracy,* 215–30. Wiarda, *Transition.*

26. Manuel Zaguirre and José M. de la Hoz, *Presente y futuro del sindicalismo* (Barcelona, 1976). Ciriaco de Vicente, *Trabajo y sindicatos, 1974–1977* (Madrid, 1977). Fishman, "Working Class Organization," 269–89, 345–54, 430–40. Pérez Díaz, *Clase obrera, orden social,* 16–19, 33–66, 88–90. Ibarra, *Movimiento obrero,* 29–33, 125–27, 539–42, 551–54.

27. Rafael Sastre Ibarreche, *Derecho sindical y transición política* (Madrid, 1987). Mario Gobbo, *The Political, Economic, and Labor Climate in Spain* (Philadelphia, 1981). Foweraker, "Role of Labor," 108–11.

28. Víctor Pérez Díaz, *Clase obrera, partidos, y sindicatos* (Madrid, 1979), 16–18, 74–77. Guinea, *movimientos obreros,* 176–77, 190–93.

29. Pérez Díaz, *Clase obrera, partidos,* 13–32; idem, *Clase obrera, orden,* 20–90. Fishman, "Working Class Organization," 30–440. Caciagli, *Elecciones y partidos,* 39–77. Penniman and Mujal-León, *Spain at the Polls.* Luis Enrique de la Villa, *Los grandes pactos colectivos a partir de la transición democrática* (Madrid, 1985). Angel Zaragoza, *Pactos sociales, sindicatos y patronal en España* (Madrid, 1988). Richard Gunther, "Spain: The Very Model of the Modern Elite Settlement," Higley and Gunther, *Elites and Democratic Consolidation,* 38–80. Rafael López-Pintor, "Mass and Elite Perspectives in the Process of Transition to Democracy," in Enrique A. Baloyra, *Comparing New Democracies: Transition and Consolidation in Mediterranean Europe and the Southern Cone* (Boulder, Colo., 1987), 79–108. Juan Antonio Sagardoy Bengoechea, *La realidad laboral española (algunas reflexiones)* (Madrid, 1976). José Luis Gómez Calcerrada, *La negociación colectiva en España durante 1978* (Madrid, 1979).

30. Eusebio M. Mujal-León, "The Spanish Communists and the Search for Electoral Space," in Penniman and Mujal-León, *Pactos colectivos,* 160–87. Miguel Satrústegui, "PSOE: A New Catch-all Party," in Wolfgang Merkel et al., *Socialist Parties in Europe II: Of Class, Populars, Catch-All* (Barcelona, 1992), 33–48. Eric Hershberg, "Transition from Authoritarianism and Eclipse of the Left: Toward a Reinterpretation of Political Change in Spain" (Ph.D. diss., University of Wisconsin—Madison, 1989); idem, "Liberal Democracy, Market-Oriented Development, and the Future of Popular Sector Representation: Lessons from Contemporary Chile and Spain" (Mar. 1994). Donald Share, *The Making of Spanish Democracy* (New York, 1985).

31. Balfour, *Labour in Barcelona,* 236–58. Fishman, "Working Class Organization," 53–280, 362–65, 430–53. Faustino Miguélez and Carlos Prieto, *Las relaciones laborales en España* (Madrid, 1991).

32. Mouzelas, *Politics,* 139–49. U.S. Department of Labor, Bureau of Labor Statistics, *Labor Law and Practice in the Kingdom of Greece* (Washington, D.C., 1968). Chris Jacchinis, "The Role of Trade Unions in the Social Development of Greece," in Everett M. Kassalow and Ukandi G. Damachi, *The Role of Trade Unions in Developing Societies* (Geneva, 1978), 51–66. George Yannopoulos, "Workers and Peasants

under the Military Dictatorship," in Richard Clogg and George Yannopoulos, *Greece under Military Rule* (London, 1972), 109–27. Rossetos Fakiolas, "Interest Groups—An Overview," in Kevin Featherstone and Dimitrios K. Katsoudas, *Political Change in Greece: Before and after the Colonels* (London, 1987), 174–88.

33. Kevin Featherstone, "PASOK and the Left," in Featherstone and Katsoudas, *Political Change,* 112–34; idem, "Introduction," in ibid., 8–12; idem, "Elections and Voting Behavior," in ibid., 34–63. Keith R. Legg, *Politics in Modern Greece* (Stanford, Calif., 1969), 116–214.

34. Stephen Rousseas, *The Death of a Democracy: Greece and the American Conscience* (New York, 1967). Stylianos Hadjiyannis, "Democratization and the Greek State," in Chilcote et al., *Transitions from Dictatorship,* 135–36. Nikolaos A. Stavrou, *Allied Politics and Military Interventions: The Political Role of the Greek Military* (Athens, 1976). "Athenian," *Inside the Colonels' Greece* (London, 1972). Nicos P. Mouzelis, *Modern Greece: Facets of Underdevelopment* (New York, 1978), 11–133.

35. P. C. Ioakimidis, "Greece: From Military Dictatorship to Socialism," in Williams, *Southern Europe Transformed,* 33–60. P. Nikiforos Diamandouros, "La transición de 1974 de un régimen autoritario a un régimen democrático en Grecia: Datos básicos e interpretación desde una perspectiva europea," in Santamaría, *Transición a la democracia,* 199–242; idem, "Regime Change and the Prospects for Democracy in Greece: 1974–1983," in O'Donnell, Schmitter, and Whitehead, *Transitions: Europe,* 138–64. Peter Schwab and George D. Frangos, *Greece under the Junta* (New York, 1973). Kohler, *Political Forces,* 98–122.

36. John Pesmazoglu, "The Greek Economy since 1967," in Clogg and Yannopoulos, *Greece under Military Rule,* 75–108. Richard Clogg and George Yannopoulos, "Editors' Introduction," in ibid., 7–22. George A. Jouganatos, *The Development of the Greek Economy, 1950–1991* (Westport, Conn., 1992), 4–92, 218–19. Dimitrios A. Germidis and María Negreponti-Delivanis, *Industrialization, Employment, and Income Distribution in Greece: A Case Study* (Paris, 1975). Yannopoulos, "Workers," 112–21.

37. George Yannopoulos, "The State of the Opposition Forces since the Military Coup," in Clogg and Yannopoulos, *Greece under Military Rule,* 163–90. Featherstone, "PASOK," 118–19.

38. Mouzelis, *Modern Greece,* 112–33.

39. Harry J. Psomiades, "Greece: From the Colonels' Rule to Democracy," in Herz, *From Dictatorship to Democracy,* 251–73. Michalis Papayannakis, "The Crisis in the Greek Left," in Howard R. Penniman, *Greece at the Polls: The National Elections of 1974 and 1977* (Washington, D.C., 1981), 130–59. Vassilis Kapetanyannis, "The Communists," in Featherstone and Katsoudas, *Political Change,* 145–73. Jouganatos, *Greek Economy,* 57–60, 92, 111, 123–26.

40. Michalis Spourdalakis, *The Rise of the Greek Socialist Party* (London, 1988); idem, "A Petty Bourgeois Party with a Populist Ideology and Catch-All Party Structure: PASOK," in Merkel et al., *Socialist Parties in Europe,* vol. 2, 97–122. Christos Lyrintzis, "PASOK in Power: The Loss of the 'Third Road to Socialism,'" in Gallagher and Williams, *Southern European Socialism,* 34–58. Angelos Elephantis, "PASOK and the Elections of 1977: The Rise of the Populist Movement," in Penniman, *Greece,* 105–29. Richard Clogg, *Parties and Elections in Greece: The Search for Le-*

gitimacy (Durham, N.C., 1987). Featherstone, "Elections," 34–60; idem, "PASOK," 122–33. Hadjiyannis, "Democratization," 131–61. Psomiades, "Greece," 258–67.

41. Guillermo O'Donnell, *Modernization and Bureaucratic Authoritarianism: Studies in South American Politics* (Berkeley, 1973).

42. For general coverage of the authoritarian period, see Thomas E. Skidmore, *The Politics of Military Rule in Brazil, 1964–85* (New York, 1988). Eduardo Viola and Scott Mainwaring, "Transitions to Democracy: Brazil and Argentina in the 1980s," *Journal of International Affairs,* no. 38 (winter 1985), 193–219.

43. Samuel A. Morley, *Labor Markets and Inequitable Growth: The Case of Authoritarian Capitalism in Brazil* (Cambridge, 1982), 6–8.

44. Kenneth Erickson, *The Brazilian Corporative State and Working-Class Politics* (Berkeley, Calif., 1977). Timothy Harding, "The Political History of Organized Labor in Brazil" (Ph.D. diss., Stanford University, 1973). John D. French, *The Brazilian Workers' ABC: Class Conflict and Alliances in Modern São Paulo* (Chapel Hill, N.C., 1992). Thomas Skidmore, *Politics in Brazil, 1930–1964: An Experiment in Democracy* (New York, 1967); idem, "Politics and Economic Policy-Making in Authoritarian Brazil, 1937–71," in Alfred Stepan, *Authoritarian Brazil* (New Haven, Conn., 1973), 3–46. Peter Flynn, *Brazil: A Political Analysis* (Boulder, Colo., 1978). Edgard Carone, *Movimento operário no Brasil,* 3 vols. (São Paulo, 1979–84). U.S. Department of Labor, Bureau of Labor Statistics, *Labor Law and Practice in Brazil* (Washington, D.C., 1967). Leonçio Martins Rodrigues, *Trabalhadores, sindicatos e industrialização* (São Paulo, 1974). Lucília de Almeida Neves, *O Comando Geral dos Trabalhadores no Brasil, 1961–1964* (Belo Horizonte, Brazil, 1981). José Alvaro Moisés, "La estrategia del nuevo sindicalismo," in Manuel Barrera and Gonzalo Falabella, *Sindicatos bajo regímenes militares: Argentina, Brasil, Chile* (Santiago, 1990), 97–132. James Payne, *Labor and Politics in Peru* (New Haven, Conn., 1965).

45. Martins, *Trabalhadores,* 88–124. José Alvaro Moisés, "Current Issues in the Labor Movement in Brazil," *Latin American Perspectives* 6:4 (fall 1979), 51–70. Henry A. Landsberger, "The Labor Elite: Is It Revolutionary?" in Seymour Martin Lipset and Aldo Solari, *Elites in Latin America* (New York, 1967), 256–300. María do Carmo C. Campello de Souza, *Estado e partidos políticos no Brasil, 1930–1964* (São Paulo, 1983). Ronald H. Chilcote, *The Brazilian Communist Party: Conflict and Integration, 1922–1972* (New York, 1974). Cilas Cerqueira, "Brazil," in Jean-Pierre Bernard, *Guide to the Political Parties of South America* (Middlesex, England, 1973), 150–235.

46. Skidmore, *Politics in Brazil,* 253–305. Erickson, *Brazilian Corporative State,* 78–117. Francisco Weffort, *O populismo na política brasileira* (Rio de Janeiro, 1978). Octavio Ianni, *Crisis in Brazil* (New York, 1970). Irving Louis Horowitz, *Revolution in Brazil* (New York, 1964). Salvador A. M. Sandoval, *Social Change and Labor Unrest in Brazil since 1945* (Boulder, Colo., 1993), 23–106. Alfred Stepan, "Political Leadership and Regime Breakdown: Brazil," in Juan J. Linz and Alfred Stepan, *The Breakdown of Democratic Regimes: Latin America* (Baltimore, 1978), 110–37. Ruth Berins Collier and David Collier, *Shaping the Political Arena: Critical Junctures, the Labor Movement, and Regime Dynamics in Latin America* (Princeton, N.J., 1991), 536–55. Leigh A. Payne, "Industrialists, Labor Relations, and the Transition to Democracy in Brazil," working paper no. 158, Kellogg Institute, Notre Dame, Apr.

1991, 1–18. Youssef Cohen, *Radicals, Reformers, and Reactionaries: The Prisoner's Dilemma and the Collapse of Democracy in Latin America* (Chicago, 1994), 76–97.

47. Raby, *Fascism and Resistance,* 263. Saturnino Braga, "La oposición y la apertura política en Brasil," in Augusto Varas, *Transición a la democracia* (Santiago, 1984), 85–100. Joan Dassin, *Torture in Brazil* (New York, 1986). Lawrence Weschler, *A Miracle, A Universe: Settling Accounts with Torturers* (New York, 1990), 5–79.

48. James L. Schlagheck, *The Political, Economic, and Labor Climate in Brazil* (Philadelphia, 1977), 29–46. Margaret Keck, "From Movement to Politics: The Formation of the Workers' Party in Brazil" (Ph.D. diss., Columbia University, 1986); published in a revised form as *The Workers' Party and Democratization in Brazil* (New Haven, Conn., 1992). Leigh A. Payne, "Working Class Strategies in the Transition to Democracy in Brazil," *Comparative Politics* 23:1 (Oct. 1990), 221–38. Thomas E. Skidmore, "The Political Economy of Policy Making in Authoritarian Brazil, 1967–1970," in Philip O'Brien and Paul Cammack, *Generals in Retreat: The Crisis of Military Rule in Latin America* (Manchester, England, 1985), 115–43.

49. Carlos A. Hasenbalg and Nelson do Valle Silva, "Industrialization, Employment, and Stratification in Brazil," in John D. Wirth, Edson de Oliveira Nunes, and Thomas E. Bogenschild, *State and Society in Brazil: Continuity and Change* (Boulder, Colo., 1987), 59–102.

50. Ibid., 71–79. Kenneth S. Mericle, "Conflict Regulation in the Brazilian Industrial Relations System" (Ph.D. diss., University of Wisconsin, 1974); idem, "Corporatist Control of the Working Class: Authoritarian Brazil since 1964," in James M. Malloy, *Authoritarianism and Corporatism in Latin America* (Pittsburgh, 1977), 303–38. María Hermínia Tavares de Almeida, "O sindicalismo brasileiro entre a conservação e a mudança," in Bernardo Sorj and María Hermínia Tavares de Almeida, *Sociedade e política no Brasil pós-64* (São Paulo, 1983), 191–214. Vilmar Faria, "Desenvolvimento, urbanização e mudanças na estrutura do emprego: A experiencia brasileira dos últimos trinta anos," in ibid., 118–63. John Humphrey, *Capitalist Control and Workers' Struggle in the Brazilian Auto Industry* (Princeton, 1982); idem, *Gender and Work in the Third World: Sexual Divisions in Brazilian Industry* (London, 1987). John Wells, "Brazil and the Post-1973 Crisis in the International Economy," in Rosemary Thorp and Laurence Whitehead, *Inflation and Stabilization in Latin America* (New York, 1979), 227–63; idem, "Industrial Accumulation and Living Standards in the Long Run: The São Paulo Industrial Working Class, 1930–1975," Working Paper Series, no. 37, Centre of Latin American Studies, University of Cambridge, 1983. Werner Baer, *The Brazilian Economy: Growth and Development,* 2d ed. (New York, 1983). Peter Evans, *Dependent Development: The Alliance of Multinational, State, and Local Capital in Brazil* (Princeton, 1979). Ronald M. Schneider, *The Political System of Brazil: Emergence of a "Modernizing" Authoritarian Regime, 1964–1970* (New York, 1971). Albert Fishlow, "Some Reflections on Post-1964 Brazilian Economic Policy," in Stepan, *Authoritarian Brazil,* 69–118. Samuel A. Morley and Gordon W. Smith, "The Effect of Changes in the Distribution of Income on Labor, Foreign Investment, and Growth in Brazil," in ibid., 119–41. José Marcio Camargo, "Brasil: Ajuste estructural y distribución de ingreso," Documentos de Trabajo, no. 308, OIT, PREALC, Oct. 1987.

51. Regis Bonelli and Pedro S. Malan, "Industrialization, Economic Growth,

and Balance of Payments: Brazil, 1970–84," in Wirth, Oliveira Nunes, and Bogenschild, *State and Society,* 13–47. Wayne A. Selcher, "Contradictions, Dilemmas, and Actors in Brazil's 'Abertura,' 1979–1985," in Wayne A. Selcher, *Political Liberalization in Brazil* (Boulder, Colo., 1986), 55–96. Werner Baer, Dan Biller, and Curtis T. McDonald, "Austerity under Different Political Regimes: The Case of Brazil," in Howard Handelman and Werner Baer, *Paying the Costs of Austerity in Latin America* (Boulder, Colo., 1989), 19–42. Payne, "Working Class Strategies," 223–27.

52. María Helena Moreira Alves, *State and Opposition in Military Brazil* (Austin, Tex., 1985), 46–47.

53. Moisés, "Current Issues." Erickson, *Brazilian Corporative State.* Schlagheck, *Political Climate,* 52–94. Sandoval, *Social Change,* 26, 107–22. Paul F. Shaw, *Manual of Labor Practices and Policies in Brazil, 1980–81* (New York, 1980). Luis F. Andrade, *The Labor Climate in Brazil* (Philadelphia, 1985). Youssef Cohen, *The Manipulation of Consent: The State and Working-Class Consciousness in Brazil* (Pittsburgh, 1989), 59–60.

54. U.S. Department of Labor, *Labor Law in Brazil,* 40. Schlagheck, *Political Climate,* 83–91. Keck, "From Movement to Politics," 134–40. Ralph Della Cava, "The 'People's Church,' the Vatican, and Abertura," in Alfred Stepan, *Democratizing Brazil: Problems of Transition and Consolidation* (New York, 1989), 143–67. Thomas C. Bruneau, *The Church in Brazil* (Austin, Tex., 1982). Scott Mainwaring, *The Catholic Church and Politics in Brazil, 1916–1985* (Stanford, Calif., 1986).

55. These figures may be exaggerated. María Hermínia Tavares de Almeida, "Novo Sindicalismo and Politics in Brazil," in Wirth, Oliveira Nunes, and Bogenschild, *State and Society,* 147–78.

56. Keck, "From Movement to Politics." Mericle, "Corporatist Control." Moreira Alves, *State and Opposition,* 182–210. Moisés, "La estrategia." José Pastore and Thomas E. Skidmore, "Brazilian Labor Relations: A New Era?" in Hervey Juris et al., *Industrial Relations in a Decade of Economic Change* (Madison, Wisc., 1985), 73–113. John Humphrey, "Auto Workers and the Working Class in Brazil," *Latin American Perspectives* 6:4 (fall 1979), 71–89. Laís Wendel Abramo, "La experiencia del enfrentamiento con la estructura sindical oficial en San Bernardo," in Barrera and Falabella, *Sindicatos,* 133–72. Youssef Cohen, "The Benevolent Leviathan: Political Consciousness among Urban Workers under State Corporatism," *American Political Science Review* 79 (1982), 46–59. Angela Mendes de Almeida and Michael Lowy, "Union Structure and Labor Organization in the Recent History of Brazil," *Latin American Perspectives* 3:1 (winter 1976), 98–119. Duarte Pereira, *Um perfil da classe operária* (São Paulo, 1981). Helios Prieto, "La emergencia de la oposición sindical en Brasil," *Debate* 3:8 (Mar.–Apr. 1979), 9–17. Amaury de Souza, "The Nature of Corporatist Representation: Leaders and Members of Organized Labor in Brazil" (Ph.D. diss., Massachusetts Institute of Technology, 1978). Celso Frederico, *Consciencia operária no Brasil* (São Paulo, 1978); idem, *A vanguardia operária* (São Paulo, 1980). Thomas C. Bruneau and Philippe Faucher, *Authoritarian Capitalism: Brazil's Contemporary Economic and Political Development* (Boulder, Colo., 1981). Thomas G. Sanders, "Decompression," in Howard Handelman and Thomas G. Sanders, *Military Government and the Movement toward Democracy in South America* (Bloomington, Ind., 1981), 145–62; idem, "Human Rights and Political Process," in ibid.,

181–206; idem, "Postscript," in ibid., 273–77. Maurice Dias David, "Control militar-corporativo en Brasil y en Chile: Funciones, consecuencias y perspectivas," Research Paper Series, no. 4, Institute of Latin American Studies, Stockholm, Mar. 1977. Transnationals Information Exchange, *Brazil: The New Militancy* (Amsterdam, 1984). Enrique A. Baloyra, "From Moment to Moment: The Political Transition in Brazil, 1977–1981," in Selcher, *Political Liberalization,* 9–54.

57. Moreira Alves, *State and Opposition,* 239–48. María Hermínia Tavares de Almeida, "Sindicalismo brasileiro e pacto social," in CLACSO, *El sindicalismo lati-noamericano en los ochenta* (Santiago, 1986), 103–20. Roque Aparecido da Silva, "Sindicatos e sociedade na palavra dos metalúrgicos," in ibid., 227–34.

58. Selcher, "Contradictions," 79–81. María Helena Moreira Alves, "Trade Unions in Brazil: A Search for Autonomy and Organization," in Edward C. Epstein, *Labor Autonomy and the State in Latin America* (Boston, 1989), 39–72. Dick Parker, "Trade Union Struggle and the Left in Latin America, 1973–1990," in Barry Carr and Steve Ellner, *The Latin American Left: From the Fall of Allende to Perestroika* (Boulder, Colo., 1993), 205–24. Stanley Gacek, "The CUT and the Brazilian Labor Situation," *Latin American Labor News* 5 (1992), 1, 5, 8–9.

59. A political survey conducted in 1972–73 discovered these attitudes. In Brazil as in the Southern Cone and Spain, the opinions of workers which were reflected in polls and interviews tended to be more moderate and cooperative than one would have expected from a study of workers' parties, leaders, proclamations, and objective deprivation. Of course, responses to pollsters under authoritarian regimes may be guarded or even deceptive. Cohen, *Manipulation of Consent;* idem, "Benevolent Leviathan." Souza, "Corporatist Representation." Keck, "From Movement to Politics," 140–41. Janice E. Perlman, *The Myth of Marginality* (Berkeley, 1976). Vera María Candido Pereira, *O coração da fábrica: Estudo de caso entre operários texteis* (Rio de Janeiro, 1979), 219–20.

60. María Andrea Loyola, *Os sindicatos e o PTB* (Petrópolis, Brazil, 1980), 14, 97–120. Candido, *Coração da fábrica,* 199–222.

61. Erickson, *Brazilian Corporative State.* Tavares, "Novo Sindicalismo," 160–74. Cohen, *Manipulation of Consent.* Selcher, "Contradictions," 70–75. Margaret E. Keck, "The New Unionism in the Brazilian Transition," in Stepan, *Democratizing Brazil,* 252–98. Bolivar Lamounier and Fernando Henrique Cardoso, *Os partidos e as eleições no Brasil* (Rio de Janeiro, 1975), esp. 15–44. Olavo Brasil Lima Junior, *Partidos políticos brasileiros* (Rio de Janeiro, 1983). Luciano Martins, "The 'Liberalization' of Authoritarian Rule in Brazil," in Guillermo O'Donnell, Philippe C. Schmitter, and Laurence Whitehead, *Transitions from Authoritarian Rule: Latin America* (Baltimore, 1986), 72–94. María Helena Moreira Alves, "Something Old, Something New: Brazil's Partido dos Trabalhadores," in Carr and Ellner, *Latin American Left,* 225–42. Fabio W. Reis, *Os partidos e o regime* (São Paulo, 1978). María D'Alva G. Kinzo, *Legal Opposition Politics under Authoritarian Rule in Brazil: The Case of the MDB, 1966–79* (London, 1988). Marcio Moreira Alves, "New Political Parties," *Latin American Perspectives* 6:4 (fall 1979), 108–20. "Interview with Luis Inácio da Silva ('Lula'), President of the Sindicato dos Metalurgicos de São Bernardo Campo," ibid., 6:4 (fall 1979), 90–100. Mario Morel, *Lula o metalúrgico* (Rio de Janeiro, 1981). Isabel Gómez de Souza, "Labor and Politics: An Analysis of the 'New Union-

ism' in Brazil" (Ph.D. diss., University of Wisconsin, 1985). Isabel Ribeiro de Oliveira Gómez de Souza, *Trabalho e política: As origens do Partido dos Trabalhadores* (Petrópolis, Brazil, 1988). Gerald Michael Greenfield, "Brazil," in Gerald Michael Greenfield and Sheldon L. Maram, *Latin American Labor Organizations* (New York, 1987), 63–128. Glaucio Ary Dillon Soares, "Elections and the Redemocratization of Brazil," in Paul W. Drake and Eduardo Silva, *Elections and Democratization in Latin America, 1980–85* (La Jolla, Calif., 1986), 273–98. David Fleischer, "Brazil at the Crossroads: The Elections of 1982 and 1985," in ibid., 299–328; idem, *Os partidos políticos no Brasil* (Brasília, 1981); idem, "Brazilian Elections in the 1980s: Transition or Transformation," in Julian Chacel, Pamela Falk, and David Fleischer, *Brazil's Economic and Political Future* (Boulder, Colo., 1988), 153–67. Douglas Chalmers and Craig Robinson, "Why Power Contenders Choose Liberalization: Perspectives from South America," *International Studies Quarterly* 26:1 (Mar. 1982), 3–36.

62. Tavares, "O sindicalismo," 212–13.

63. Keck, "From Movement to Politics," 43–45, 315–25. Martins, *Trabalhadores,* 124–50. Wanderley Guilherme dos Santos, *Poder e política* (Rio de Janeiro, 1978). Fernando Henrique Cardoso, "The Authoritarian Regime at the Crossroads: The Brazilian Case," working paper no. 93, Latin American Program, Wilson Center, 1981. María Helena Moreira Alves, "Interclass Alliances in the Opposition to the Military in Brazil: Consequences for the Transition Period," in Susan Eckstein, *Power and Popular Protest: Latin American Social Movements* (Berkeley, Calif., 1989), 278–98. Sebastião C. Velasco e Cruz, "De Castelo a Figueiredo: Una visión histórica de la 'apertura,'" in Isidro Cheresky and Jacques Chonchol, *Crisis y transformación de los regímenes autoritarios* (Buenos Aires, 1985), 33–50. Bolivar Lamounier, "Dilemas y perspectivas de la consolidación democrática en Brasil," in ibid., 51–62.

64. Alain Touraine, *Actores sociales y sistemas políticos en América Latina* (Santiago, 1987), 210–12. Salvador Antonio Mireles Sandoval, "General Strikes in Brazil, 1980–1989," *Latin American Labor News* (1990), 2, 3, 11–13; idem, *Social Change,* 153–96. Payne, "Working Class Strategies," 228–29.

65. Thomas Bruneau, "Brazil's Political Transition," in Higley and Gunther, *Elites and Democratic Consolidation,* 257–81.

66. Skidmore, *Politics of Military Rule,* 289–98. Laís W. Abramo, "Movimiento sindical, transição e consolidação democratica no Brasil" (Santiago, 1989, mimeographed), 117–22. Keck, "New Unionism." María do Carmo Campello de Souza, "The Brazilian 'New Republic' under the 'Sword of Damocles,'" in Stepan, *Democratizing Brazil,* 351–94. Peter Swavely, "Organized Labor in Brazil," in Lawrence S. Graham and Robert H. Wilson, *The Political Economy of Brazil: Public Policies in an Era of Transition* (Austin, Tex., 1990). William C. Smith, "The Political Transition in Brazil: From Authoritarian Liberalization and Elite Conciliation to Democratization," in Enrique A. Baloyra, *Comparing New Democracies: Transition and Consolidation in Mediterranean Europe and the Southern Cone* (Boulder, Colo., 1987), 179–240. Mark Steven Langevin, "Development by Division: The Brazilian Labor Movement under Democracy" (1994). Frances Hagopian and Scott Mainwaring, "Democracy in Brazil: Problems and Prospects," *World Policy Journal* 4 (1987), 485–514.

67. Jeffry A. Frieden, *Debt, Development, and Democracy: Modern Political Economy and Latin America, 1965–1985* (Princeton, 1991), 95–137. Jorge G. Castañeda,

Utopia Unarmed: The Latin American Left after the Cold War (New York, 1993), 143–55. Abramo, "Movimiento," 87, 122–28. Payne, "Industrialists."

FIVE : Uruguay, 1973–1984

1. Alfredo Errandonea and Daniel Costabile, *Sindicato y sociedad en el Uruguay* (Montevideo, 1969). Ruth Berins Collier and David Collier, *Shaping the Political Arena: Critical Junctures, the Labor Movement, and Regime Dynamics in Latin America* (Princeton, 1991), 640–66. For a survey of Uruguayan politics, see Martin Weinstein, *Uruguay: Democracy at the Crossroads* (Boulder, Colo., 1988).

2. Juan Rial, "El movimiento sindical uruguayo ante la redemocratización" (Montevideo, 1986), 2–5. Germán D'Elía and Armando Miraldi, *Historia del movimiento obrero en el Uruguay desde sus orígenes hasta 1930* (Montevideo, 1984). Wladimir Turiansky, *El movimiento obrero uruguayo* (Montevideo, 1973).

3. By contrast, only some 20 percent of Chile's manufacturing proletariat toiled in establishments with fewer than twenty-five workers. Errandonea and Costabile, *Sindicato y sociedad.* Jorge Notaro, *La política económica en el Uruguay, 1968–1984* (Montevideo, 1984), 138.

4. Walter Cancela and Alicia Melgar, *El desarrollo frustrado: 30 años de economía uruguaya, 1955–1985* (Montevideo, 1985), 17. Luis Macadar, *Uruguay 1974–1980: ¿Un nuevo ensayo de reajuste económico?* (Montevideo, 1982), 16–43. Rosa Alonso Eloy and Carlos Demasi, *Uruguay, 1958–1968: Crisis y estancamiento* (Montevideo, 1986). Charles Gillespie, "Desentrañando la crisis de la democracia uruguaya," in Charles Gillespie et al., *Uruguay y la democracia,* 3 vols. (Montevideo, 1984), vol. 1, 109–40.

5. On the fear of the Cuban Revolution that gripped elites in Latin America, see Thomas C. Wright, *Latin America in the Era of the Cuban Revolution* (New York, 1991). Errandonea and Costabile, *Sindicato y sociedad,* esp. 73–132, 170–79. Turiansky, *El movimiento obrero,* 178–83. Martín Gargiulo, "El desafío de la democracia: La izquierda política y sindical en el Uruguay post-autoritario" (1986). Juan Rial, *Partidos políticos, democracia y autoritarismo,* 2 vols. (Montevideo, 1984). Gustavo Cosse, "Notas acerca de la clase obrera, la democracia y el autoritarismo en el caso uruguayo," in Gillespie et al., *Uruguay y la democracia,* vol. 1, 87–107; idem, "Clase obrera, democracia y autoritarismo," in Carlos H. Filgueira et al., *Movimientos sociales en el Uruguay de hoy* (Montevideo, 1985), 77–120. Ronald H. McDonald, "Electoral Politics and Uruguayan Political Decay," *Inter-American Economic Affairs* 26:1 (summer 1972), 25–45; idem, "The Rise of Military Politics in Uruguay," ibid., 28:4 (spring 1975), 25–43. Germán d'Elía, *El movimiento sindical* (Montevideo, 1969). Howard Handelman, "Labor-Industrial Conflict and the Collapse of Uruguayan Democracy," *Journal of Inter-American Studies and World Affairs* 23:4 (Nov. 1981), 371–94. Luis Carlos Benvenuto et al., *Uruguay hoy* (Buenos Aires, 1971). U.S. Department of Labor, Bureau of Labor Statistics, *Labor Law and Practice in Uruguay* (Washington, D.C., 1971), 30–36.

6. Luis González, "Political Parties and Redemocratization in Uruguay," Centro de Informaciones y Estudios del Uruguay; Documento de Trabajo (CIESU/DT), no. 83, [1984?], 10. Juan Rial, "Los partidos políticos tradicionales: Restauración o renovación," in Gillespie et al., *Uruguay y la democracia,* vol. 1, 193–227.

7. Rial, "El movimiento," 50–51. Gargiulo, "El desafío." Turiansky, *El movimiento obrero*, 9.

8. César A. Aguiar, "La doble escena: Clivajes sociales y subsistema electoral," in Gillespie et al., *Uruguay y la democracia*, vol. 1, 14–45. Cosse, "Notas." McDonald, "Electoral Politics." Gargiulo, "El desafío." Howard Handelman, "Politics and Plebiscites: The Case of Uruguay," working paper no. 89, Latin American Program, Wilson Center, 1982.

9. Romeo Pérez, "La izquierda en la fase post-autoritaria," in Gillespie et al., *Uruguay y la democracia*, vol. 2, 130–47. Gerónimo de Sierra et al., *Partidos políticos y clases sociales en el Uruguay* (Montevideo, 1972). Miguel Aguirre Bayley, *El Frente Amplio: Historia y documentos* (Montevideo, 1985). González, "Political Parties," 10. Gargiulo, "El desafío."

10. Howard Handelman, "Prelude to Elections: The Military's Legitimacy Crisis and the 1980 Constitutional Plebiscite in Uruguay," in Paul W. Drake and Eduardo Silva, *Elections and Democratization in Latin America, 1980–1985* (La Jolla, Calif., 1986), 201–14; idem, "Labor-Industrial Conflict." Juan Rial, "Crisis y caída de la democracia en el Uruguay: Hacia el autoritarismo, 1968–1973," CIESU/DT, no. 72, 1984. Charles Guy Gillespie, *Negotiating Democracy: Politicians and Generals in Uruguay* (Cambridge, 1991), 37–40; idem, "Desentrañando."

11. Edy Kaufman, *Uruguay in Transition: From Civilian to Military Rule* (New Brunswick, N.J., 1979), 38–65. Martin Weinstein, *Uruguay: The Politics of Failure* (Westport, Conn., 1975). Handelman, "Labor-Industrial Conflict"; idem, "Politics." Cosse, "Notas."

12. Servicio Paz y Justicia Uruguay, *Uruguay nunca más: Informe sobre la violación a los derechos humanos (1972–1985)* (Montevideo, 1989), esp. 25–26. Gargiulo, "El desafío," 14.

13. Handelman, "Labor-Industrial Conflict." Henry Finch, "The Military Regime and Dominant Class Interests in Uruguay, 1973–1983," in Philip O'Brien and Paul Cammack, *Generals in Retreat: The Crisis of Military Rule in Latin America* (Manchester, 1985), 89–114. Guillermo O'Donnell, *Modernization and Bureaucratic Authoritarianism: Studies in South American Politics* (Berkeley, 1973). David Collier, *The New Authoritarianism in Latin America* (Princeton, 1979).

14. Lawrence Weschler, *A Miracle, A Universe: Settling Accounts with Torturers* (New York, 1990), 147.

15. The data in the foregoing discussion are drawn from the following: M.H.J. Finch, *A Political Economy of Uruguay since 1870* (New York, 1981); idem, "Stabilization Policy in Uruguay since the 1950s," in Rosemary Thorp and Laurence Whitehead, *Inflation and Stabilization in Latin America* (New York, 1979), 144–80. Howard Handelman, "Economic Policy and Elite Pressures in Uruguay," in Howard Handelman and Thomas G. Sanders, *Military Government and the Movement toward Democracy in South America* (Bloomington, Ind., 1981), 237–72; idem, "Labor-Industrial Conflict"; idem, "Politics." Alberto Bension and Jorge Caumont, *Política económica y distribución del ingreso en el Uruguay, 1970–1976* (Montevideo, 1976). James Hanson and Jaime de Melo, "The Uruguayan Experience with Liberalization and Stabilization, 1974–1981," *Journal of Interamerican Studies and World Affairs* 25:4 (Nov. 1983), 477–507. Walter Cancela, "Políticas de estabilización en

Uruguay: La inflación acompañada," *Cuadernos del CLAEH* 52 (1989/4), 39–54. Joseph Ramos, *Neoconservative Economics in the Southern Cone of Latin America, 1973–1983* (Baltimore, 1986), 24–33. Danilo Veiga, "Urban Decay and Restructuring: Montevideo in the 80s" (Montevideo, 1988), 9–11. Luis Stolovich, *La cuestión salarial en el Uruguay* (Montevideo, 1990), 23–45. Alfredo Errandonea, *Las clases sociales en el Uruguay* (Montevideo, 1989), 102–3, 112–18. Macadar, *Uruguay,* 186–242. Cancela and Melgar, *El desarrollo,* 17, 47–65.

16. Manufacturing had absorbed 22 percent of the economically active population in 1963. The data in the foregoing discussion are drawn from the following: U.S. Department of Labor, *Labor Law in Uruguay,* 18. Macadar, *Uruguay,* 57–59, 72–113, 186–208, 266–69. Notaro, *La política.* Alfredo Picerno and Pablo Mieres, *Uruguay, indicadores básicos* (Montevideo, 1983), 8–9. Uruguayan industrialists claimed that employment in manufacturing rose absolutely from 221,900 in 1973 to 265,000 in 1980, although their numbers disagreed with those of some other sources. Cámara de Industrias del Uruguay, Departamento de Estudios Económicos, *La política económica y la industria nacional, 1972–1980* (Montevideo, 1980), 57.

17. Jorge Notaro, "La escenografía económica del drama político. Uruguay hacia marzo de 1985," in Gillespie et al., *Uruguay y la democracia,* vol. 1, 141–64. Picerno and Mieres, *Uruguay,* 8, 44–45. Handelman, "Labor-Industrial Conflict"; idem, "Economic Policy."

18. Notaro, "La escenografía," 151–61. Cancela and Melgar, *El desarrollo,* 56.

19. José Pedro Alberti, "Las políticas de los actores en la negociación salarial," *Cuadernos del CLAEH* 52 (1989/4), 55–73. Naciones Unidas, Comisión Económica para América Latina (CEPAL), *La evolución de la economía y la política económica en Uruguay en el período 1981–1984* (n.p., 1985). Veiga, "Urban Decay." Cancela and Melgar, *El desarrollo,* 50–51. Errandonea, *Las clases,* 94–103.

20. Martín Gargiulo, "El movimiento sindical uruguayo: De la reactivación a la concertación," in Gillespie et al., *Uruguay y la democracia,* vol. 3, 61–80. Veiga, "Urban Decay," 40.

21. Gerónimo de Sierra, "Los sindicatos en la transición democrática uruguaya" (Montevideo, Aug. 1989). Alejandro Portes, Silvia Blitzer, and John Curtis, "The Urban Informal Sector in Uruguay: Its Internal Structure, Characteristics, and Effects," *World Development* 14:6 (1986), 727–41. Macadar, *Uruguay,* 174–79, 224–25. Augusto Longhi and Luis Stolovich, *La dinámica del mercado laboral uruguayo* (Montevideo, 1991).

22. Organization of American States, *Report on the Situation of Human Rights in Uruguay* (Washington, D.C., 1978). Amnesty International, *Political Imprisonment in Uruguay* (London, 1979). Weinstein, *Uruguay,* 67–68. Martín Gargiulo, "The Uruguayan Labor Movement in the Post-Authoritarian Period," in Edward C. Epstein, *Labor Autonomy and the State in Latin America* (Boston, 1989), 219–46; idem, "El desafío."

23. Latin America Bureau, *Uruguay: Generals Rule* (London, 1980), 45–48; idem, *Unity Is Strength: Trade Unions in Latin America. A Case for Solidarity* (London, 1980), 126–28. Enrique Rodríguez, *Uruguay: Un movimiento obrero maduro* (Montevideo, 1988), 12.

24. Jorge Luis Lanzaro, *Sindicatos y sistema político* (Montevideo, 1986), 87–88.

Cosse, "Notas." Rial, *Partidos políticos,* vol. 1. Kaufman, *Uruguay in Transition,* 40–41, 80. Latin America Bureau, *Uruguay.* Howard Handelman, "Military Authoritarianism and Political Change," in Handelman and Sanders, *Military Government,* 215–36; idem, "Labor-Industrial Conflict." Ruth Berins Collier and David Collier, "Inducements versus Constraints: Disaggregating Corporatism," *American Political Science Review* 73:4 (Dec. 1979), 967–86.

25. Lanzaro, *Sindicatos,* 107–8.

26. Servicio, *Uruguay nunca más,* 374–75, 381–82. De Sierra, "Los sindicatos." Latin America Bureau, *Uruguay,* 48, 56.

27. Luis E. González, "Uruguay, 1980–1981: An Unexpected Opening," *Latin American Research Review* 18:3 (1983), 63–76. Carlos H. Filgueira, "Movimientos sociales en la restauración del order democrático: Uruguay, 1985," in Filgueira et al., *Movimientos,* 9–50. Gargiulo, "El desafío."

28. In Spanish, the confederation's name was Plenario Intersindical de Trabajadores–Convención Nacional de Trabajadores. *El Día,* May 2, 1983; ibid., Apr. 24, 29, 1984.

29. Lanzaro, *Sindicatos,* 108–13. Gargiulo, "El movimiento"; idem, "El desafío." Gerónimo de Sierra, "Uruguay: Sindicatos en primera línea," *Sindicalismo y Democracia* (Aug. 1989), 33–35; idem, "Los sindicatos."

30. Aguirre Bayley, *El Frente,* 46–47. González, "Political Parties," 41–46. Rodríguez, *Uruguay,* 250–54.

31. Aguirre Bayley, *El Frente,* 48–55. Servicio, *Uruguay nunca más,* 375. Juan Rial, "La izquierda partidaria frente a la redemocratización: ¿Hacia una integración negativa?" CIESU/DT, no. 109, 1985.

32. Rodríguez, *Uruguay,* 7. Rial, *Partidos políticos,* vol. 2, 83–84.

33. Luis González, "The Legitimation Problems of Bureaucratic-Authoritarian Regimes: The Cases of Chile and Uruguay" (June 1983); idem, "Uruguay, 1980–1981." Cosse, "Notas." Kaufman, *Uruguay in Transition.* McDonald, "Rise of Military Politics." De Sierra, "Los sindicatos." Charles G. Gillespie, "Activists and Floating Voters: The Unheeded Lessons of Uruguay's 1982 Primaries," in Drake and Silva, *Elections,* 215–44.

34. Juan Rial, "Uruguay," in Gerald Michael Greenfield and Sheldon L. Maram, *Latin American Labor Organizations* (New York, 1987), 701–26; idem, "El movimiento," 8–11, 50–61. *La Hora,* Aug. 21, Oct. 13, 15, 16, 1984.

35. Rial, *Partidos políticos,* vol. 1, 124–30. *El Día,* Jan. 15, 1984; ibid., Jan. 16, 1984; ibid., May 2, 1984; ibid., Aug. 20, 1984; ibid., Feb. 26, 1985.

36. De Sierra, "Los sindicatos."

37. Centro de Informaciones y Estudios del Uruguay, *7 enfoques sobre la concertación* (Montevideo, 1984). Martín Gargiulo, "El movimiento sindical uruguayo en los '80: ¿Concertación o confrontación?" in CLACSO, *El sindicalismo latinoamericano en los ochenta* (Santiago, 1986), 167–80. Rodríguez, *Uruguay,* 284–85.

38. Juan Rial, "Concertación y gobernabilidad: Proyecto, acuerdo político y pacto social. La reciente experiencia uruguaya," CIESU/DT, no. 124, 1985; idem, "Transición hacia la democracia y restauración en el Uruguay, 1985–1989" (Montevideo, 1990). Gerónimo de Sierra, "Los sindicatos en la transición democrática

uruguaya," in Guillermo Campero and Alberto Cuevas, *El sindicalismo latinoamericano en los 90* (Santiago, 1991), vol. 1, 241–67. Filgueira, "Movimientos," 11–13. *El Día,* Dec. 16, 19, 1984; ibid., July 28, 1985.

39. Aguirre Bayley, *El Frente,* 61–78. Rial, "La izquierda," 4–6.

40. Juan Rial, "The Uruguayan Elections of 1984: A Triumph of the Center," in Drake and Silva, *Elections,* 245–71; idem, "Notas preliminares acerca de los resultados de las elecciones del 25 de noviembre de 1984 en el Uruguay," CIESU/DT, no. 87, Jan. 1985. Pablo Mieres, "Los partidos uruguayos: Imágenes y desafíos," *Cuadernos del CLAEH* 32 (1984/4), 7–27. Carina Perelli, "25 de noviembre: Los programas partidarios," *Cuadernos de Historia y Política* (CIEP) 4 (Nov. 1984). Charles G. Gillespie, "Uruguay's Transition from Collegial Military-Technocratic Rule," in Guillermo O'Donnell, Philippe C. Schmitter, and Laurence Whitehead, *Transitions from Authoritarian Rule: Latin America* (Baltimore, 1986), 173–95.

41. Gerónimo de Sierra, "La izquierda de la transición," in Gillespie et al., *Uruguay y la democracia,* vol. 2, 149–60. Gargiulo, "El desafío," 15–20. Gillespie, "Activists," 233. Rial, "Uruguayan Elections," 253–55, 267–68. Cosse, "Clase," 95. Pablo Mieres, "Democratización en Uruguay: Disyuntivas para la izquierda," *Opciones* 10 (Jan.–Apr. 1987), 29–55.

42. The strong blue-collar vote for the FA had as important a role as did that for the Spanish PSOE. The positive effect of unionization (union density) on class-based voting has also been common in Western Europe. Luis E. González, *Political Structures and Democracy in Uruguay* (Notre Dame, Ind., 1991), 121–27, 133–34. Gillespie, "Activists," 228–41. Rial, "Uruguayan Elections," 267–68.

43. Rial, "La izquierda," 6–10.

44. Hugo Fernández Faingold, minister of labor, Colorado Party, interview by author, Montevideo, Sept. 1985. Fernando Filgueira, "El movimiento sindical uruguayo en la encrucijada: De la restauración a la transformación democrática" (Montevideo, 1990), 2. Rodríguez, *Uruguay,* 298–305. Alberti, "Las políticas," 55–56. Rial, "Transición." Stolovich, *La cuestión,* 47–49, 55–60. Weinstein, *Uruguay,* 102–4. Gillespie, *Negotiating,* 222–27. Under Sanguinetti, unemployment fell from 14 percent to 9 percent. Gargiulo, "Uruguayan Labor Movement," 233.

45. Interviews with Socialist trade union and PIT-CNT leaders: Eduardo Fernández, Guillermo Alvarez, and Daniel Martínez (these interviews were conducted by the author in Montevideo, Sept. 1985). Arturo S. Bronstein, "The Evolution of Labour Relations in Uruguay: Achievements and Challenges," *International Labour Review* 128:2 (1989), 195–212. Filgueira, "El movimiento," 2.

46. Errandonea, *Las clases,* 135–36. Rial, "El movimiento," 16–31, 153. Gargiulo, "El movimiento"; idem, "Uruguayan Labor Movement," 231.

47. *La Hora,* Nov. 11, 12, 14, 1984. Jorge Chargas and Mario Tonarelli, "Paros generales en Uruguay," *Latin American Labor News* 2–3 (1990), 17. Jorge Balbis, "Huelgas generales en el Uruguay de los '80," ibid., 4 (1991), 13–15. Filgueira, "El movimiento." Rial, "El movimiento," 44, 79–90, 95–101, 135–55, 116. Gargiulo, "El desafío," 12–14. Cancela, "Políticas," 47–48. Alberti, "Las políticas," 55–57. For polling data, see Equipos, "Los sindicatos," 23–27, 54. Gillespie, *Negotiating,* 222–27. Weinstein, *Uruguay,* 102–4.

48. Oscar Ermida Uriarte, *Sindicatos en libertad sindical* (Montevideo, 1985), 7. Alberti, "Las políticas," 71–72. Rial, "El movimiento," 44. Survey results can be found in Equipos, "Los sindicatos," 21–22.

49. Gargiulo, "El desafío," 14. Filgueira, "Movimientos," 13–14. El Centro Uruguay Independiente, *Sindicatos y partidos, sus relaciones* (Montevideo, 1989), 19–28.

50. Juan Raúl Ferreira of the Blanco Party, interview by author, Montevideo, Sept. 1985. Percentages of union delegates are given in Rial, "El movimiento," 50–74; idem, "La izquierda," 10–13. Equipos, "Los sindicatos," 35–37. El Centro Uruguay Independiente, *Sindicatos*. Dick Parker, "Trade Union Struggle and the Left in Latin America, 1973–1990," in Barry Carr and Steve Ellner, *The Latin American Left: From the Fall of Allende to Perestroika* (Boulder, Colo., 1993), 205–24.

51. Equipos, "Los sindicatos," 8–24. González, *Political Structures*, 132–35.

52. Rial, "La izquierda," 10–18. Carina Perelli and Juan Rial, "El discreto encanto de la social-democracia en el Uruguay," CIESU/DT, no. 86, 1985. Angel Cocchi, "Los partidos políticos y la historia reciente," *Cuadernos de Orientación Electoral*, 2, PEITHO (1989).

53. Rial, *Partidos políticos*. Carina Perelli and Juan Rial, "El fin de la restauración: La elección del 26 de noviembre de 1989," *Cuadernos de Orientación Electoral*, 10, PEITHO (Apr. 1990).

SIX : Chile, 1973–1990

1. For the political history of Chile, see Brian Loveman, *Chile: The Legacy of Hispanic Capitalism,* 2d ed. (New York, 1988). For a synopsis, consult Paul W. Drake, "The Historical Setting," in Rex A. Hudson, *Chile: A Country Study* (Washington, D.C., 1994), 1–58.

2. Ruth Berins Collier and David Collier, "Inducements versus Constraints: Disaggregating 'Corporatism,'" *American Political Science Review* 73:4 (Dec. 1979), 967–86; idem, *Shaping the Political Arena: Critical Junctures, the Labor Movement, and Regime Dynamics in Latin America* (Princeton, 1991), 507–22, 536–41, 555–65.

3. Jaime Ruiz-Tagle, *El sindicalismo chileno después del plan laboral* (Santiago, 1985), 8–14. Javier Martínez and Eugenio Tironi, *Las clases sociales en Chile: Cambio y estratificación, 1970–1980* (Santiago, 1985). Guillermo Campero and José A. Valenzuela, *El movimiento sindical chileno en el capitalismo autoritario (1973–1981)* (Santiago, 1981), 7–15. Guillermo Campero, "Los actores sociales y la clase política," Documento de Trabajo, ILET (Santiago, n.d.); idem, "El movimiento sindical chileno en el capitalismo autoritario: Un intento de reflexión y perspectiva," in Manuel Barrera and Gonzalo Falabella, *Sindicatos bajo regímenes militares: Argentina, Brasil, Chile* (Santiago, 1990), 175–218. Alan Angell, *Politics and the Labour Movement in Chile* (London, 1972). J. Samuel Valenzuela, "The Chilean Labor Movement: The Institutionalization of Conflict," in Arturo Valenzuela and J. Samuel Valenzuela, *Chile: Politics and Society* (New Brunswick, N.J., 1976), 135–71. Manuel Barrera and J. Samuel Valenzuela, "The Development of the Labor Movement Opposition to the Military Regime," in J. Samuel Valenzuela and Arturo Valenzuela, *Military Rule in Chile: Dictatorship and Oppositions* (Baltimore, 1986), 230–69. Ernesto Moreno

Beauchemin, *Historia del movimiento sindical chileno: Una visión cristiana* (Santiago, 1986). Homero Ponce Molina, *Historia del movimiento asociativo laboral chileno* (Santiago, 1986). Silas Cerqueira, "Chile," in Jean Pierre-Bernard et al., *Guide to the Political Parties of South America* (Middlesex, 1973), 236–76. Timothy R. Scully, *Rethinking the Center: Party Politics in Nineteenth- and Twentieth-Century Chile* (Stanford, Calif., 1992).

4. Campero and Valenzuela, *El movimiento*, 8–14. Manuel Castells, *La lucha de clases en Chile* (Buenos Aires, 1974), 426–29. Francisco Zapata S., "The Chilean Labor Movement under Salvador Allende, 1970–1973," *Latin American Perspectives* 3:1 (winter 1976), 85–97. Angell, *Politics*, 84–85, 216–19.

5. Small-scale interviews normally turned up the same working-class attitudes as did polls. Peter Winn, "Loosing the Chains: Labor and the Chilean Revolutionary Process, 1970–1973," *Latin American Perspectives* 3:1 (winter 1976), 70–84; idem, "Oral History and the Factory Study: New Approaches to Labor History," *Latin American Research Review* 14:2 (1979), 130–40. James Petras, "Nationalization, Socioeconomic Change, and Popular Participation," in Valenzuela and Valenzuela, *Chile: Politics*, 172–200. Maurice Zeitlin and James Petras, "The Working Class Vote in Chile," *British Journal of Sociology* 21 (Mar. 1970), 16–29. James W. Prothro and Patricio E. Chaparro, "Public Opinion and the Movement of Chilean Government to the Left, 1952–72," in Valenzuela and Valenzuela, *Chile: Politics*, 67–114. Robert Ayres, "Unidad Popular and the Chilean Electoral Process," in ibid., 30–66. Alejandro Portes, "Occupation and Lower-Class Political Orientation in Chile," in ibid., 201–37. Susan Beth Tiano, "Authoritarianism, Class Consciousness, and Modernity: Working-Class Attitudes in Argentina and Chile" (Ph.D. diss., Brown University, 1979). Claire V. Brooks, "Political Behavior in a Conflict Society: Social Bases of Electoral Support for the Chilean Left" (Ph.D. diss., University of Kansas, 1979). C. Lalive and J. Zylberberg, "Dichotomie sociale et pluralisme culturel: La dispersion politique de la classe ouvrière chilienne," *Cahiers Internationaux de Sociologie* 59 (July-Dec. 1975), 255–72. J. Zylberberg and C. Lalive, "Corporatism—Populism—Socialism: The Political Culture of the Chilean Workers," *Canadian Journal of Latin American Studies* 4:8 (1979), 172–90. Henry A. Landsberger, "The Labor Elite: Is It Revolutionary?" in Seymour M. Lipset and Aldo Solari, *Elites in Latin America* (New York, 1967), 256–300. Henry A. Landsberger and Tim McDaniel, "Hypermobilization in Chile, 1970–1973," *World Politics* 28 (July 1976), 502–41. Brian H. Smith and José Luis Rodríguez, "Comparative Working-Class Behavior: Chile, France, and Italy," *American Behavioral Scientist* 18:1 (Sept. 1974), 59–96. Kenneth P. Langton and Ronald Rapoport, "Social Structure, Social Context, and Partisan Mobilization: Urban Workers in Chile," *Comparative Political Studies* 8:3 (Oct. 1975), 318–44. Liliana de Riz, *Sociedad y política en Chile: De Portales a Pinochet* (Mexico, 1979).

6. Paul W. Drake, *Socialism and Populism in Chile, 1932–52* (Urbana, Ill., 1978). Arturo Valenzuela, *The Breakdown of Democratic Regimes: Chile* (Baltimore, 1978), 6, 53–54, 85–87. César Caviedes, *The Politics of Chile: A Sociogeographical Assessment* (Boulder, Colo., 1979), 265–73. Enzo Faletto, "Algunas características de la base social del Partido Socialista y del Partido Comunista, 1958–1973," FLACSO [Facultad Latinoamericano de Ciencias Sociales], no. 97, Sept. 1980.

7. Karen L. Remmer, "Political Demobilization in Chile, 1973–1978," *Comparative Politics* 12:3 (Apr. 1980), 277–82.

8. Guillermo Campero and René Cortázar, "Logics of Union Action in Chile," working paper no. 85, Kellogg Institute, Oct. 1986. Peter Winn, *Weavers of Revolution: The Yarur Workers and Chile's Road to Socialism* (New York, 1986); idem, "Loosing."

9. Arturo Valenzuela, "Political Constraints to the Establishment of Socialism in Chile," in Valenzuela and Valenzuela, *Chile: Politics*, 1–29; idem, *Breakdown*. Ian Roxborough et al., *Chile: The State and Revolution* (New York, 1974). Dale Johnson, *The Chilean Road to Socialism* (Garden City, N.J., 1973). Stefan De Vylder, *Allende's Chile: The Political Economy of the Rise and Fall of the Unidad Popular* (New York, 1976). Edy Kaufman, *Crisis in Allende's Chile* (New York, 1988). Barbara Stallings, *Class Conflict and Economic Development in Chile* (Stanford, Calif., 1978). Paul E. Sigmund, *The Overthrow of Allende and the Politics of Chile, 1964–1976* (Pittsburgh, 1977). Les Evans, *Disaster in Chile* (New York, 1974). Juan Espinosa and Andrew Zimbalist, *Economic Democracy* (New York, 1978). Janine Miguel, "Proceso de gestación y desarrollo histórico del movimiento laboral chileno," Research Paper Series, no. 16, Institute of Latin American Studies, Stockholm, Sept. 1979. Jorge Giusti, "Participación y organización de los sectores populares en América Latina: Los casos de Chile y Perú," *Revista Mexicana de Sociología* 34:1 (Jan.–Mar. 1972), 39–64. Sergio Bitar, *Chile, Experiment in Democracy* (Philadelphia, 1986). Sergio Bitar and Crisóstomo Pizarro, *La caída de Allende y la huelga de El Teniente* (Santiago, 1986). Landsberger and McDaniel, "Hypermobilization." Youssef Cohen, *Radicals, Reformers, and Reactionaries: The Prisoner's Dilemma and the Collapse of Democracy in Latin America* (Chicago, 1994), 98–118. Winn, "Loosing."

10. Karen L. Remmer, *Military Rule in Latin America* (Boston, 1989), 111–206; idem, "Political Demobilization." James Warren Wilson, "Freedom and Control: Workers' Participation in Management in Chile, 1967–1975," 4 vols. (Ph.D. diss., Cornell University, 1979). Organización Mundial del Trabajo, *La situación sindical en Chile* (Geneva, 1975). Genaro Arriagada, "Ideology and Politics in the South American Military (Argentina, Brazil, Chile, and Uruguay)," working paper no. 55, Latin American Program, Wilson Center, 1979; idem, *Pinochet: The Politics of Power* (Winchester, Mass., 1988). Ascanio Carvallo, Manuel Salazar, and Oscar Sepúlveda, *La historia oculta del régimen militar* (Santiago, 1988). David E. Hojman, *Chile after 1973: Elements for the Analysis of Miltary Rule* (Liverpool, 1985). Phil O'Brien and Jackie Roddick, *Chile: The Pinochet Decade* (London, 1983). Samuel Chavkin, *Storm over Chile* (Westport, Conn., 1985). Manuel Antonio Garretón, "The Political Evolution of the Chilean Military Regime and Problems in the Transition to Democracy," in Guillermo O'Donnell, Philippe C. Schmitter, and Laurence Whitehead, *Transitions from Authoritarian Rule: Latin America* (Baltimore, 1986), 95–122. Augusto Varas, *Los militares en el poder: Régimen y gobierno militar en Chile, 1973–1986* (Santiago, 1987). Pamela Constable and Arturo Valenzuela, *A Nation of Enemies: Chile under Pinochet* (New York: 1991). Mary Helen Spooner, *Soldiers in a Narrow Land: The Pinochet Regime in Chile* (Berkeley, 1994). Lois Hecht Oppenheim, *Politics in Chile: Democracy, Authoritarianism, and the Search for Development* (Boulder,

Colo., 1993). Raúl Rettig G., et al., *Informe de la Comisión Nacional de Verdad y Reconciliación* (Santiago, 1991).

11. Alan Angell, "Unions and Workers in the 1980s," in Paul W. Drake and Iván Jaksic, *The Struggle for Democracy in Chile, 1982–90* (Lincoln, Neb., 1991), 188–210. Manuel Barrera, Helia Henríquez, and Teresita Selamé, *Sindicatos y estado en el Chile actual* (Santiago, 1985), 55–57. For a praiseful account of the social security reform, see José Piñera, *El casabel al gato: La batalla por la reforma previsional* (Santiago, 1991). Ruiz-Tagle, *El sindicalismo,* 13–14. Martínez and Tironi, *Las clases.* For further sources of economic data, see n. 16, below.

12. Although all sources agree that there was a drop in industrial employment under the military regime, figures vary. For example, the government's own data showed the national workforce in the industrial sector plummeting from 776,000 in 1972 to 590,000 in 1980. República de Chile, Ministerio de Economía, Fomento y Reconstrucción, Instituto Nacional de Estadísticas, *Estadísticas laborales, 1979–1981* (n.p., n.d.), 7; idem, *Estadísticas laborales, 1982–1985* (n.p., n.d.). Jaime Gatica Barros, *Deindustrialization in Chile* (Boulder, Colo., 1989). Also see the series of publications by the Oficina Internacional del Trabajo, Programa Regional del Empleo para América Latina y el Caribe: OIT, PREALC, "Monetarismo global y respuesta industrial: El caso de Chile," Documentos de Trabajo, no. 232, Mar. 1984; idem, "Fuentes del cambio en la estructura del sector industrial chileno: 1967–1982," Documentos de Trabajo, no. 274, Mar. 1986; idem, "Una nota sobre el impacto de la liberalización y apertura financiera sobre el sector manufacturero chileno: 1974–1982," Documentos de Trabajo, no. 275, Apr. 1986; idem, "La caída del empleo manufacturero: Chile, 1979–83," Documentos de Trabajo, no. 298, May 1987. For further sources on industry and employment, consult n. 16, below.

13. Alvaro Díaz, "Chile: Nuevas tecnologías y su impacto en los trabajadores," Documento de Trabajo, no. 88, SUR, Jan. 1988.

14. Campero and Valenzuela, *El movimiento,* 35–86. Barrera, Henríquez, and Selamé, *Sindicatos,* 57. Sergio Arancibia et al., "Los trabajadores y los cambios en la estructura económico-social del país" (Santiago, 1988), 2–3, 50–62. Helia Henríquez, "La reconstitución del sindicalismo durante el régimen militar: Análisis de algunos sectores urbanos," in CLACSO, *El sindicalismo latinoamericano en los ochenta* (Santiago, 1986), 245–64.

15. Francisco Zapata, "Nationalisation, Copper Miners, and the Military Government in Chile," in Thomas Greaves and William Culver, *Miners and Mining in the Americas* (Manchester, England, 1985), 257–76.

16. From the huge bibliography on economic changes and data under Pinochet, the following publications are particularly recommended: Campero and Valenzuela, *El movimiento.* Barrera, Henríquez, and Selamé, *Sindicatos,* esp. 80–82. Cristina Hurtado-Beca, "Chile, 1973–1981: Desarticulación y reestructuración autoritaria del movimiento sindical," *Boletín de Estudios Latinoamericanos y del Caribe* 31 (Dec. 1981), 91–117. René Cortázar, "Austerity under Authoritarianism: The Neoconservative Revolution in Chile," in Howard Handelman and Werner Baer, *Paying the Costs of Austerity in Latin America* (Boulder, Colo., 1989), 43–63. Javier Martínez and Eugenio Tironi, "La clase obrera en el nuevo estilo de desarrollo: Un enfoque es-

tructural," in Manuel Antonio Garretón et al., *Chile, 1973–198?* (Santiago, 1983), 105–32; idem, *Las clases.* Alvaro Bardón M., Camilo Carrasco A., and Alvaro Vial G., *Una década de cambios económicos: La experiencia chilena, 1973–1983* (Santiago, 1985). Alejandro Foxley, *Latin American Experiments in Neoconservative Economics* (Berkeley, 1983). Ricardo Ffrench-Davis, "Políticas de comercio exterior en Chile: 1973–1978," working paper no. 67, Latin American Program, Wilson Center, 1980. Joseph Ramos, *Neoconservative Economics in the Southern Cone of Latin America, 1973–1983* (Baltimore, 1986), 12–23. Gary M. Walton, "Focusing on Chilean Economic Policy," in Gary M. Walton, *The National Economic Policies of Chile* (Greenwich, Conn., 1985), 1–10. René Cortázar, "Distributive Results in Chile, 1973–1982," in ibid., 79–106. Daniel L. Wisegarver, "Economic Regulation and Deregulation in Chile, 1973–83," in ibid., 145–202. Sebastian Edwards, "Economic Policy and the Record of Economic Growth in Chile, 1973–1982," in ibid., 11–46. Sebastian Edwards and Alejandra Cox Edwards, *Monetarism and Liberalization: The Chilean Experiment* (Cambridge, 1987); idem, "The Economy," in Hudson, *Chile,* 137–96. Roberto Zahler, "Recent Southern Cone Liberalization Reforms and Stabilization Policies: The Chilean Case, 1974–1982," *Journal of Interamerican Studies and World Affairs* 25:4 (Nov. 1983), 509–62. Patricio Meller, René Cortázar, and Jorge Marshall, "Employment Stagnation in Chile: 1974–1978," *Latin American Research Review* 16:2 (1981), 144–55. Patricio Meller and Andrés Solimano, "Desempleo en Chile: Interpretación y políticas económicas alternativas," in Alejandro Foxley et al., *Reconstrucción económica para la democracia* (Santiago, 1983), 149–88. Pilar Vergara, *Auge y caída del neoliberalismo en Chile* (Santiago, 1985). Peter Hakim and Giorgio Solimano, *Development, Reform, and Malnutrition in Chile* (Cambridge, 1978). Markos Mamalakis, *The Growth and Structure of the Chilean Economy* (New Haven, Conn., 1976). Juan Gabriel Valdés, *La Escuela de Chicago: Operación Chile* (Buenos Aires, 1989). Philip J. O'Brien, "The New Leviathan: The Chicago School and the Chilean Regime, 1973–1980," Occasional Papers, no. 38, Institute of Latin American Studies, University of Glasgow, 1982; idem, "Authoritarianism and the New Orthodoxy: The Political Economy of the Chilean Regime, 1973–1982," in Philip O'Brien and Paul Cammack, *Generals in Retreat: The Crisis of Military Rule in Latin America* (Manchester, England, 1985), 144–83. Alvaro García, "The Political Economy of the Rise and Fall of the Chicago Boys: Chile, 1973–83," Working Paper Series, no. 38, Centre of Latin American Studies, University of Cambridge, 1983. Sholeh A. Maani, "Chilean Unemployment: An Estimation of the Probability of Employment for Males," *Inter-American Economic Affairs* 37:1 (summer 1983), 67–81. Nicolás Flaño and Gustavo Jiménez, *Empleo, política económica y concertación: ¿Qué opinan los empresarios?* (Santiago, 1987). Laurence Whitehead, "Inflation and Stabilization in Chile, 1970–77," in Rosemary Thorp and Laurence Whitehead, *Inflation and Stabilization in Latin America* (New York, 1979), 65–109. Eduardo Silva, "The Political Economy of Chile's Regime Transition: From Radical to Pragmatic Neoliberal Policies," in Drake and Jaksic, *Struggle,* 98–107; idem, "Capitalist Coalitions and Economic Policymaking in Authoritarian Chile, 1973–1988" (Ph.D. diss., University of California, San Diego, 1991). Gatica, *Deindustrialization.*

17. Guillermo Campero, "Las nuevas condiciones en las relaciones del trabajo y la acción política en Chile," *Revista Mexicana de Sociología* 41:2 (Apr.–June 1979),

481–93; idem, *Entre la sobrevivencia y la acción política: Las organizaciones de pobladores en Santiago* (Santiago, 1987). Faletto, "Características."

18. The data in the foregoing discussion are from the following sources: Manuel Barrera and Alberto Bastías, "Cambios en la relación entre sistema económico y sindical: El caso de Chile," Materiales de Discusión, no. 12, Centro de Estudios Sociales (hereafter, CES), Aug. 1989. Barrera, Henríquez, and Selamé, *Sindicatos,* 50–54. Alberto Bastías, "Factores que inciden en la precarización del empleo: El caso de la gran minería del cobre," Materiales de Discusión, no. 5, CES, Aug. 1988. Rodrigo Baño, "Notas sobre organizaciones de desocupados," Documento de Trabajo, no. 297, FLACSO, June 1986. OIT, PREALC, "Determinantes estructurales y coyunturales de la producción en la industria manufacturera chilena: 1969–1983," Documentos de Trabajo, no. 249, Sept. 1984. Angell, "Unions," 189–91. Arancibia et al., "Los trabajadores," 7–8. Edwards and Edwards, "Economy." República de Chile, Ministerio de Economía, Fomento y Reconstrucción, Instituto Nacional de Estadísticas, *Boletín de estadísticas laborales, 1986* (n.p., n.d.), 76–85. Alejandro Foxley, "Después del monetarismo," working paper no. 12, Kellogg Institute, Mar. 1984. Carlos Huneeus, *Los chilenos y la política* (Santiago, 1987), 37–52.

19. Eduardo Silva, "Capitalist Coalitions"; idem, "Political Economy." Gatica, *Deindustrialization,* 130–33. Edwards and Edwards, "Economy," 338–39. Arancibia et al., " Los trabajadores," 5–7. Felipe Larraín, "The Economic Challenges of Democratic Development," in Drake and Jaksic, *Struggle,* 276–301. OIT, PREALC, "Nuevos antecedentes sobre la desindustrialización chilena," Documentos de Trabajo, no. 307, Oct. 1987. Carlos Vignolo, "De la desindustrialización a una nueva industrialización para Chile," Materiales de Discusión, no. 147, CED [Centro de Estudios Democraticos], Sept. 1986. For a very positive assessment of the dictatorship's economic and social achievements, see David E. Hojman, *Chile: The Political Economy of Development and Democracy in the 1990s* (Pittsburgh, 1993). Tarsicio Castañeda, *Combating Poverty: Innovative Social Reforms in Chile during the 1980s* (San Francisco, 1992). Barry P. Bosworth, Rudiger Dornbusch, and Raul Laban, *The Chilean Economy: Policy Lessons and Challenges* (Washington, D.C., 1994).

20. Jaime Ruiz-Tagle, "Sindicalismo y estado en el régimen militar chileno," Documento de Trabajo, no. 51, Programa de Economía del Trabajo, Sept. 1986; idem, "Trade Unionism and the State under the Chilean Military Regime," in Edward C. Epstein, *Labor Autonomy and the State in Latin America* (Boston, 1989), 73–100.

21. Patricia Politzer, *Miedo en Chile* (Santiago, 1985), 90–93, 269–82.

22. In 1987 the government formalized these 1978–79 laws by decreeing an official Labor Code. Manuel Antonio Garretón, *Dictaduras y democratización* (Santiago, 1984). José Piñera, *La revolución laboral en Chile,* 2d ed. (Santiago, 1990). Barrera and Valenzuela, "Opposition." Arturo Valenzuela and J. Samuel Valenzuela, "Party Oppositions under the Chilean Authoritarian Regime," in Valenzuela and Valenzuela, *Military Rule,* 184–229. Remmer, "Political Demobilization." Wilson, "Freedom." Vergara, "Neoliberalismo," 134–56, 215–30. One of the best sources of data on unions is Campero and Valenzuela, *El movimiento.* For other key sources, see n. 26, below.

23. *El Mercurio,* July 25, 1980; ibid., Sept. 3, 1980; ibid., Dec. 10, 1980. Patricio Cueto Román, *Derecho laboral y transición democrática: El caso español y el caso chileno* (Santiago, 1990), 27–30, 100–118. Piñera, *La revolución.*

24. Both the Ten and the CNS traced their roots back to preliminary organizational efforts in 1975. The CNS evolved into a new version of the CUT in 1988. Barrera and Valenzuela, "Opposition." Interviews by author with Group of Ten leaders José Ruiz di Giorgio (president of the National Confederation of Petroleum Workers and a Director of the National Workers' Command) and Eduardo Ríos (president of the Maritime Workers Union and of the CDT), Santiago, Dec. 1984. *El Mercurio,* Aug. 12, 19, 1981; ibid., Dec. 16, 1981; ibid., Dec. 8, 1982. On the CDT, see R. Jiliberto, *Libertad sindical o sindicalizar la libertad?* (Santiago, 1986).

25. For an example of visits from international trade union organizations, see *El Mercurio,* Oct. 27, 1982. Guillermo Campero, "El sindicalismo internacional y la redemocratización de Chile," Materiales para Discusión, no. 12, CED, Aug. 1984.

26. Barrera, Henríquez, and Selamé, *Sindicatos,* 84. All these sections on labor unions rely heavily on Campero and Valenzuela, *El movimiento.* Campero and Cortázar, "Logics." Ruiz-Tagle, "Sindicalismo"; idem, *El sindicalismo.* Hurtado-Beca, "Chile." Valenzuela and Valenzuela, "Party Oppositions." Wisegarver, "Regulation." Manuel Barrera, "Política laboral y movimiento sindical chileno durante el régimen militar," working paper no. 66, Latin American Program, Wilson Center, 1980; idem, interview by author, Santiago, Aug. 1989. Barrera and Valenzuela, "Opposition," 230–69. Gonzalo Falabella, "Labour in Chile under the Junta," working paper no. 4, Institute of Latin American Studies, University of London, July 1981; idem, "La diversidad en el movimiento sindical chileno bajo el régimen militar," in Barrera and Falabella, *Sindicatos,* 219–82. Brian Loveman, "Chile," in Gerald Michael Greenfield and Sheldon L. Maram, *Latin American Labor Organizations* (New York, 1987), 129–78. Patricio Frías, *El movimiento sindical chileno en la lucha por la democracia, 1973–1988* (Santiago, 1989). Jacqueline Roddick, "Chile," in Jean Carriere, Nigel Haworth, and Jacqueline Roddick, *The State, Industrial Relations, and the Labour Movement in Latin America* (New York, 1989), 178–262. Jacqueline Roddick and Nigel Haworth, "Tres cambios de rumbo en la política laboral del gobierno militar en Chile, 1973–1979," in Bernardo Gallitelli and Andres A. Thompson, *Sindicalismo y regímenes militares en Argentina y Chile* (Amsterdam, 1982), 293–330. Nigel Haworth and Jackie Roddick, "Labour and Monetarism in Chile, 1975–1980," *Bulletin of Latin American Research* 1:1 (Oct. 1981), 49–62. Benny Pollack, "Comentarios preliminares sobre el plan laboral y el nuevo sistema de pensiones en Chile: Sus alcances como instrumento de control social," in Gallitelli and Thompson, *Sindicalismo,* 281–91. Bjorn Feuer, "Mining Unionism, Political Democracy, and Revealed Preferences—The Quid Pro Quo of Labour Relations in Bolivia, Chile, and Peru, 1950–80," *Economic and Industrial Democracy* 12:1 (Feb. 1991), 97–118. Agustín Quevedo and Francisco Tapia, "El marco de las relaciones laborales en Chile durante el régimen militar," Materiales de Discusión, no. 14, CES, Dec. 1989. Janine Miguel, "La nueva institucionalidad laboral de los regímenes de seguridad nacional: La experiencia chilena," Research Papers Series, no. 33 Institute of Latin American Studies, Stockholm, Feb. 1982; idem, "La defensa de los derechos y libertades de los trabajadores chilenos y sus organizaciones sindicales ante los organismos internacionales," Research Papers Series, no. 31 Institute of Latin American Studies, Stockholm, June 1981. Thomas G. Sanders, "Chilean Self-Management Cooperatives during the Military Regime," *American University Field Service Reports* 49 (1979), 1–15. Karen L. Remmer, "Public

Policy and Regime Consolidation: The First Five Years of the Chilean Junta," *Journal of Developing Areas* 13 (July 1979), 441–62; idem, "Political Demobilization." Francisco Rojas Aravena, *Autoritarismo y alternativas populares en América Latina* (San Jose, Costa Rica, 1982). Manuel Antonio Garretón, "Transformación social y refundación política en el capitalismo autoritario," in ibid., 141–58. Tomás Moulián, "Dictaduras hegemonizantes y alternativas populares," in ibid., 159–80. Carlos Portales, "La izquierda y la alternativa democrática," in ibid., 203–15. Augusto Varas, "Crisis política y alternativas democráticas: Límites y perspectivas de la izquierda chilena," in ibid., 181–202. Howard Handelman and Thomas G. Sanders, *Military Government and the Movement toward Democracy in South America* (Bloomington, Ind., 1981). Brian H. Smith, *The Church and Politics in Chile: Challenges to Modern Catholicism* (Princeton, 1982); idem, "Old Allies, New Opponents: The Church and the Military in Chile, 1973–1979," working papers, no. 68, Latin American Program, Wilson Center, 1981. Ernesto Moreno Beauchemin, *Sindicalismo y democracia* (Santiago, 1987). Ernesto Moreno and Rodolfo Bonifaz, "Las organizaciones sindicales y el contexto autoritario," *Estudios Sociales* 40 (1984), 71–116. Carlos A. González Moya, *Nuevo código del trabajo* (Santiago, [1988?]). Wilson, "Freedom." Angell, "Unions," 189–208.

27. José Ruiz di Giorgio, interview, in Centro de Estudios Sociales, "Unidad: Problemas actuales del movimiento sindical" (n.p., n.d.), 4. Guillermo Pérez, interview by author, Santiago, 1984.

28. Manuel Antonio Garretón, *Reconstruir la política* (Santiago, 1987); idem, "Popular Mobilization and the Military Regime in Chile: The Complexities of the Invisible Transition," in Susan Eckstein, *Power and Popular Protest: Latin American Social Movements* (Berkeley, 1989), 259–77. Gonzalo de la Maza and Mario Garcés, *La explosión de las mayorías: Protesta nacional, 1983–1984* (Santiago, 1985). Iván Valenzuela, "Conflictos en la gran minería del cobre, 1973–1983," in CLACSO, *El sindicalismo,* 265–94. Carlos Huneeus, "La política de la apertura y sus implicancias para la inauguración de la democracia en Chile," *Revista de Ciencia Política* 7:1 (1985), 25–84. Patricio Frías F., *Prácticas y orientaciones del movimiento sindical en la lucha por la democracia* (Santiago, 1986). Gonzalo Falabella and Guillermo Campero, "Los sindicatos en la transición a la democracia en Chile," in Guillermo Campero and Alberto Cuevas, *El sindicalismo latinoamericano en los 90* (Santiago, 1991), 133–64. Mario Albuquerque and Victor Zuñiga, *Democracia, participación, unidad* (Santiago, 1987). Barrera, Henríquez, and Selamé, *Sindicatos,* 150–52. Barrera and Valenzuela, "Opposition." Ruiz-Tagle, *El sindicalismo,* 3, 191–99. Politzer, *Miedo,* 178–83. *Temas Laborales* 5 (Oct. 1984).

29. Cathy Schneider, "The Mobilization at the Grassroots: Shantytowns and Resistance in Authoritarian Chile" (Ph.D. diss., Cornell University, 1989). Peter Winn and María Angélica Ibáñez, "Textile Entrepreneurs and Workers in Pinochet's Chile, 1973–1989," Papers on Latin America, no. 15, Institute of Latin American and Iberian Studies, Columbia University, 1990.

30. Mario dos Santos et al., *Concertación social y democracia* (Santiago, 1985). José Ruiz di Giorgio and José Ruiz dos Santos, "Concertación social: Un camino posible y necesario," Materiales para Discusión, no. 43, CED, Nov. 1984. Guillermo Pérez V., "Sindicalismo y redemocratización: Posibilidades y alcances de la con-

certación social," Materiales para Discusión, no. 50, CED, Nov. 1984. Guillermo Campero, "Trabajadores, empresarios y concertación social para la democracia," Materiales para Discusión, no. 48, CED, Nov. 1984. Gonzalo Falabella, "El rol de los sindicatos en la transición a la democracia en Chile" (Santiago, 1989). Flaño and Jiménez, *Empleo.* Falabella and Campero, "Los sindicatos," 142–62.

31. Data on unionization vary among sources, but the general patterns are consistent. Between the early 1970s and the late 1980s, the number of unions had shrunk less than the number of union members because the average number of members per union had diminished sharply, as unions became generally smaller and weaker. Angell, "Unions," 192–93. Ruiz-Tagle, *El sindicalismo,* 18–20.

32. Huneeus, *Los chilenos,* 114–16.

33. Falabella, "El rol," 27. Angell, "Unions," 205–8. Barrera, Henríquez, and Selamé, *Sindicatos,* 150–52. CES, "Unidad," 12–26; idem, "Problemas actuales del movimiento sindical" (n.p., n.d.). Rodrigo Baño, *Lo social y lo político* (Santiago, 1985). Garretón, *Dictaduras.* Quevedo and Tapia, "El marco," 13.

34. Guillermo Campero, "El sindicalismo en la actual crisis: Orientaciones y alternativas," in Isidro Cheresky and Jacques Chonchol, *Crisis y transformación de los regímenes autoritarios* (Buenos Aires, 1985), 129–42. Cristina Hurtado Beca, "Régimen autoritario y sectores populares urbanos en Chile: Transformación de las relaciones sociales (1973–1983)," in ibid., 103–28. Ponce, *Historia,* 278–79.

35. CES, "Unidad," 35–36.

36. Barrera and Valenzuela, "Opposition." Valenzuela and Valenzuela, "Party Oppositions." Falabella, "Labour." Remmer, "Political Demobilization." Wilson, "Freedom."

37. *El Socialista* 9 (Apr. 1981); ibid., 18 (June 1982); ibid., 19 (July 1982); ibid., 21 (Oct. 1982). Carlos Altamirano, *Dialéctica de una derrota* (Mexico, 1977). Carlos Bascuñán Edwards, *La izquierda sin Allende* (Santiago, 1990), 71–100, 161–79. Benny Pollack and Herman Rosenkranz, *Revolutionary Social Democracy: The Chilean Socialist Party* (New York, 1987). Angel Flisfisch et al., *El futuro democrático de Chile: 4 visiones políticas* (Santiago, 1985), 165–206. Tomás Moulián, "La crisis de la izquierda," in Garretón et al., *Chile,* 301–16. Martínez and Tironi, "La clase." Rojas, *Autoritarismo.* Interviews with Sergio Bitar, Guillermo Campero, Manuel Antonio Garretón, Heraldo Muñoz, Eduardo Ortiz, and Carlos Portales, Santiago, 1984–90.

38. Luis Corvalán, "Terminar con la dictadura es una exigencia nacional" (Santiago, 1980, mimeographed); idem, "El partido es y debe ser un conglomerado vivo" (Santiago, 1980, mimeographed); idem, "Nuestra línea es elaborada colectivamente" (Santiago, 1981, mimeographed). Carmelo Furci, *The Chilean Communist Party and the Road to Socialism* (London, 1984), 136–68. Augusto Varas, *El Partido Comunista en Chile* (Santiago, 1988). Juraj Domic K., *Política militar del Partido Comunista de Chile* (Santiago, 1988). Gustavo Jiménez F., "El Partido Comunista de Chile en el contexto del sistema de partidos y de la transición política," *Estudios Sociales* 52 (1986), 21–69. Bascuñán, *La izquierda,* 34–55.

39. Carlos Bascuñán, Edgardo Boeninger, Alejandro Foxley, Carlos Huneeus, and Sol Serrano, interviews by author, Santiago, 1984–88. Campero and Valenzuela, *El movimiento.* Valenzuela and Valenzuela, "Party Oppositions." Arturo Valenzuela, "Six Years of Military Rule in Chile," working paper no. 109, Latin American Pro-

gram, Wilson Center, 1982. Manuel Antonio Garretón, "Institucionalización y oposición en el regimen autoritario chileno," working paper no. 59, Latin American Program, Wilson Center, 1980; idem, "Evolución política y problemas de la transición a la democracia en el régimen militar chileno," FLACSO (Santiago), no. 148, June 1982; idem, *Dictaduras,* 82–93; idem, "The Political Opposition and the Party System under the Military Regime," in Drake and Jaksic, *Struggle,* 211–50. Francisco Zapata S., "Los mineros del cobre y el gobierno militar en Chile entre 1973 y 1981," *Boletín de Estudios Latinoamericanos y del Caribe* 32 (June 1982), 39–47. Carmelo Furci, "The Chilean Communist Party (PCCH) and Its Third Underground Period, 1973–1980," *Bulletin of Latin American Research* 2:1 (Oct. 1982). Alan Angell and Susan Carstairs, "The Exile Question in Chilean Politics," *Third World Quarterly* 9:1 (Jan. 1987), 148–67. Michael Fleet, *The Rise and Fall of Chilean Christian Democracy* (Princeton, 1985). "Chile: Autocrítica y reafirmación de la izquierda," *Cuadernos de Marcha* 1:6 (Mar.–Apr. 1980), 3–104. Eugenio Ortega, "La oposición en períodos de transición a la democracia: El caso de Chile," in Augusto Varas, *Transición a la democracia* (Santiago, 1984), 171–82. Brian Loveman, "Military Dictatorship and Political Opposition in Chile, 1973–86," *Journal of Inter-American Studies and World Affairs* 28:4 (winter 1986–87), 1–38.

40. Manuel Barrera, "La coyuntura política pre-plebiscito en Chile y los actores sociales más significativos," Materiales de Discusión, no. 8, CES, Nov. 1988. Manuel Barrera, interview by author, Santiago, Oct. 1988. Clodomiro Almeyda, "Interacción de lo político y sindical en Chile," Materiales de Discusión, no. 9, CES, Mar. 1989. Frías, *El movimiento,* 100–105.

41. Patricio Tupper, *89/90 Opciones políticas en Chile* (Santiago, 1987). Richard Friedmann, *1964–1988: La política chilena de la A a la Z* (Santiago, 1988). Norbert Lechner, José Joaquín Brunner, and Angel Flisfisch, *Partidos y democracia* (Santiago, 1985). CES, "Unidad," 2–3, 17–19. Baño, *Lo social,* 141–61.

42. Paul W. Drake, *Socialismo y populismo: Chile, 1936–1973* (Valparaíso, 1992). Jorge Arrate, *La fuerza democrática de la idea socialista* (Santiago, 1985). Jorge Arrate and Paulo Hidalgo, *Pasión y razón del socialismo chileno* (Santiago, 1989). Ricardo Lagos, *Democracia para Chile, proposiciones de un socialista* (Santiago, 1985); idem, *Hacia la democracia* (Santiago, 1987). *La renovación socialista: Balance y perspectivas de un proceso vigente* (Santiago, 1987). Clodomiro Almeyda, *Reencuentro con mi vida* (Santiago, 1988). Sergio Bitar, *Chile para todos* (Santiago, 1988). Hernán Vodanovic, *Un socialismo renovado para Chile* (Santiago, 1988). Aniceto Rodríguez, *Unidad y renovación, dialéctica para la victoria* (Santiago, 1991). Ignacio Walker, *Socialismo y democracia: Chile y Europa en perspectiva comparada* (Santiago, 1990). Eduardo Ortiz, "El proyecto socialista y el tema de la democracia," *Opciones* 10 (Jan.–Apr. 1987), 76–100. Bascuñán, *La izquierda,* 161–79, 188–89.

43. On both the Socialists and the Communists, see Brian Loveman, "The Political Left in Chile, 1973–1990," in Barry Carr and Steve Ellner, *The Latin American Left: From the Fall of Allende to Perestroika* (Boulder, Colo., 1993), 23–40. A. E. Fernándes Jilberto, *Dictadura militar y oposición política en Chile* (Amsterdam, 1985), 277–432. Luis Guastavino, *Caen las catedrales* (Santiago, 1991). Varas, *El Partido.* Jiménez, *El Partido Comunista.*

44. Alejandro Foxley, *Para una democracia estable* (Santiago, 1985); idem, *Chile y*

su futuro: Un país posible (Santiago, 1987). Andrés Zaldívar, *Por la democracia ahora y siempre* (Santiago, 1987). Angell, "Unions," 193. Barrera, "La coyuntura," 21–23; idem, interview by author, Santiago, Aug. 1989.

45. Angell, *Politics,* 84–85, 216–19; idem, "Unions," 198–200. Zapata, "Chilean Labor Movement." Frías, *El movimiento,* 113–24.

46. Central Unitaria de Trabajadores, *Propuesta para la transición a la democracia* (Santiago, 1989). Angell, "Unions," 198–200. Ruiz-Tagle, *El sindicalismo,* 5.

47. Garretón, "Political Opposition," 226–32. Paul W. Drake and Arturo Valenzuela, "The Chilean Plebiscite: A First Step toward Redemocratization (Report by the International Commission of the Latin American Studies Association to Observe the Chilean Plebiscite)," *LASA Forum* 19:4 (winter 1989), 18–36. César N. Caviedes, *Elections in Chile: The Road toward Redemocratization* (London, 1991).

48. Paul W. Drake and Iván Jaksic, "Transformation and Transition in Chile, 1982–90," in Drake and Jaksic, *Struggle,* 13–16. Joseph S. Tulchin and Augusto Varas, *From Dictatorship to Democracy: Rebuilding Political Consensus in Chile* (Boulder, Colo., 1991).

49. Fernando Echeverría Bascuñán and Jorge Rojas Hernández, *Añoranzas, sueños, realidades: Dirigentes sindicales hablan de la transición* (Santiago, 1992). Jorge Rojas Hernández, "Movimiento sindical chileno en la transición a la democracia," Documento de Trabajo, no. 140, CES, 1993, 1–77. Manuel Antonio Garretón, *Propuestas políticas y demandas sociales,* 3 vols. (Santiago, 1989), vol. 2, 39, 103–8. Concertación de Partidos por la Democracia, *Programa de gobierno* (Santiago, 1989). Gonzalo Falabella, "Chile: Sus sueños por verse," *Sindicalismo y Democracia* 1 (Aug. 1989), 15–17. Patricio Frías Fernández, "El movimiento sindical chileno en el primer año de transición a la democracia (1990–1991)," Documento de Trabajo, no. 84, Programa de Economía del Trabajo, May 1991, 1–50. Alejandro Foxley, *La economía política de la transición* (Santiago, 1994). James Petras and Fernando Ignacio Leiva, *Democracy and Poverty in Chile* (Boulder, Colo., 1994). Edward Epstein, "Labor and Political Stability in the New Chilean Democracy: Three Illusions," *Revista de Economía y Trabajo* 1:2 (July-Dec. 1993), 1–34. Silva, "Capitalist Coalitions," 361–69. Cueto Román, *Derecho laboral,* 30–36, 121–42. Edwards and Edwards, "Economy," 336–37. Central Unitaria de Trabajadores, *Propuesta. La Epoca,* July 23, 1990. *La Nación,* Sept. 10, 1992.

50. Gonzalo Falabella, "Labor's Odd Man Out," *Hemisfile* 2:2 (Mar. 1991), 1–2, 12. Eric Hershberg, "Liberal Democracy, Market-Oriented Development, and the Future of Popular Sector Representation: Lessons from Contemporary Chile and Spain" (1994), 20–27.

51. Unionization in the United States also accounted for about 16 percent of the economically active population. Manuel Barrera, "Consideraciones acerca de la relación entre política y movimiento sindical: El caso de Chile," Materiales de Discusión, no. 6, CES, Oct. 1988; idem, "Política económica y democratización en Chile: Sus efectos sobre los trabajadores" (1992). Barrera, Henríquez, and Selamé, *Sindicatos,* 12–14. Guillermo Campero, "El sindicalismo ante la democratización," *Mensaje* 378 (May 1989), 143–46. Oscar Guillermo Garretón, "Cambios estructurales y movimiento sindical en Chile," Materiales de Discusión, no. 10, CES, Mar. 1989. Angell, "Unions," 205–8. *El Mercurio,* Apr. 7, 1993.

52. Barrera, "Política," 23–24. Francisco Zapata, "The End of the Honeymoon: The Chilean Labor Scene," *Latin American Labor News* 5 (1992), 9; idem, "Transición democrática y sindicalismo en Chile" (1992). Jaime Ruiz-Tagle, "Desafíos del sindicalismo chileno frente a la flexibilización del mercado del trabajo" (1992). J. Samuel Valenzuela and Volker Frank, "The Labor Movement and the Return to Democratic Government in Chile," *Latin American Labor News* 5 (1992), 9–11.

53. More than any other group, unions elicited the highest percentage who had no opinion about them (17%), while 60 percent found them to be "good" or "very good," and 23 percent "bad" or "very bad." Centro de Estudios de la Realidad Contemporánea, "Evaluación del primer año del gobierno democrático" (Mar. 1991).

54. Epstein, "Labor." Zapata, "End of the Honeymoon."

55. Loveman, "Political Left," 35–38. Arturo Valenzuela, "Government and Politics," in Hudson, *Chile,* 197–274. *El Mercurio,* Sept. 8, 1992.

56. Gerardo L. Munck, "Democratic Stability and Its Limits: An Analysis of Chile's 1993 Elections," *Journal of Interamerican Studies and World Affairs* 36:2 (summer 1994).

57. Alain Touraine, *Actores sociales y sistemas políticos en América Latina* (Santiago, 1987), 210. Angell, "Unions," 205–8. Falabella, "El rol." Ruiz-Tagle, *El sindicalismo,* 3–5. Winn and Ibáñez, "Textile Entrepreneurs," 16–18. Barrera, "Consideraciones."

SEVEN : Argentina, 1976–1983

1. The phrase "reciprocal blockade" comes from Marcelo Cavarozzi, *Autoritarismo y democracia (1955–1983)* (Buenos Aires, 1983).

2. Ibid.; Marcelo Cavarozzi, "Political Cycles in Argentina since 1955," in Guillermo O'Donnell, Philippe C. Schmitter, and Laurence Whitehead, *Transitions from Authoritarian Rule: Latin America* (Baltimore, 1986), 19–48. Guillermo O'Donnell, *Modernization and Bureaucratic Authoritarianism: Studies in South American Politics* (Berkeley, 1973); idem, "Estado y alianzas en la Argentina, 1956–1976," Documento de Trabajo, no. 5, Centro de Estudios de Estado y Sociedad (CEDES), 1976; idem, *Bureaucratic Authoritarianism: Argentina, 1966–1973, in Comparative Perspective* (Berkeley, 1988). Carlos H. Waisman, *Reversal of Development in Argentina* (Princeton, 1987). Ruth Berins Collier and David Collier, *Shaping the Political Arena: Critical Junctures, the Labor Movement, and Regime Dynamics in Latin America* (Princeton, 1991), 331–50, 484–97, 721–42. Ronaldo Munck, Ricardo Falcón, and Bernardo Gallitelli, *Argentina: From Anarchism to Peronism. Workers, Unions, and Politics, 1855–1985* (London, 1987). William C. Smith, *Authoritarianism and the Crisis of the Argentine Political Economy* (Stanford, Calif., 1989). Peter G. Snow and Luigi Manzetti, *Political Forces in Argentina,* 3d ed. (Westport, Conn., 1993). Luigi Manzetti, *Institutions, Parties, and Coalitions in Argentine Politics* (Pittsburgh, 1993). Pablo Pozzi, *Oposición obrera a la dictadura (1976–1982)* (Buenos Aires, 1988), 26–33. O'Donnell's *Bureaucratic Authoritarianism* examines in detail a less thorough attempt by the armed forces to subdue the labor movement, an episode that will not be covered here.

3. Héctor Palomino, *Cambios ocupacionales y sociales en Argentina, 1947–1985* (Buenos Aires, 1988), 90–95; idem, "Democratización y crisis: Los dilemas del sindi-

calismo argentino," in Guillermo Campero and Alberto Cuevas, *El sindicalismo lati-noamericano en los noventa* (Santiago, 1991), 25–60.

4. Juan Carlos Torre, "The Meaning of Current Workers' Struggles," *Latin American Perspectives* 1:3 (fall 1974), 73–81; idem, "El movimiento obrero y el último gobierno peronista (1973–1976)," *Crítica y Utopía* 6 (1982), 99–134; idem, *Los sindicatos en el gobierno, 1973–1976* (Buenos Aires, 1983), 16. Gerardo Luis Munck, "State Power and Labor Politics in the Context of Military Rule: Organized Labor, Peronism, and the Armed Forces in Argentina, 1976–1983" (Ph.D. diss., University of California, San Diego, 1990), 54–59. Osvaldo Calello and Daniel Parcero, *De Vandor a Ubaldini*, 2 vols. (Buenos Aires, 1984). Santiago Senén González, *El sindicalismo después de Perón* (Buenos Aires, 1971). Alvaro Abós, *La columna vertebral: Sindicatos y peronismo* (Buenos Aires, 1983). Gary Wynia, *Argentina in the Postwar Era* (Albuquerque, 1978). Liliana de Riz, *Retorno y derrumbe: El último gobierno peronista* (Mexico, 1981), 118–29. Rubén Rotondaro, *Realidad y cambio en el sindicalismo* (Buenos Aires, 1971). Daniel James, "Power and Politics in Peronist Trade Unions," *Journal of Interamerican Studies and World Affairs* 20:1 (Feb. 1978), 3–36; idem, *Resistance and Integration: Peronism and the Argentine Working Class, 1946–76* (Cambridge, 1988). Iris Martha Roldán, *Sindicatos y protesta social en la Argentina: Un estudio de caso. El sindicato de luz y fuerza de Córdoba (1969–1974)* (Amsterdam, 1978). Juan José Taccone and Alberto Delfico, *Historia y política en el sindicalismo argentino*, 2 vols. (Buenos Aires, 1986). Beatriz S. Balvé, *Los nucleamientos político-ideológicos de la clase obrera: Composición interna y alineamientos sindicales en relación a gobiernos y partidos. Argentina, 1955–1974* (Buenos Aires, 1990). Rubén Zorrilla, *Estructura y dinámica del sindicalismo argentino* (Buenos Aires, 1974); idem, *El liderazgo sindical argentino: Desde sus orígenes hasta 1975* (Buenos Aires, 1983); idem, *Líderes del poder sindical* (Buenos Aires, 1988). Arturo Fernández, *Ideologías de los grupos dirigentes sindicales (1966–1973)*, 2 vols. (Buenos Aires, 1986). Richard D. Mallon and Juan V. Sourrouille, *Economic Policy-Making in a Conflict Society: The Argentine Case* (Cambridge, 1975). Ricardo Sidicario, "Consideraciones sociológicas sobre las relaciones entre el peronismo y la clase obrera en la Argentina, 1943–1955," *Boletín de Estudios Latinoamericanos y del Caribe* 31 (Dec. 1981), 43–60. Roberto P. Korzeniewicz, "The Labor Movement in Argentina, 1887–1973" (Ph.D. diss., State University of New York, Binghamton, 1989). Paul G. Buchanan, "State Corporatism in Argentina: Labor Administration under Perón and Onganía," *Latin American Research Review* 20:1 (1985), 61–96. Samuel Baily, *Labor, Nationalism, and Politics in Argentina* (New Brunswick, 1967). Guido Di Tella, *Perón-Perón, 1973–1976* (Buenos Aires, 1983), 184. Torcuato Di Tella, "Working-Class Organization and Politics in Argentina," *Latin American Research Review* 16:2 (1981), 33–56; idem, *El sistema político argentino y la clase obrera* (Buenos Aires, 1964). Sebastiao C. Velasco e Cruz, "Estado, sindicato e instabilidade política: Argentina, 1955–1970," *Dados* 15 (1977), 43–59. Elizabeth Jelin, "Conflictos laborales en la Argentina, 1973–1976," *Revista Mexicana de Sociología* 2 (Apr.–June 1978), 421–63. Oscar Cornblit, "Política y sindicatos," in Carlos A. Floria and Marcelo Montserrat, *Pensar la república* (Buenos Aires, 1977), 143–61. Marcelo Cavarozzi, "Unions and Politics in Argentina, 1955–1962," working paper no. 63, Latin American Program, Wilson Center, 1982; idem, "Consolidación del sindicalismo peronista y emergencia de la formula política Argentina durante el gobierno

frondizista," *Estudios Cedes* 2:7/8 (1979); idem, *Autoritarismo.* Waisman, *Reversal.* Palomino, "Democratización," 35–37; idem, *Cambios,* 98–99.

5. Cavarozzi, "Unions and Politics." Darío Cantón, *Elecciones y partidos políticos en la Argentina* (Buenos Aires, 1973). Darío Cantón and Jorge R. Jorrat, "Occupation and Vote in Urban Argentina: The March 1973 Presidential Election," *Latin American Research Review* 13:1 (1978), 146–57. Manuel Mora y Araujo, "La estructura sindical del peronismo: Un análisis electoral inter-provincial," *Desarrollo Económico* 56 (Jan.–Mar. 1975). Manuel Mora y Araujo and Ignacio Llorente, *El voto peronista* (Buenos Aires, 1980). Manuel Mora y Araujo and Peter H. Smith, "Peronism and Economic Development: The 1973 Elections," in Frederick C. Turner and José Enrique Miguens, *Juan Perón and the Reshaping of Argentina* (Pittsburgh, 1983), 147–70. Susan Beth Tiano, "Authoritarianism, Class Consciousness, and Modernity: Working-Class Attitudes in Argentina and Chile" (Ph.D. diss., Brown University, 1979).

6. Abós, *La columna,* 81–93. Marcelo Cavarozzi, "Peronism and Radicalism: Argentina's Transitions in Perspective," in Paul W. Drake and Eduardo Silva, *Elections and Democratization in Latin America, 1980–85* (La Jolla, Calif., 1986), 143–74. Deolindo F. Bittel, *Qué es el peronismo* (Buenos Aires, 1983). Vicente Palermo, "Movimientos sociales y partidos políticos: Aspectos de la cuestión en la democracia emergente en la Argentina," in Elizabeth Jelin, *Movimientos sociales y democracia emergente,* 2 vols. (Buenos Aires, 1987), 2, 132–75. Ronaldo Munck, *Politics and Dependency in the Third World: The Case of Latin America* (London, 1984), 145–68.

7. Thomas C. Wright, *Latin America in the Era of the Cuban Revolution* (New York, 1991). Donald C. Hodges, *Argentina, 1943–1987: The National Revolution and Resistance* (Albuquerque, 1988). Di Tella, *Perón,* 113, 327.

8. Torre, *Los sindicatos.* Di Tella, *Perón,* 83–85.

9. José Enrique Miguens, "The Presidential Elections of 1973 and the End of an Ideology," in Turner and Miguens, *Perón,* 147–70. Di Tella, *Perón,* 93–95, 109–11. Santiago Senén González, *Diez años de sindicalismo argentino (de Perón al Proceso)* (Buenos Aires, 1984), 9–16.

10. Paul H. Lewis, *The Crisis of Argentine Capitalism* (Chapel Hill, N.C., 1990), 423–24. Pozzi, *Oposición obrera,* 41–47. Di Tella, *Perón,* 184–86. Santiago Senén González, *El poder sindical* (Buenos Aires, 1978); idem, *Diez años,* 17–18.

11. De Riz, *Retorno,* 20–25, 94–97. Torre, *Los sindicatos;* idem, "Workers' Struggles." Jelin, "Conflictos." Di Tella, *Perón.* Senén, *El poder,* 127–29. Lewis, *Crisis,* 437–41. Marcelo Cavarozzi, "Argentina at the Crossroads," working paper no. 115, Latin American Program, Wilson Center, 1982; idem, "The Recurrence of Authoritarianism and the Prospects of Democracy in Argentina" (1982); idem, *Autoritarismo,* 51–60. Julio Godio, *El movimiento obrero argentino (1955–1990): Venturas y desventuras de la columna vertebral desde la resistencia hasta el menemismo* (Buenos Aires, 1991), 225–303. Arturo Fernández, *Las prácticas sociales del sindicalismo (1976–1982)* (Buenos Aires, 1985), 42–47. Oscar R. Cardoso and Rodolfo Audi, *Sindicalismo: El poder y la crisis* (Buenos Aires, 1982), 77–116. Gary W. Wynia, "Workers and Wages: Argentine Labor and the Incomes Policy Problem," in Turner and Miguens, *Perón,* 33–54. Juan Carlos D'Abate, "Trade Unions and Peronism," in ibid., 55–75. Louise Doyon, "El crecimiento sindical bajo el peronismo," *Desarrollo*

Económico 57 (Apr.–June 1975). North American Congress on Latin America, *Argentina in the Hour of the Furnaces* (New York, 1975). Richard Gillespie, *Soldiers of Perón: Argentina's Montoneros* (New York, 1983). Adolfo Canitrot, "La viabilidad económica de la democracia: Un análisis de la experiencia peronista, 1973–1976," *Estudios Sociales* 11 (May 1978). Juan Perón, *El gobierno, el estado, y las organizaciones libres del pueblo* (Buenos Aires, 1975).

12. Adolfo Gilly, "Las Malvinas, una guerra del capital," in Alberto J. Pla et al., *La década trágica: Ocho ensayos sobre la crisis argentina, 1973–1983* (Buenos Aires, 1984), 155–228. Alvaro Abós, *Las organizaciones sindicales y el poder militar (1976–1983)* (Buenos Aires, 1984). David Pion-Berlin, *The Ideology of State Terror: Economic Doctrine and Political Repression in Argentina and Peru* (Boulder, Colo., 1989), 111–18. Donald C. Hodges, *Argentina's "Dirty War": An Intellectual Biography* (Austin, Tex., 1991). Argentine National Commission on the Disappeared, *Nunca Más* (New York, 1986). Eduardo Luis Duhalde, *El estado terrorista argentino* (Buenos Aires, 1983). John Simpson and Jana Bennett, *The Disappeared and the Mothers of the Plaza* (New York, 1985). Marysa Navarro, "The Personal Is Political: Las Madres de Plaza de Mayo," in Susan Eckstein, *Power and Popular Protest: Latin American Social Movements* (Berkeley, 1989), 241–58. Enrique Vázquez, *PRN La última: Origen, apogeo y caída de la dictadura militar* (Buenos Aires, 1985). Gustavo Beliz, *CGT, el otro poder* (Buenos Aires, 1988), 98. Mario Balzán and Silvia Mercado, *Oscar Smith: El sindicalismo peronista ante sus límites* (Buenos Aires, 1987). Fernández, *Las prácticas*, 55–60. Pozzi, *Oposición obrera*, 155–57. G. Munck, "State Power," 93–94.

13. Pion-Berlin, *State Terror*, 97–123. Fernández, *Las prácticas*, 26–42. Hodges, *Argentina's "Dirty War,"* 124–71. Eduardo Jozami, "La política antinflacionaria," in Eduardo Jozami, Pedro Paz, and Juan Villarreal, *Crisis de la dictadura argentina: Política económica y cambio social, 1976–1983* (Buenos Aires, 1985), 107–96. Ronaldo Munck, "Capital Restructuring and Labour Recomposition under a Military Regime: Argentina, 1976–83," in Roger Southall, *Trade Unions and the New Industrialization of the Third World* (London, 1988), 121–43.

14. Comisión Económica para América Latina (CEPAL), *Precios, salarios y empleo en la Argentina* (Santiago, 1984), 136. Héctor L. Dieguez and Pablo Gerchunoff, "La dinámica del mercado laboral urbano en la Argentina, 1976–1981," *Desarrollo Económico* 24:93 (Apr.–June 1984), 3–39. Edward C. Epstein, "Labor Populism and Hegemonic Crisis in Argentina," in Edward C. Epstein, *Labor Autonomy and the State in Latin America* (Boston, 1989), 13–38. Lewis, *Crisis,* 472–73. Other sources on prices and wages are listed in n. 16, below.

15. The data in the foregoing discussion are from the following sources: CEPAL, *Precios,* 125–30. Pozzi, *Oposición obrera,* 50–56. Palomino, *Cambios,* 116. Bernardo Gallitelli and Andrés A. Thompson, "La situación laboral en la Argentina del 'Proceso,' 1976–1981," in Bernardo Gallitelli and Andrés A. Thompson, *Sindicalismo y regímenes militares en Argentina y Chile* (Amsterdam, 1982), 141–90. Julio Godio, Héctor Palomino, and Achim Wachendorfer, *El movimiento sindical argentino (1880–1987)* (Buenos Aires, 1988), 72–81. Francisco Delich, "Después del diluvio, la clase obrera," in Alain Rouquié, *Argentina, hoy* (Mexico, 1982), 129–50. Daniel C. Fernández, "Las luchas obreras en la Argentina moderna," *Cuadernos Políticos* 31

(Jan.–Mar. 1982), 41–57. Information on industry, employment, and unions can also be gleaned from the sources cited in n. 16, below.

16. Walter Little, "Argentine Labour Crisis since 1976" (1982). Adolfo Canitrot, "Teoría y práctica: Liberalismo, política anti-inflacionaria y apertura económica en la Argentina, 1976–1981," *Estudios Cedes* 3:10 (1981); idem, "La política de apertura económica (1976–1981) y sus efectos sobre el empleo y el salario: Un estudio macroeconómico," Estudios y Documentos de Trabajo sobre Recursos Humanos, Empleo y Remuneraciones, Ministerio de Trabajo de la Nación, Apr. 1983. William C. Smith, "Reflections on the Political Economy of Authoritarian Rule and Capitalist Reorganization in Contemporary Argentina," in Philip O'Brien and Paul Cammack, *Generals in Retreat: The Crisis of Military Rule in Latin America* (Manchester, England, 1985), 37–88. Joseph Ramos, *Neoconservative Economics in the Southern Cone of Latin America, 1973–1983* (Baltimore, 1986), 34–43. Jorge Schvarzer, *La política económica de Martínez de Hoz* (Buenos Aires, 1986). J. Figueiredo et al., *Empleo y salarios en América Latina* (Petrópolis, Brazil, 1985), 16–29. Aldo Ferrer, "La economía argentina bajo una estrategia 'preindustrial,' 1976–1980," in Rouquié, *Argentina,* 105–28. Juan M. Villarreal, "Changes in Argentine Society: The Heritage of the Dictatorship," in Monica Peralta-Ramos and Carlos H. Waisman, *From Military Rule to Liberal Democracy in Argentina* (Boulder, Colo., 1987), 69–96. Larry A. Sjaastad, "Argentine Economic Policy, 1976–81," in Guido Di Tella and Rudiger Dornbusch, *The Political Economy of Argentina, 1946–83* (Pittsburgh, 1989), 254–75. Rudiger Dornbusch, "Argentina after Martínez de Hoz," in ibid., 286–315. David G. Erro, *Resolving the Argentine Paradox: Politics and Development, 1966–1992* (Boulder, Colo., 1993), 104–13. OIT, PREALC, "Monetarismo global y respuesta industrial: El caso de Argentina" (1983). Guillermo Almeyra, "La clase obrera en la Argentina actual," in Pla, *La década trágica,* 27–44. Alberto Spagnolo and Oscar Cismondi, "Argentina: El proyecto económico y su carácter de clase," in ibid., 45–76. Gilly, "Las Malvinas," 165–86. Palomino, "Democratización"; idem, *Cambios,* 100–101, 108–11. Jozami, Paz, and Villarreal, *Crisis.* Lewis, *Crisis,* 448–75, 481. Senén, *Diez años,* 77–80. Alejandro Foxley, *Latin American Experiments in Neoconservative Economics* (Berkeley, 1983), 120–23.

17. Alejandro Dabat, "El derrumbe de la dictadura," in Pla, *La década trágica,* 127–54. Senén, *Diez años,* 120, 153. Palomino, *Cambios,* 102–5, 111. Lewis, *Crisis,* 482–83.

18. Some vacillation between atomization and co-optation as the best way to bring labor to heel also characterized the Onganía dictatorship in the late 1960s. Buchanan, "State Corporatism," 77–78. Smith, *Authoritarianism,* 101–61.

19. G. Munck, "State Power," 103–4.

20. Ronaldo Munck, "Restructuración del capital y recomposición de la clase obrera en Argentina desde 1976," in Gallitelli and Thompson, *Sindicalismo,* 191–228. G. Munck, "State Power," 100–103, 120–21. Ricardo Falcón, "Conflicto social y régimen militar: La resistencia obrera en Argentina (marzo, 1976–marzo, 1981)," in Gallitelli and Thompson, *Sindicalismo,* 124–26.

21. Fernández, *Las prácticas,* 59, 69–82.

22. Di Tella, *Perón,* 57. Fernández, "Las luchas."

23. For a short time in 1979, the two organizations dissolved and merged into the United Conduction of Argentine Workers (CUTA). However, the CUTA remained sorely divided between the hard-liners from the Twenty-five and the soft-liners from the CNT, and it quickly fell apart. Senén, *Diez años,* 142–46, 154–57. Pozzi, *Oposición obrera,* 68–163. G. Munck, "State Power," 90–123.

24. Senén, *Diez años,* 155–56.

25. Organization of American States, Inter-American Commission on Human Rights, *Report on the Situation of Human Rights in Argentina* (Washington, D.C., 1980). Epstein, "Labor," 26–27. Little, "Argentine Labour Crisis." Senén, *Diez años,* 58–186. Falcón, "Conflicto social." Gallitelli and Thompson, "La situación." Godio, *El movimiento obrero,* 307–86. Delich, "Después del diluvio," 129–50. Pozzi, *Oposición obrera,* 157–63. Canitrot, "Teoría." Pion-Berlin, *State Terror,* 116–18. Abós, *Las organizaciones.* Beliz, *CGT,* 53–63. Cavarozzi, "Argentina"; idem, *Autoritarismo.* G. Munck, "State Power," 119–225. Hector Capraro et al., "Argentina: Economía y política en los años setenta," in Pla, *La década trágica,* 77–104. Martin Edwin Andersen, *Dossier Secreto: Argentina's Desaparecidos and the Myth of the "Dirty War"* (Boulder, Colo., 1993), 175–83. Juan Carlos D'Abate, *El antipoder sindical* (Buenos Aires, 1980). Arturo C. Piccoli et al., *Sindicalismo y política* (Buenos Aires, 1982). David R. Decker, *The Political, Economic, and Labor Climate in Argentina* (Philadelphia, 1983).

26. Fernández, *Las prácticas,* 82–90. Decker, *Political Climate,* 83–93. Alvaro Abós, *Los sindicatos argentinos: Cuadro de situación, 1984* (Buenos Aires, 1985), 112–13; idem, *Las organizaciones,* 29–33. Beliz, *CGT,* 129–30. Daniel Parcero, *La CGT y el sindicalismo latinoamericano* (Buenos Aires, 1987), 182–92. G. Munck, "State Power," 122–23, 196. Senén, *Diez años,* 72–91, 118–23, 154, 159.

27. Beliz, *CGT,* 146–63. Senén, *Diez años,* 90, 143, 156, 161, 197–98. Fernández, *Las prácticas,* 102. Abós, *Las organizaciones,* 82–84. Hodges, *Argentina's "Dirty War,"* 242–44.

28. Falcón, "Conflicto social." Gallitelli and Thompson, "La situación," 162–70. Francisco Delich, "Desmovilización social, reestructuración obrera y cambio sindical," in Peter Waldman and Ernesto Garzón Valdés, *El poder militar en la Argentina (1976–1981)* (Frankfurt, 1982), 101–15. León E. Bieber, "El movimiento laboral argentino a partir de 1976," in ibid., 116–22. Andrés Thompson, "Las luchas sociales en la Argentina (1976–1983)," in Isidoro Cheresky and Jacques Chonchol, *Crisis y transformación de los regímenes autoritarios* (Buenos Aires, 1985), 85–102. Isidoro Cheresky, "Hacia la Argentina postautoritaria," in ibid., 21–32. Héctor Cordone and Pablo Forni, "Argentina: Las huelgas generales durante la última década," *Latin American Labor News* 4 (1991), 1–2, 7. G. Munck, "State Power," 99–105, 122–23, 127–28. Pozzi, *Oposición obrera,* 70–166. Fernández, *Las prácticas.* Abós, *La columna,* 9–10, 140–43.

29. Pozzi, *Oposición obrera,* 95–102. Senén, *Diez años,* 158–59, 165–70. Hodges, *Argentina,* 203–5. G. Munck, "State Power," 191–93. Gilly, "Las Malvinas," 197–203. Abós, *Las organizaciones,* 140–45.

30. Piccoli et al., *Sindicalismo,* 113. Dabat, "El derrumbe," 140–51. Pozzi, *Oposición obrera,* 24–26. Senén, *Diez años,* 187–200. Abós, *La columna,* 7–9. Lewis, *Crisis,* 474.

31. Vicente Palermo, *Democracia interna en los partidos* (Buenos Aires, 1986), 34–35, 84–87. Cavarozzi, "Peronism and Radicalism"; idem, "Recurrence." Deolindo F. Bittel, *Peronismo y dictadura* (Buenos Aires, 1983). Gilly, "Las Malvinas," 207.

Senén, *Diez años,* 157. Little, "Argentine Labour Crisis." Organization of American States, *Human Rights.* Piccoli et al., *Sindicalismo.*

32. G. Munck, "State Power," esp. 201–2. Gilly, "Las Malvinas."

33. Lisberth Haas, "Argentina," in Gerald Michael Greenfield and Sheldon L. Maram, *Latin American Labor Organizations* (New York, 1987), 1–24. Dabat, "El derrumbe," 145–52. Beliz, *CGT,* 99–102, 127. Palermo, *Democracia interna,* 114–16.

34. Adolfo Gilly, "Argentina después de la dictadura," in Pla, *La década trágica,* 228–52. Ricardo Gaudio and Héctor Domeniconi, "Las primeras elecciones sindicales en la transición democrática," *Desarrollo Económico* 26:103 (Oct.–Dec. 1986), 423–54.

35. The electoral and polling data in the foregoing discussion are from the following sources: Edgardo Raúl Catterberg, "Las elecciones del 30 de octubre de 1983: El surgimiento de una nueva convergencia electoral," *Desarrollo Económico* 25:98 (July–Sept. 1985), 259–67; idem, *Los Argentinos frente a la política* (Buenos Aires, 1989), 106–15, 123–27. Mora Cordeu, Silvia Mercado, and Nancy Sosa, *Peronismo, la mayoría perdida* (Buenos Aires, 1985). Torcuato S. Di Tella, "The October 1983 Elections in Argentina," *Government and Opposition* 19:2 (spring 1984), 188–92. Luis González Esteves and Ignacio Llorente, "Elecciones y preferencias políticas en la capital federal y Gran Buenos Aires: El 30 de octubre de 1983," in Natalio R. Botana et al., *La argentina electoral* (Buenos Aires, 1985), 39–73. Francisco Delich, *Metáforas de la sociedad argentina* (Buenos Aires, 1986), 149–56. Alfredo Errandonea, "Algunas hipotesis sobre el cambio sociopolítico en la Argentina actual," in Daniel R. García Delgado, *Los cambios en la sociedad política (1976–1986)* (Buenos Aires, 1987), 11–29. Carlos Waisman, "The Legitimation of Democracy under Adverse Conditions: The Case of Argentina," in Peralta-Ramos and Waisman, *From Military Rule,* 97–112. Jorge Raúl Jorrat, "Las elecciones de 1983: ¿'Desviación' o 'realineamiento'?" *Desarrollo Económico* 26:101 (Apr.–June 1986), 89–119. Manuel Mora y Araujo, "The Nature of the Alfonsín Coalition," in Drake and Silva, *Elections and Democratization,* 175–88. David Rock and Susanne E. Avellano, "The Argentine Elections of 1983: Significance and Repercussions," in ibid., 189–99. Leticia Maronese, Ana Cafiero de Nazar, and Víctor Waisman, *El voto peronista '83: Perfil electoral y causas de la derrota* (n.p., 1985). Darío Cantón, *El pueblo legislador: Las elecciones de 1983* (Buenos Aires, 1986). Manuel Alcántara Saez, *Elecciones y consolidación democrática en Argentina: 1983–1987* (Costa Rica, 1988). Peter Ranis, "View from Below: Working-Class Consciousness in Argentina," *Latin American Research Review* 26:2 (1991), 133–56. Gilly, "Argentina," 239–48. Cavarozzi, "Peronism and Radicalism," 156–59, 169–72.

36. Beliz, *CGT,* 104–7, 118–19. Alvaro Abós, "Sindicalismo, autonomía y política," in Jelin, *Movimientos,* vol. 2, 113–31.

37. Godio, Palomino, and Wachendorfer, *El movimiento,* 78–88. Data on unionization in Argentina—as throughout Latin America—are subject to manipulation, interpretation, and debate. Although sources disagree on precise numbers, they agree on trends, particularly that there was a surge in membership in 1973–76, a decline in 1976–83, and recuperation during 1984–85. Abós, *Los sindicatos,* 23–34, 67–72.

38. In that same 1984 poll, 55 percent of the public viewed the armed forces positively, but only 12 percent saw their leaders the same way. Catterberg, *Los Argentinos,* 88. Palermo, "Movimientos," 150–51. Ranis, "View," 152.

39. Peter Ranis, *Argentine Workers: Peronism and Contemporary Class Consciousness* (Pittsburgh, 1992), 6–7, 116–27, 136–53.

40. Gaudio and Domeniconi, "Elecciones sindicales." Waisman, "Legitimation," 105–6. Godio, *El movimiento obrero,* 392–401. Abós, *Los sindicatos,* 109–10. Héctor Palomino, "El movimiento de democratización sindical," in Elizabeth Jelin, *Los nuevos movimientos sociales,* 2 vols. (Buenos Aires, 1985), vol. 2, 36–60.

41. Lewis, *Crisis,* 480–81. Hodges, *Argentina,* 246–50. Beliz, *CGT,* 118. Héctor Palomino, "Argentina: Dilemas y perspectivas del movimiento sindical," *Nueva Sociedad* 83 (May-June 1986), 89–102. Godio, Palomino, and Wachendorfer, *El movimiento,* 84–85. Abós, *Los sindicatos,* 31–34.

42. Liliana De Riz, Marcelo Cavarozzi, and Jorge Feldman, *Concertación, estado y sindicatos en la Argentina contemporánea* (Buenos Aires, 1987). Carlos Alberto Floria, "Dilemmas of the Consolidation of Democracy in Argentina," in Enrique A. Baloyra, *Comparing New Democracies: Transition and Consolidation in Mediterranean Europe and the Southern Cone* (Boulder, Colo., 1987), 153–78.

43. Héctor Palomino, "Argentina 1984–1990: Huelgas generales política y crisis," *Latin American Labor News* 2 and 3 (1990), 19–20; idem, "Democratización," 25–26, 33–34. Beliz, *CGT,* 118. Epstein, "Labor," 28–29. Erro, *Argentine Paradox,* 136–54. Cordone and Forni, "Argentina." Marcelo Cavarozzi and María Grossi, *De la reinvención democrática al reflujo político y la hyperinflación* (Buenos Aires, 1989). Ernesto S. Ceballos, *Historia política del movimiento obrero argentino (1944–1985)* (Buenos Aires, 1985), 130–33. Mario Damill and Roberto Frenkel, *Hiperinflación y estabilización: La experiencia argentina reciente* (Buenos Aires, 1990); idem, *Malos tiempos: La economía argentina en la década de los ochenta* (Buenos Aires, 1990). Roberto Frenkel, interview by author, San Diego, 1992. Bernardo Grinspun, *La evolución de la economía argentina desde diciembre 1983 a septiembre de 1989* (Buenos Aires, 1990). República de Argentina, Ministerio de Trabajo, Dirección Nacional de Recursos Humanos y Empleo, "La subutilización de la mano de obra en el Gran Buenos Aires: Evolución y tendencias" (Dec. 1986). Adriana Marshall, "The Fall of Labor's Share in Income and Consumption: A New 'Growth Model' for Argentina?" in William L. Canak, *Lost Promises: Debt, Austerity, and Development in Latin America* (Boulder, Colo., 1989), 47–68. William C. Smith, "Heterodox Shocks and the Political Economy of the Democratic Transition in Argentina and Brazil," in ibid., 138–68.

44. Palomino, "Democratización." Abós, "Sindicalismo," 116–19. Beliz, *CGT.* Snow and Manzetti, *Political Forces,* 131–36. Erro, *Argentine Paradox,* 143–44. Leopoldo Mármora, "La posición de los sindicatos en la democracia actual," in Ernesto Garzón Valdes, Manfred Mols, and Arnold Spitta, *La nueva democracia argentina* (Buenos Aires, 1988), 153–72. Ricardo Gaudio and Andrés Thompson, *Sindicalismo peronista, gobierno radical* (Buenos Aires, 1990).

45. Liliana de Riz, "Notas sobre parlamento y partidos en la Argentina de hoy," in Hilda Sábato and Marcelo Cavarozzi, *Democracia, orden político y parlamento fuerte* (Buenos Aires, 1984), 118–26. Abós, "Sindicalismo," 115. Godio, *El movimiento obrero,* 387–453.

46. Palermo, "Movimientos," 152–56. Alvaro Abós, *El posperonismo* (Buenos Aires, 1986); idem, *Las organizaciones.* Cordeu, Mercado, and Sosa, *Peronismo.*

Guido Di Tella, "Fuerzas armadas y democratización en Argentina," in Augusto Varas, *Transición a la democracia* (Santiago, 1984), 101–12. Alberto van Klaveren, "Instituciones y concertación política en Argentina," in ibid., 137–46. Cavarozzi, "Peronism and Radicalism," 156–59.

47. Abós, *El posperonismo.* Liliana de Riz, *La Argentina de Alfonsín: La renovación de los partidos y el parlamento* (Buenos Aires, 1989). James W. McGuire, "Union Political Tactics and Democratic Consolidation in Alfonsín's Argentina, 1983–1989," *Latin American Research Review* 27:1 (1992), 37–74.

48. Always small, the Argentine left—principally socialists and communists—was weakened even more by the dictatorship and by the discrediting of the guerrillas, not to mention the Communists' support for the military regime. Leftists claimed at most 3–4 percent of the electorate. Donald C. Hodges, "The Argentine Left since Perón," in Barry Carr and Steve Ellner, *The Latin American Left: From the Fall of Allende to Perestroika* (Boulder, Colo., 1993), 155–70. Albero Kohen, *La izquierda y los nuevos tiempos* (Buenos Aires, 1987). William Ratliff and Roger Fontaine, *Changing Course: The Capitalist Revolution in Argentina* (Stanford, Calif., 1990). Paul Berks, "The Decline of Militant Unionism in Argentina: The Case of the Auto Workers' Union" (Masters thesis, University of California, San Diego, 1993). Víctor De Genaro, Agustín Amicone, and Andrés Thompson, "Argentina: La recesión del poder sindical," *Sindicalismo y Democracia* 6 (Jan. 1993), 6–8. Godio, *El movimiento obrero,* 378–80, 438–53. Erro, *Argentine Paradox,* 185–86, 195–213. Snow and Manzetti, *Political Forces,* 48–51, 139–40. Ranis, *Argentine Workers,* 214–19. Edward C. Epstein, *The New Argentine Democracy: The Search for a Successful Formula* (Westport, Conn., 1992).

49. Edward C. Epstein, "Labor-State Conflict in the New Argentine Democracy: Parties, Union Factions, and Power Maximizing," in Epstein, *Argentine Democracy,* 124–56. Abós, *Las organizaciones,* 96–107. Palomino, "Argentina." Pozzi, *Oposición obrera,* 176–80. G. Munck, "State Power," 270–73.

E I G H T : Labor Movements after Capitalist Authoritarianism

1. Throughout this book, the term *redemocratization* simply indicates that the pre- and postauthoritarian governments were much more democratic than the intervening regime; the regime's successor did not necessarily constitute a restoration of the status quo ante or an unlimited democracy, any more than the dictatorship's predecessor was always a paragon of democratic virtue. On political democratization, see the following: Guillermo O'Donnell, Philippe C. Schmitter, and Laurence Whitehead, *Transitions from Authoritarian Rule,* 4 vols. (Baltimore, 1986). D. L. Raby, *Fascism and Resistance in Portugal: Communists, Liberals, and Military Dissidents in the Opposition to Salazar, 1941–1974* (Manchester, England, 1988), 266–68. Gonzalo Falabella, "Epílogo," in Manuel Barrera and Gonzalo Falabella, *Sindicatos bajo regímenes militares: Argentina, Brazil, Chile* (Santiago, 1990), 283–318. Kevin J. Middlebrook, "Prospects for Democracy: Regime Transformation and Transitions from Authoritarian Rule," working paper no. 62, Latin American Program, Wilson Center, Sept. 1979, 1–26. Enrique Baloyra, *Comparing New Democracies: Transition and Consolidation in Mediterranean Europe and the Southern Cone* (Boulder, Colo.,

1987). James M. Malloy and Mitchell A. Seligson, *Authoritarians and Democrats: Regime Transition in Latin America* (Pittsburgh, 1987). Larry Diamond, Juan Linz, and Seymour Martin Lipset, *Democracy in Developing Countries,* 3 vols. (Boulder, Colo., 1988). Larry Diamond and Marc F. Plattner, *The Global Resurgence of Democracy* (Baltimore, 1993). Samuel P. Huntington, *The Third Wave: Democratization in the Late Twentieth Century* (Norman, Okla., 1991). Robert A. Pastor, *Democracy in the Americas: Stopping the Pendulum* (New York, 1989). Marcelo Cavarozzi and Manuel Antonio Garretón, *Muerte y resurrección: Los partidos políticos en el autoritarismo y las transiciones del cono sur* (Santiago, 1989). Paul W. Drake, "International Factors in Democratization," Estudios / Working Papers, no. 56, Instituto Juan March, Nov. 1994. Paul W. Drake and Eduardo Silva, *Elections and Democratization in Latin America, 1980–85* (La Jolla, Calif., 1986).

    2. Gonzalo Falabella, "El rol de los sindicatos en la transición a la democracia en Chile" (Santiago, 1989).

    3. Victor Pérez Díaz, *Clase obrera, orden social, y conciencia de clase* (Madrid, 1980). Joan M. Nelson, *Intricate Links: Democratization and Market Reforms in Latin America and Eastern Europe* (New Brunswick, N.J., 1994); idem, *A Precarious Balance: Democratic and Economic Reforms in Eastern Europe and Latin America,* 2 vols. (San Francisco, 1994). Luis Carlos Bresser Pereira, José María Maravall, and Adam Przeworski, *Economic Reforms in New Democracies: A Social-Democratic Approach* (Cambridge, 1993).

    4. J. Samuel Valenzuela, "Labor Movements in Transitions to Democracy: A Framework for Analysis," *Comparative Politics* 21:4 (July 1989), 445–72.

    5. James W. McGuire, "Union Political Tactics and Democratic Consolidation in Alfonsín's Argentina, 1983–1989," *Latin American Research Review* 27:1 (1992), 37–74. Valenzuela, "Labor Movements," 449–69. Guillermo O'Donnell and Philippe C. Schmitter, *Transitions from Authoritarian Rule: Tentative Conclusions about Uncertain Democracies* (Baltimore, 1986). Leigh A. Payne, "Working Class Strategies in the Transition to Democracy in Brazil," *Comparative Politics* 23:1 (Oct. 1990), 221–38. "Panorama: El nervio de la modernización sindical," *Sindicalismo y Democracia* 4 (Nov. 1991), 4–7. Gian Primo Cella, "Negociación colectiva en América Latina: Un difícil camino," *Sindicalismo y Democracia* 4 (Nov. 1991), 8–11. Robert M. Fishman, "Working Class Organization and Political Change: The Labor Movement and the Transition to Democracy in Spain" (Ph.D. diss., Yale University, 1985), 362–65, 421–89; also published as *Working-Class Organization and the Return to Democracy in Spain* (Ithaca, N.Y. 1990).

    6. Paul G. Buchanan, "Reconstituting the Institutional Bases of Consent: Notes on State-Labor Relations and Democratic Consolidation in the Southern Cone," working paper no. 160, Kellogg Institute, Notre Dame, May 1991, 1–43. Adam Przeworski, *Democracy and the Market: Political and Economic Reforms in Eastern Europe and Latin America* (Cambridge, 1991), 184–86. María Grossi and Mario R. Dos Santos, "La concertación social: Una perspectiva sobre instrumentos de regulación económico-social en procesos de democratización," *Crítica y Utopía* 9 (1983), 127–48. Valenzuela, "Labor Movements."

    7. Edward C. Epstein, "Conclusion: The Question of Labor Autonomy," in

Edward C. Epstein, *Labor Autonomy and the State in Latin America* (Boston, 1989), 275–90.

8. Paul W. Drake, "Debt and Democracy in Latin America, 1920s-1980s," in Barbara Stallings and Robert Kaufman, *Debt and Democracy in Latin America* (Boulder, Colo., 1989), 39–58. Fernando Limongi and Adam Przeworski, "Democracy and Development in South America, 1946–1988," Estudio/Working Paper, no. 55, Instituto Juan March, Feb. 1994, 1–32.

9. Lawrence Weschler, *A Miracle, A Universe: Settling Accounts with Torturers* (New York, 1990).

10. Scott Mainwaring, Guillermo O'Donnell, and J. Samuel Valenzuela, *Issues in Democratic Consolidation: The New South American Democracies in Comparative Perspective* (Notre Dame, Ind., 1992).

11. Wolfgang Merkel et al., *Socialist Parties in Europe II: Of Class, Populars, Catch-All* (Barcelona, 1992).

12. Jorge G. Castañeda, *Utopia Unarmed: The Latin American Left after the Cold War* (New York, 1993), 38–39, 172–74, 474–76. Marcelo Cavarozzi, "The Left in Latin America: The Decline in Socialism and the Rise of Political Democracy," in Jonathan Hartlyn, Lars Schoultz, and Augusto Varas, *The United States and Latin America in the 1990s: Beyond the Cold War* (Chapel Hill, N.C., 1992), 101–27. Barry Carr and Steve Ellner, *The Latin American Left: From the Fall of Allende to Perestroika* (Boulder, Colo., 1993). (In Carr and Ellner, *Latin American Left,* see especially the following: Steve Ellner, "Introduction: The Changing Status of the Latin American Left in the Recent Past," 1–22. Dick Parker, "Trade Union Struggle and the Left in Latin America, 1973–1990," 205–24.) Thomas C. Wright, *Latin America in the Era of the Cuban Revolution* (New York, 1991).

13. "Democracy comes, democracy goes, but trade unions endure." Bjorn Feuer, "Mining Unionism, Political Democracy, and Revealed Preferences—The Quid Pro Quo of Labour Relations in Bolivia, Chile, and Peru, 1950–80," *Economic and Industrial Democracy* 12:1 (Feb. 1991), 97–118. Stanley G. Payne, "La oposición a las dictaduras en Europa Occidental: Una perspectiva comparativa," in Javier Tusell, Alicia Alted, and Abdón Mateos, *La oposición al régimen de Franco,* 2 vols. (Madrid, 1990), 1:63–64. Raby, *Fascism and Resistance,* 267–68.

Index

Library of Congress Cataloging-in-Publication Data

Drake, Paul W., 1944–
    Labor movements and dictatorships : the Southern Cone in comparative perspective /
Paul W. Drake.
        p.   cm.
    Includes bibliographical references (p.   ) and index.
    ISBN 0-8018-5326-5 (hardcover : alk. paper), — ISBN 0-8018-5327-3 (pbk. : alk. paper)
    1. Labor movement—Southern Cone of South America—History—20th century.
2. Trade-unions—Southern Cone of South America—Political activity—History—20th
century.   3. Authoritarianism—Southern Cone of South America—History—20th century.
4. Southern Cone of South America—Politics and government.
HD8259.S65D7   1996
322'.2'098—dc20   96-790